In pra

Beings Be Fed

"In *May All Beings Be Fed*, Dana takes you into the vulnerable and intimate tale of her life. With her sense of wonder and awe for the world around her, she paints a colorful portrait of her world, as vibrant and wild as the jungle, filled with interesting creatures of both the two legged and four legged variety. Her tale will amaze you, captivate your imagination, and open your heart for this little girl named Yaya as she learns to navigate a world that is often confusing, and grows into a woman that learns to dance with it all. Truly a fun and entertaining read!"

Sam Liebowitz, author, *Everyday Awakening: You Are More Powerful Than You Know.*

"Dana Humphrey's inner light seems to pour out of her and fill the room. It's a treat to discover more of Dana's wise, joyous lens on life in this book."

Elsie Maio, Board Advisor and Expert Commentator on the authentic Evolution to a Wellbeing Economy

"From the little girl invisible to others reluctantly wearing the beige dress, to the brave, vibrant young woman shaving her head in ceremony of true self love and expression.... Yaya's journey is filled with invaluable life lessons. It gave me the tools and motivation to set the butterfly within me free!!!"

Renée Sunshine

"Dana is a hotshot! She is dependable, very upbeat and fun!"

Ann Fry, author, *Sixty, Sexy, Sassy and Free*

"Dana, just like your custom magic wands, your book is the epitome of Big "Stick" Energy! You are powerful and your creations are full of BIG MAGIC."

Kaí Cole Henderson

"Dana and I go way back to 2008, when she was a wee little publicist, just getting started in NYC. We've grown together professionally and spiritually, from tv segments to travel, through all these years. I've been able to see her transformation first hand, and now you get to read all the juicy details, revealed publicly for the first time! What can I say, "Me Gusta!""

Jorge Bendersky, Celebrity Dog Groomer, Star of NBC's show Pooch Perfect, and author *DIY Dog Grooming, From Puppy Cuts to Best in Show: Everything You Need to Know, Step by Step.*

"I LOVED reading about Dana's life story and her very unique quarantine situation during the pandemic. WOW! Dana really knows how to turn every challenging situation into a positive one. Life for sure has its ups and downs, but it's so important to count your blessings as we pass through this world. Dana does just that as she expresses her journey in a very creative and captivating memoir."

Rebecca Symon

"Amazing women and true person to the core."

Jocelyn Mizrahi

"Dana is unbelievable! She has the professional energy and pizazz to make just about anything she works on a success."

Thomas Hollowell, author, *The Complete Idiot's Guide to Barefoot Running and Allah's Garden: A True Story of a Forgotten War in the Sahara Desert of Morocco, and The Everything Travel Guide to Ireland*

"Dana's book is a Positive Transformational Disruption! If there is someone who can share how to discover living your authentic life, it's Dana Humphrey. She's a diamond among gems; creative, dependable, and has your best interest at heart."

Sheryl Matthys, Founder of FetchaDate.com & author of *Leashes and Lovers*

"Energetic, well networked, genuine and hardworking. This is Dana in a bundle. She is a great pride to women entrepreneurs, a successful person and a free spirit."

Richard Fallah, Founder, Vbout.com

May All Beings Be Fed: Playing with Consciousness

A Memoir

By Dana Humphrey

Published by
Hybrid Global Publishing
301 E 57th Street
4th Floor
New York, NY 10022

Manufactured in the United States of America, or in the United Kingdom when distributed elsewhere.

Humphrey, Dana.
May All Beings Be Fed: Playing with Consciousness
     ISBN: 978-1-957013-04-6
     eBook: 978-1-957013-05-3
     LCCN: 2021922970

Cover design by: Natasha Clawson
Copyediting by: Dea Gunning
Interior design by: Suba Murugan
Author photo by: Emma Pion-Berlin

www.danahumphrey.com

I dedicate this book to all the women struggling with emotional abuse, gaslighting and codependency.

May you learn to love yourself fully and unconditionally and break old patterns of behavior and accept that life is happening for you.

Contents

Foreword

This is a story of one woman's coming of age story, her dark night of the soul, her hero's journey to wholeness.

Along the way, she tackles mental health, suicidal thoughts, sex, tantra, travel, ayahuasca, queerness, drugs, ancestral baggage and domestic violence. You have been warned.

After discovering and experiencing many healing modalities from breathwork to plant medicine to yoga, and through paying attention and listening to her inner child, Yaya heals and learns to trust her wise inner shaman.

Acknowledgments

I am grateful for the many partners and lovers that I have had to teach me about myself and my patterns. To be a mirror to shape my human evolution.

Grateful for my therapist David Rinaldi for coaching me on Ho'oponopono (a Hawaiian practice of reconciliation and forgiveness) and connecting with and loving my inner child.

Sam Liebowitz for displaying an unwavering example of unconditional love.

My YouTube support family: Lisa A. Romano for her amazing YouTube videos that showed me the light during a dark period.

Ross Rosenberg "the self-love deficit guy" for his YouTube videos, for helping me understand the Human Magnet Syndrome.

Dr Ramani for her YouTube videos and explanations.

Dr. Gabor Mate for his talks on addiction and attachment which have deeply shaped my understanding of the world and myself.

For the development and encouragement for this book I would like to thank:

Joan Pelzer for her friendship and real support during all the hardships and victories.

Joe Fox for his coaching mentorship.

Rebecca Secchiano for her ongoing diligence, hard work, great ideas and assistance for all my wild ideas and projects.

For my publishing partner Karen Strauss for mentoring me and encouraging me from the very beginning in my author's journey.

Naketa Thigpin, my amazing friend and life and business coach for inspiring me and empowering me to self-validate, let go, PAUSE and find my bold balance and permission to be selfish, so I may serve from a full cup.

My Capricorn sister, Sally Montiano for her steady and solid presence in my turbulent life in my 20s.

Neva Talladen, my editing partner and patient, understanding writer, thank you for riding this publishing wave with me and making it fun.

Kamala Devi for their mastermind book course making this possible and openness to partner and co-create with me.

To my sister Andrea for her love and encouragement.

To my parents, Leila and Thomas Humphrey for supporting my travels and growth.

And to all who want the best from life and are willing to step out of their comfort zone and take chances.

Prologue

There are three Cs in life: cats, cookies, and champagne. At least, that's what it felt like at my going away party. It was a clear day in Guatemala, on the expansive wooden platform deck at Eagle's Nest, and I could see straight through to the rippling lake water, volcanoes, and the neighboring barrios. We painted whiskers and put cat ears on each other. The glitter was overflowing.

This sounds like any other party that spontaneously erupts in a wet jungle. Except that it wasn't. The sun was high in the sky when we started because we knew we had to go before the 6pm curfew. It was the summer of 2020, and the COVID pandemic had reached everywhere. This tropical paradise was no exception.

In this moment, I felt so light and free. My almost-bare scalp was still a new sensation, and I couldn't stop feeling it with my hands every chance I got, the memory of the full moon ceremony still lingering in my mind.

In the winter of 2020, the year that most people refer to as the 'before times' (B.C. as in Before COVID), I flew to Guatemala, and promptly got stuck there. There were worse places to be, and the uncertainty of what was happening there, along with the fact that there wasn't much anyone could do about it, made it all feel so destined to be – that I, along with the dozen or so people from different parts of the world, were called to be 'stuck' on that lake.

Looking back, I can see that I took that journey not just for the retreat that I had originally signed for, but because I was following an instinct that I've always had since childhood, and it has carried me through all my life experience. I was called to be there.

Whatever giant forces have always moved the world in one direction or another, there will always be some things that shake loose and go their own way. And with the heavy shroud of the pandemic enveloping everything, I felt like I was one of those things that got shaken out into that corner of Guatemala, left to roll how I pleased.

Then again, it's always seemed to be the case for most of my life. I lived in the same world as everyone else, but it sometimes felt like I was thrown just off-orbit, touching the surface, and moving in my own direction.

During the full moon ceremony, one month before, I shaved my head. What started as a joke became a self-fulfilling prophecy, and a lesson on the power of words.

If we're still here by May, I'll shave my head, I said then. And through the inspiration of a neighbor, the joke turned into a rite of passage, an unexpected shedding of myself.

Part of me thinks it wasn't a very pivotal moment in my life; that it was a moment of self-expression more than a major decision. But I know that the ritual would forever stay with me: burying part of my hair to represent the past, burning some in honor of the present, and donating the rest as a legacy to the future.

My closely shaved hair grew into a Mohawk, which certainly didn't look as 'no-big-deal' as I thought, either. When I got back to New York, it was friends and people who had known me for years who seemed to feel the impact, almost more than I did. Then again, hair has always been, and would always be, considered a symbol more than a body part. As inessential a head of hair is to human survival, it's become the stuff of the greatest legends: a source of superhuman strength, a display of guile, a tool for oppression, a feared instrument of sin.

All of my life, I've never given much thought to my own head of hair. But I've always worn and used it as I was expected, from the length, style, color – and as spontaneous and intuitive as the hair ceremony was, I have to admit that there was a part of me at work there, too, shaking loose into my own trajectory, manifesting and symbolizing the shift inside me through the letting go of my hair.

My friends had quite the reaction:

According to Connie, "It felt like an invisible veil was lifted, and we could simply be in our humanness even more greatly together."

My business partner said, "You've definitely come into more of who you are, from what I've seen -- calmer, more content, and happier!"

Capricorns are notorious for not wanting to explain themselves. I think I've always brewed the narration of my life story privately in my head. But it was shortly after coming home from Guatemala that I began putting it into words.

People tell their life stories for different reasons. But I believe for most, as it is for myself, it's because the telling makes it real (yes, *it happened*), and because the story is sometimes the only gift we have in our power to give in return for the privilege of living in this beautiful world.

I'm telling my story as the 'herstory' of Yaya, the girl that I was, and how my given name was pronounced when I first emerged into the world. It's a true story as much as any story could ever really be true. But we live in a world with social contracts, after all, and some truths I have to own up to before we go any further:

1. The events I narrate here are from my memories and my perspective. They are impressions and feelings in the moment, which are genuine and important – if not more so – than the things as they happened. The conversations are most likely

not verbatim, and should be considered as approximations. These exchanges are me saying, "It went a little something like this..."

2. These stories aren't always told in a chronological sequence. My telling is not meant as a historical reference, but a telling of major events that have shaped me as Yaya.

3. I'm sharing this story out of need and out of love. The title of this memoir, "May All Beings Be Fed," has become a lens that I see the world by. And while I am fulfilling my mission to share my story, I am conscious of making sure that the people I mention here are not maligned or harmed. I've only used real names for those who have consented, but the major characters have been renamed, and in certain cases, combined into a composite character without altering my personal experience, impressions, and insights. All beings deserve a chance to thrive, not just survive, and so, like the spider I leave in the corner of my ceiling as it spins, I've also made sure that these people who have been part of my story may continue undisturbed in their own corners.

4. Lastly, however true the impact of my experience with my family (specifically, my mother), I love them unconditionally, and always will. I will always be grateful to them. True love exists only in truth, and my retelling of my memories of them and with them are told from how it has affected me, and at times, transformed me.

This story is about my self-reflection, not a criticism or tool for accusation. I've done my best to give context, but since this is a memoir, and not a historical text, the story has been confined to my personal impressions and memory of events.

All this aside, the story which lay dormant inside me has finally sprouted and bloomed, thanks to the shedding of my cells through my hair, and the shedding of the world before now.

My hope is that my story of how I overcame what I went through will resonate and serve as someone else's survival guide, and that the (mis)adventures of Yaya will be as fun and fulfilling as it has all been for me so far.

CHAPTER ONE

Origins

One of these things is not like the other.

You know the saying, 'Life's a journey, not a destination?' Well, for the girl called Yaya, life started out as a series of journeys, which began, as all journeys do, with the source of her life: her parents.

Before they became her parents, in their own corners of Canada, Tom, who was from Ontario, and Leila, who was from Calgary, were raised in families that were not so ideal for them as children. Tom's mother (Yaya's grandmother) and Leila's mother (who Yaya would come to know as "Mormor") were both fastidious women who were spiritual in their own specific ways. One was devoted to religion, and the other was deep into the mystical, owing to her gypsy roots.

Both mothers believed in the virtue of tough love, which suited their mercurial tempers. These mood swings would bring on both verbal and physical lashings for the young Tom and Leila in their separate corners of Canada.

They wouldn't meet until much later at a party, when they had both moved away from their childhood homes, and they each had sensible, reliable jobs that they made sure had as little to do with anything religious or mystical. When both decided that they were compatible enough, they did the other sensible thing: get married.

As planned, Tom's career as a geologist took off, which gave him and Leila opportunities to travel and live comfortably in other countries. The next logical step for them was to have children of their own.

They conceived Yaya in the heat of Cameroon and carried on with their vacation plans, with Yaya in Utero, spending a few months in the sacred mountains of Peru.

Her parents made it just in time to the certainty of a securely sterile Calgary hospital, with the doctor and nurses dancing in and out like Mariachis with forceps to pull Yaya out into the world.

Tom and Leila must have suspected that Yaya would be different, as she seemed to be made from all the things they were running away from, even then.

Resistance would be a recurring theme throughout Yaya's life. Even as a kid, she was strong-willed with a stubborn streak, and didn't always find it easy to embrace change.

This quality became especially obvious as her father's work took the family to the UK, and her parents often took the whole family to explore and travel Europe. There were so many landlocked countries close enough for them to reach through driving or riding the train.

By the time Yaya was three years old, her passport had logged 30 countries, making travel a comfort zone for her. She had started her childhood in London with regular trips to various cities in Scotland, Italy, or France. She was so used to motion that sometimes her Mom would drive her around the block in her car seat just to lull her to sleep.

The family always seemed to be moving from one place to another. The more she got used to the coming-and-going of life in transit, the more she longed for constant presence and stillness, which, in her adult years, she would equate to being loved.

Yaya was walking confidently in the street, bangs blowing against her forehead as her parents walked just a few steps faster than her on the gray sidewalks. She looked up at her Mom and Dad and thought, *maybe I can push the stroller today?* She took the pacifier out of her mouth and brushed it against her itchy wool tights and asked, "May I please push my sister today?" They were on a side street near Hyde Park, where the London traffic was subdued yet steady and geese flew overhead. "Sure," her Mom replied, and let Yaya take the reins of the stroller's handlebars.

Yaya quickly pointed up at the winged creatures overhead and called out to her parents, "Pigeons!" pointing and exclaiming, meanwhile, wanting to rid her life of her pesky new attention-seeking younger sister, she pushes the stroller horizontally off the sidewalk and into the middle of the road. She keeps walking, now with a bit more of a pep in her step. "That's not where we put your little sister," Mom snipped sternly and loudly with pursed lips.

Yaya was going through her own cycle of jealousy and didn't live in a household where she could verbalize this. There was a shared belief in their family, that there was a lack of love in the world.

Yaya loved going to preschool at the nearby Jewish synagogue on their street. She was a non-Jewish shiksa, who loved singing the songs and playing the jingling instruments and clanging tambourines in a circle with the other little kids.

But her Mom wasn't always so enthusiastic about life in London. It was an unfamiliar city that she was trying to navigate with her two very young children, all without a strong support network.

One day, whilst out shopping with her Mom at Marks & Spencer's, Yaya saw some challah bread, usually saved for Shabbat, grabbed it and started munching on it. What followed would be one of Yaya's lasting childhood memories of her Mom: the quick scolding, the pointed reminder that it was her fault, and that she, a small child, was 'ruining it.' From then on, Yaya learned to be afraid of disapproval as she thought this would mean having love withheld from her.

She saw how different things were for the other kids at her preschool. When she went to a schoolmate's fourth birthday party, she was blown away that his home had a butler, and that they had a game room, a big bouncy house, and their very own movie room.

This was one of the few times Yaya would tell her Dad, "When I grow up, I want to be Jewish."

When Yaya's parents announced they would be moving from London to California, Yaya, as expected, gave a hard "no" to this concept. Hands on her five-year-old hips, she proclaimed that she was not going to go.

But after her parents explained that California was "like Italy," with lots of sunshine and gelato, she eased up. Although she didn't want to miss her friends and leave the life she knew, she became more and more excited about the promise of this life across the pond.

In the Spring of 1989, they arrived in the Bay Area in California. Yaya was plopped into the last few months of the school year in kindergarten at Green Valley Elementary School. Yaya was a trained observer, she would watch her family, her classmates and soak in the climate of behaviors before reacting. She suddenly had new words to learn. "Mum" was "Mom," and "rubbish" was "trash," and there was pressure to conform and speak like a Valley Girl.

On her first day of show-and-tell she knew she had one chance to make a good first impression and hopefully be liked by her peers. She had debated bringing dolls or cool toys, and decided that yummy food to share with the class would be the best way to be remembered fondly. So she brought in her last prized box of her favorite cereal, which to her surprise they couldn't buy in the USA: Shreddies, the sweetened shredded breakfast cereal which tasted good with or without milk. She suspected the other kids may be sugar addicts like herself, and want some of this tasty goodness. Yaya's Mom was on a permanent health kick and this was the most outrageous form of junk food they could have.

At their temporary transition apartment in San Ramon, Yaya makes friends with a tall neighbor girl a few years her senior. She's into New Kids on the Block and other really cool American things. Yaya is impressed by her and wants to hangout. When her new friend suggests rollerblading, Yaya is a "hell, yes!" She excitedly goes to ask her Mom, who says, "No."

Well, that wasn't the vibe she was going for, so Yaya straps on the skates and goes out anyway. After a few laps around the apartment complex, she falls into some gravel and scrapes up her knee pretty badly. Afraid to seek help from her Mom, in fear of punishment for disobeying, she sneaks into the bathroom, climbs on the toilet seat to reach up to the cabinet to get some large Band-Aids and sits back on the tile floor, to fix up the wound herself. She pulls her spandex shorts down to her shin to hide the area. The wound is now covered, uncleaned and full of pebble rocks, which heals leaving a bump and a permanent lifelong scar.

It's now first grade and Yaya is eager to impress her new teacher and her fellow classmates with her brilliance. Mrs. Pearl asks the class to define the word: knickers. *Yes,* Yaya thinks, *it's my time to shine.* She shoots her fingertips into the air and reaches her arm up with enthusiasm, hoping to be called on first by the teacher.

"Yes, go ahead," Mrs. Pearl says.

Yaya excitedly reports, "Knickers are underwear."

According to her British upbringing, this is a very matter of fact, truthful statement. Of course, because she said, "underwear," the young kids are now snickering and laughing and the teacher tells her that she is wrong. *WHAT?* She shuts down from the embarrassment.

At recess break she goes to her dingy cubby and rearranges her stuff, feeling gloomy about the prospect of playing with other kids after her major unjustified defeat today.

Why was the world so unfair? she thought. *When would she catch her break?*

5

Well, soon after thinking this, her Mom found out that they were reciting the Pledge of Allegiance every morning at school and quickly put a stop to that. She writes Mrs. Pearl a note declaring that her Canadian daughter would not be participating in this ridiculous American ritual each day. One more ding for Yaya's goal to be a chameleon and fit-in like the other 1st graders.

Yaya befriended Mei, a calm well-behaved Chinese girl, their parents wanted them to be friends. On Chinese New Year, Mei taught the class how to use chopsticks. She offered a show-and-tell where each child got a set of chopsticks and got to practice holding them and using them. This skill would stay with Yaya through her life, an asset, a little cooler than being able to tie your shoes.

Yaya fiercely lacked community and despised spending too much time at home alone with her family. She quickly found out from a few sparse Easter and Christmas visits, that church was a place of fun! There was singing, other kids, nice adults, clean bathrooms, and most importantly, there was cake with frosting.

She started asking to go to church every Sunday. Deciding this was a wholesome and respectable activity, her Mom obliged, taking the girls to church on the weekends. Yaya loved belting out loudly in worship and enjoyed the community vibe, happily saying hello and smiling to greet their neighbors.

These moments from her childhood prompted her Mom to call her, "Moana." Like the Disney character, young Yaya's headstrong and journey-loving nature was bursting out of her. Unlike her parents, Yaya always had strong opinions, taking pride in herself. To her parents' dismay, Yaya was very much her grandmas' granddaughter: an intercessor and a heretic by nature.

Even in childhood games, Yaya did things differently. While the other girls were playing with dolls, or playing regular tag, she would run and jump over the drawbridge, playing Kissy Monsters, a kind of tag game that Yaya would play with the boys, except instead of a touch, she 'tagged' the boys she caught with a kiss.

The fight on what to wear to school was a daily conundrum. Yaya's Mom had her brunette hair in a bowl cut and insisted she wear muted colors like yellow and beige and green. She was seven years old and stymied from self-expression in all areas of her life, especially visually. Yaya was a child of the 80s and dreamed of wearing the hot pink spandex she sometimes saw on the music videos on MTV or Vh1.

There was one light yellow dress with many ruffles and very faint bumble bees on it that they would often agree to compromise on for Yaya to wear to class. Yaya's Mom wanted her to look proper, with frilly socks and Mary Jane shoes, and often a Laura Ashley floral dress to match with either her or her sister. Yaya wanted to break free into her own style and experiment with bold color and texture.

One afternoon, Yaya's sister Andrea and her friend Ashley got into the toys. They took every vestibule of toys, dumped them clearly on the floor, and mixed up all the games, Lego, dolls, puzzles and books. We are talking about every single craft bin in the closet and toy boxes and books under the bunk beds.

Yaya always thought that Ashley was trouble, but nobody really listened to her. She often felt invisible. The naughty duo were laughing and having a child's party in a sea of toys in Andrea's room. Yaya definitely felt the need to tell on these mischievous scoundrels as she was a truth teller.

To Yaya's surprise the naughty girls barely got in any trouble. *What was going on?* She was thoroughly confused. If one thing was out of place in her room she would be punished, but when her sister made a mess to the extreme, it was like nothing happened? She was pissed off.

She took her frustration and channeled it into a project, convincing her Dad to hang a hammock with her in the yard, creating a place of respite to go when she was feeling upset. She was her Daddy's brown-eyed girl and usually could coral him into doing projects, especially if they were construction oriented. Clearly, Andrea was the Golden Child and Yaya was just going to have to get used to it. The hammock installation cooled her down from the confirmation in her mind that there was clearly a double standard in the parenting around there.

Another project that Yaya and her Dad completed was a life-size, two-story playhouse in the backyard, complete with a toy stove, kitchen, and a sturdy ladder to the roof. The roof was tarped with bright blue that the homeowner's association didn't like, as you could see a small part of it in the front yard and on the main street. They asked Yaya's family to take it down, but her Dad refused. Yaya admired him for it.

* * *

It's the wee hours of Christmas morning, still dark out. Yaya tiptoes to the living room and switches out a gift from Santa for her sister, for a lump of coal, which she has been saving up from the barbecue. She had learned in class that bad kids get coal and good kids get toys. Since Andrea had been naughty and not been punished, now was her chance to make things just in the world.

She wrote on the stuffed piggy that Santa had left, "from Yaya." Yaya was in a dark place. She was not aware of the consequences of her actions. She had recently gotten angry at school and used her child's play scissors to cut off another girl's braid. After that, she knew for sure she didn't like being in trouble, and learned to be stealthier in her mischief.

Andrea woke up excited to have a new piggy to snuggle with. She was an easy kid and was going through an 'I love pigs' phase. She collected beanie baby pigs and piggy banks and wore pig themed sweatshirts. She was also going through a migraine phase, eventually deciphered as a cheese allergy, Yaya would later learn to diagnose it as a result of being under the pressure of their family dynamic.

* * *

"We came all the way here to see this?" Yaya exclaims as they peek over the Grand Canyon's red rocks right at sunset. The parents were all clicking away with their Nikons, while Yaya's Dad was taking a camcorder video of the scenery, describing the geography and geological details, and specifically avoiding the kid's pleas to be included in the shot.

They had belayed down some sand canyons earlier that day and Yaya was physically tired. She chose to ride in the RV with the country music with one of the other families. There were four families traveling together, and she would mix and match who she rode with to get a break from her own family, which she thought was boring. The radio station they were blasting that day mentioned that Easter was coming, and alluded to the fact that the Easter Bunny wasn't real.

Impressionable Yaya heard this, scrunched up her face and at the next rest stop, billowed out of the sliding door of the RV and demanded, hand on hips, that her parents tell her the truth about the Easter Bunny, Santa and the Tooth Fairy, right here, right now. *This was their chance to redeem themselves of these lies they had told.*

The other kids were all younger and within earshot and her parents didn't want to disclose the whole truth to her in her moment of anguish. She knew she was being lied to and she didn't like it one bit.

In her disappointment and frustration, the idea that parents were not to be trusted stayed with her. She started to feel the 'us vs. them' mentality when it came to the adults, and sided with 'team kids.'

Back in Danville, Yaya got to have her first all-American girl sleepover, even though she was technically still a green card holder. They built a fort downstairs with soft blue woven blankets and light cotton sheets. After a broccoli and pork dinner with chopsticks with Mei's family and baby sister, they got ready for bed.

They turned down the lights and put their heads on the pillows and Yaya heard "Tick Tock." The clock was ticking. After what felt like hours of agony, and from thrusting around the various pillow options on top of her head, she decided to scavenge around the downstairs very quietly on tiptoe to find the culprit. She found not one, but many clocks.

Wall clocks, alarm clocks, watches. She tried covering them in items. She quietly snuck back into the covers on their children's made sleeping area in the corner by the sofas. The tick-tocking was now less vibrant, but still audible. The next morning after a not-so-restful sleep, they enjoyed a fresh croissant and orange juice before Yaya was picked up to go back home.

It was the 90s, and Yaya's Dad got the Humphrey family a desktop computer, complete with dial-up internet. Yaya got two computer games to play: Lemmings and Oregon Trail. Following the leader off the side of the cliff in the Lemmings game was an early lesson for Yaya about following her own path and a reminder to not blindly follow. She would press the arrow buttons to make the Lemmings avoid upcoming disasters. Later she would play Oregon Trail, saving families from scurvy and plagues and weather - all with small clicks and quick choices.

Later on, she would use this to chat on AOL with friends and random pen pals, create a Myspace and be an early adopter to online dating with Match.com. The one phone line had to serve the four of their competing interests, for talking on the phone, and for the computer's dial-up modem for the internet. Yaya would often pick up the phone and kick her Dad off of his precious Wi-fi and his anger would flare up into an explosion of word hatred.

Amid all of this happening as she was growing up, Yaya started to have one nightmare that would play nightly on repeat. She would be in a barn that was her house, which caught on fire, and she would climb up the ladder and reach a place where she became stranded and she would scream (and wake herself up from the dream) but in the dream, no noise would come.

Anxiety can cause bad dreams.

CHAPTER TWO

Yaya Pushes the Boundaries

Birds of a feather fly together.

The girls were watching one of their favorite programs on TV 'Full House' sitting in front of the brown suede couch on the floor on the beige and orange wooly rug, next to each other with the antique wooden coffee table pulled up to their necks. They were multi-tasking, coloring and watching TV, and wanted to be closer to the supplies - they didn't usually sit so close to each other.

The brand new crayon box had every color in the rainbow and beyond - 128 flavors to choose from. Yaya was looking for Burnt Sienna and pulled the carton over her head to see better, when all the colors flew out and onto the girl's heads. Mom wasn't around and the two sisters busted into hysterical laughter for the next eighteen minutes. They were rolling around on the floor with the fresh crayons, completely cracking up. The new game became stuffing the box back with crayons and repeating the scenario again, by lifting the box over their heads, having more crayons fall out, and then bursting into more laughter. Eventually, Mom found them with their silly game and they went back to less laughing and more coloring. Yaya was seeing how playing with Andrea could actually be fun!

It was good timing, as Andrea and Yaya were about to become travel companions. They board the plane, bags checked, being overlooked by a tall, suited, middle-aged airline lady with brown curly hair. They each had a small brightly colored backpack with their essentials; gum, crayons, coloring books and beanie babies. Mom and Dad had dropped them off at the airport on their way to Bali, sending them off to Grandma and Grandpa Humphrey's in Ontario, Canada.

The airline lady asked them to buckle in tightly and offered them an animal cracker snack, which they gladly accepted. After the plane took off, they wanted to spit-out their gum and started breaking it up into parts, to then wad-up in their fingers and toss randomly at passengers, sitting in the seat's behind or near them. They would then burst into a fit of the giggles and shush each other. This was fun for a while, until someone was onto them and asked them to please stop.

At Grandma's they got to play street hockey out front with the cousins, Sandy and Sam. The foursome of cousins would go through the attic of goodies, and take leftover chocolate mousse batter to the old school bus parked in the back of the yard to make "chocolate poo." Grandma and Aunt Audrey took the girls to church and asked them to accept Jesus into their hearts.

Going home, they had a problem. The girls got held up at immigration and Mom got a call in the wee hours of the morning asking if she would like her children back. They brought the groggy young sisters into a holding room, asked them some questions, and gave them some juice boxes. They eventually got to be released to fly back to California.

On routine trips to the grocery store, their Mom would attach them together with Velcro cuffs, and release responsibility to Yaya. In Hebrew, the older sister or sibling is known as 'the guardian.' Yaya grew up thinking that she was responsible for Andrea, as well as for parenting herself. Later in dating, this would show up as her taking responsibility for others too, and picking the wrong partners. Strong, bold Yaya didn't need Mom and she became hyper-independent. What you resist, persists.

Yaya experienced her first earthquake drill and fire drill at school that year. "Stop, drop and roll," or find a door-frame, were the tricks they had learned in class. They had just moved into their new house in the Whitegate neighborhood and Yaya was in the bathroom playing solo pool Barbie in the sink, while Andrea and Mom were outside by the actual pool. Meanwhile, the biggest quake of the century struck in northern California and Yaya remembered what to do and found the doorway to get covered.

As soon as the floor and house stopped moving, Yaya ran outside to check on her Mom and sister. Here she finds her Mom gasping and her sister safely sitting with her doll. The entire pool was making a tidal wave and pouring into the yard full of grass and rose bushes and patio furniture.

The Humphrey house was more of a museum than a place where two kids were being raised. There were geodes and amethysts on display next to African masks and rugs from all their travels. Her Dad alone had been to over 180 countries.

Yaya would beckon her younger sister to play a little game they coined, "Queen and Slave" on these large Indonesian lounge pillows they had. Of course, Yaya, the older sister, always got to go first.

They would bust out the light gold wooden costume chest in their Mom's room, placing fluffy tutus on their heads and wrapping fun fabrics around them as skirts. Mom would be stirring her homemade pasta sauce in the kitchen, glancing at the girls every once and a while, happy they weren't fighting. Yaya would make requests, which Andrea would then obey and follow. This game went on until it was time for dinner, when they had to magically put the costumes away and close up the game until next time.

Yaya and her sister had a babysitter named Joy. Joy would bring a bag of fun things to do and play, she was fairy-like; blonde, tiny and slender with crimped wavy, wimpy hair. They preferred the boys as babysitters, the Kent sons, as they were both charming and cute and fun to play with. Their least favorite sitter was the piano teacher, who would make ramen and chat on the phone.

Playing piano helped Yaya learn to read sheet music, and then when she quit to take up the trumpet, she had a musical foundation. The trumpet had only three keys so Yaya thought it might be easier than piano, less buttons, and more breath. She thought she could handle that, as she could hold her breath for a long time while swimming.

The girls had joined the Sun Devils swim team to practice and compete among other kids. Yaya remembers an awards night, right before they announced "most improved," she had a psychic feeling in her belly that for sure they would call her name, and seconds later they did.

Once playing soccer turned up in the passion department, playing music was less of a priority. Yaya finally dumped her brass instrument, to her Dad's dismay, after a few years of unhappily playing music, around fifth grade.

Swim team remained one of their favorite summer activities. Yaya swam competitively for Freestyle and Breaststroke. She had a friend from the Sun Devils named Heather. The two of them would hang out after swim practice in Walnut Creek. Heather had a huge house, and she was a few years older than Yaya. Plus, she had an older brother with a huge porn collection, which the two of them would get into once in a while. This would forever mold, shape and change Yaya's future sex life.

Yaya hid most of her creative ideas, and buried her personal life in her journals. She taught herself to write in her journal, under the covers, in the dark.

Yaya's Mom notices she has a knack for the arts and for drawing, and gets her private lessons with an artist woman down the street. A family neighbor friend, Amanda Carter and her share the lessons

14

and they get big paper and learn to draw still life, inanimate objects, and body parts, all with fine charcoal pencils.

Yaya also had a need to read, and she would visit the librarian every few days, to stock up on some new adventures. Yaya had adapted a dissociation response to flee the pain of everyday life. She preferred to space out in her own worlds, in daydreams or escape into the worlds of others in books, and she quickly learned the way to be seen was through achievement.

She would eat her healthy lunch in the cafeteria and then return to the classroom to read. Sometimes Eddie would be there, a tall and lanky boy, ready to hold the door closed to prevent her from getting into the room. He probably had a crush on her, but at the time it was unclear, and it was a rather annoying, silly game they would play.

Yaya would escape to the brave trails that Harriet Tubman or Ramona & Beezus were making. Yaya was fascinated with these women who bravely sought out their freedom through their own talents.

Yaya had entered a phase where all she wanted was to retreat inward, to go into herself and reflect. These were her heaviest day-dreaming days. She would sit and stare out the window, thinking about *Les Misérables* and other bits of theater, songs and stories she had been introduced to. She would dream of a Castle on a Cloud, or imagine that she had powers like Roald Dahl's *Matilda* or the girl in the *Magic Finger*, or wish to be able to fly through the air like Gonzo the Muppet. She prayed for the power to fly.

She wondered if life was just one big *Truman Show*. When would the bubble burst? It was an awkward phase and the beginning of her lucid dreaming.

Yaya loves hearing "What's Love Got to Do with It?" by Tina Turner on the radio. Halloween is coming up and she begs her Mom to be able to dress up as Tina. "Sure," her Mom says, with surprisingly zero push back.

So the hunt begins, Yaya gets fishnet stockings for her third grader hairy legs and tiny black high heels, that she can actually walk in, a leather black skirt and matching leather jacket. She even finds a real microphone she can lip sync with.

Soon after, Yaya's Mom gets a part-time job as the P.E. assistant at Green Valley Elementary School. Yaya felt mortified. Mom is now around to add a watchful eye on the girl's happenings at school, as well as at home. Yaya breaks the rules just once and follows the other kids up the slide, and they all get pink slips from the principal.

On the weekends, Mom would attend a Jazzercise class at the local Grange Hall with about a hundred other women. Yaya assumed they were all Moms. The girls would tag along for the workout class, although they were supposed to be in daycare in the trailer on the side.

Yaya was very aware of her curvy body size and shape, and often got told by her mean Mormor that she was fat. So, she would wear her Mom's scrunch-socks and workout leotards and make a spot next to her, to join the workout, hoping to drop some pounds.

Yaya got some brand new construction-worker-orange, high-top sneakers just in time for the fourth grade. Instead of getting teased for wearing boy shoes, the boy in her class who was wearing the same sneakers, was being teased for having 'girl' shoes. Yaya felt smug that she wasn't the one being picked on, for once. That night, the boy's Mom called asking her to please stop wearing the orange sneakers because her son was being teased. Yaya refused.

The girls were walking home from school and they ran across the front lawn to meet their Mom in the yard who had a tiny pug puppy in the palm of her hand. They desperately wiggled like the puppy to hold it and pet him. Yaya's persistence of asking for a dog had really paid off. They had identified a pug because they were small, but had big personalities and all the books said they don't shed - *ha - yeah right*. At night they would put the baby gate up and section him off in the kitchen. Winston Bogart Humphrey, they named him, had a box with a pink blankie and he would howl and cry. They tried putting on classical music for him to enjoy and soothe him as they all retreated to their various bedrooms - with the doors open.

During recess, Yaya would take a break from reading her books and play soccer with the boys out in the field. There was news recently about a humpback whale named Humphrey that got stuck in the Bay, which spurs one of the boys to tease her and call her, "Hump-for-Free." A few days later, she ends up accidentally tripping one of the most popular boys, while playing defense to keep the soccer ball, and he breaks his arm. This earns her some street cred and she stops being teased or called any humiliating names.

Later on, as an adult many years later, she would enjoy being called a "fat slut" in humiliation play in BDSM (Bondage, Discipline, Dominance and Submission, Sadism and Masochism).

On Sundays, the girls would often wake up to Mom whistling in the kitchen, whipping up some Danish crepes from her heritage, sometimes sipping on a beer - the leftover portion used from getting the crepes to bubble and pop. Dad would be playing the radio, usually KFOG or his own mix of CCR (Creedence Clearwater Revival). He would sit in his fine leather rocking chair from Costa Rica, while Mom would playfully decorate the table with various syrups, jams, and yogurts for toppings. After breakfast, Dad would teach the girls about Jiu Jitsu and have them try a few poses.

Mom and Dad would wink and smooch each other in front of the girls, in between sips of fresh hot coffee. Yaya and her sister were privy to knowing something was different, and some deep feeling that things were going to be okay. Then Dad would leave for weeks, sometimes months for work, and Mom would get quiet and spend a lot of time in her bedroom. *How dare he leave her alone with Mom for so long?*

They are off for a tour de Calgary to visit old friends and get the green card situation worked out for the Humphrey family of four. The need to be seen was getting louder and Yaya became the self-appointed ring leader of a variety show that Andrea and her created, and they would loop in new kids at each stop on the tour. They would source local fabrics and tutus and built a cardboard box frame, so the audience appeared to be peering into a TV screen. They were visiting old college roommates of Yaya's parents, and socializing with their kids. Day by day, co-creating new shows with different kinds of people of various ages and varying desires to participate.

Back in Danville, it was school-yearbook-photo-day and Yaya wanted to sport the brightly colored women's shorts suit that Aunt Audrey and Grandma had bought for her, complete with over-sized front buttons and ladies' shoulder pads. Normally she would wear 'No Fear' shirts, which gave her courage to try to embody the messages she purchased with her allowance, or from selling home-made holiday cards.

Her tight, half-ponytail bounced as she twitched to smile for the camera against the chiseled blue school photo backdrop. Today she had prevailed against the war with her mother - regarding what to wear - and she was feeling cheeky.

* * *

Dark chocolate, milk chocolate, imported chocolate, cherry chocolate, Häagen-Dazs chocolate... it didn't really matter the flavor, strain or brand too much, the Humphrey's were an all-around, chocolate-loving family. Maybe it was their European roots, or their addiction to sugar, but chocolate was a favorite in the Humphrey household. Their 14 pound pug, Winston, was no exception.

He saw the way they passed the carefully wrapped box around from Mom to sister to Yaya, and eventually it landed under the fresh green pine tree they had picked out earlier in the week. As they gathered their Grandma-knit scarves, windbreakers and mismatched mittens to head to downtown Danville, for caroling and hot cider night, Winston casually retreated to his bed, a hard plastic crate, where the front door gate was always open.

He had musty pink and brown towels in there with a blue baby blanket for extra creature comforts. It was early December and the night was crisp and chilly, but it never got too severe in this northern California sheltered suburb. Her Mom walked out the back door and into the garage, whistling in her high-pitched 'let's go' whistle that her sister and her would recognize in any crowd, her signature sound.

Yaya grabbed a Costco brand gummy fruit snack baggie out of the pantry, said a quick goodbye to Winston and put up the cream colored baby gate they had bought at a yard sale. She hopped into the front seat of their maroon wood-paneled minivan, loudly claiming "shot-gun" before her younger sister could get to it. Dad was out of town for geology work, as usual, probably in Nigeria or Laos on one of his six-week long business trips overseas.

Mom pushed her pre-recorded church musical tape into the van's cassette holder and started belting out her part. She was a 2nd soprano at the church, and the choir was getting ready for the upcoming birthday sermon on December 25th.

Yaya spaced-out the car window, daydreaming and watching the sidewalk and streets she'd seen 1000's of times before. It was a small town, so she would scour the faces of people and dogs passing and walking or biking, checking for a classmate or familiar neighbor. Within a few minutes, they passed the high school, middle school and two elementary schools and they were pulling into Lucky's parking lot, one of their regular local grocery chain stores. Although they weren't making a purchase, they parked here and hastily got out to march the two blocks down to the bleachers full of carolers. Her Mom never casually moved, it was always a speed-walk.

First things first, Yaya had her eye on the warm cider queue while her Mom bee-lined it to her choir ensemble. Andrea followed Yaya to the steaming beverage station. A jolly, fully-make-up faced woman with a Santa Hat and jingling bell necklace, smiled with her plump red lips and handed each of them a short Styrofoam cup, halfway filled with a delicious dark cider liquid. They were handed some photo-copied limp pages of sheet music too.

They turned around, and ran into their friends and neighbors, the Carters. They chatted, sang, and socialized and eventually reconnected with their Mom in front of the chain restaurant, 'Cocoa's' big teal blue sign. There were no cell phones or hand held communication devices at this time, but the three of them had an unspoken agreement that they would find each other and meet up to return home after the event. (There were many unspoken arrangements in their special family unit).

The garage door creaked open with that heavy familiar metal scraping sound, she slammed her car door closed, (not for any particular reason, perhaps some untapped rage) and whooshed into the house.

Oh no. The baby gate was astray on the middle of the kitchen tile floor and there were little crispy black papers throughout the dining room, kitchen AND living room. Winston was smugly sitting on the shaggy rug, uncharacteristically not coming to greet them with a friendly bark and cute little wag of his stubby curled tail.

"Auhhh," her Mom gasped. "That gluttonous little shit."

"No! Bad dog," she declared over and over again.

"Mom, this whole box is empty," Yaya said, lifting up the velvety red chocolate box they had gingerly set under the tree a short time before. She walked over to the dewy glass sliding door and let the bloated and uncomfortable dog out for a bathroom break. He slowly waddled down the three brick steps into the dark garden.

"Do you remember what happened to Lydia's dog?" she asked her Mom.

"Not really," she mumbled. "What kind of dog is she again?"

"A Chesapeake Bay Retriever. Well, she ate just one little Hershey kiss, and had to get her stomach pumped. Think about it Mom, she is a big dog and that is a small bit of chocolate. Winston is about a fourth her size and consumed the whole box."

"We are NOT going to the vet tonight, you can be sure of that," her Mom raged.

"Okay," Yaya shrugged and started walking down the hallway to join her sister in the small blue bathroom for the nightly ritual of teeth and hair brushing.

This was the way sickness and injury was dealt with around there. It was generally unwelcome and dealt with later, only if absolutely necessary.

Fortunately, Winston was a real trooper and a card carrying member of the Humphrey clan - they woke up the next day to a perfectly happy, normally breathing pug.

* * *

Yaya discovered the local theater. She performed in a few plays with the local Mormon Mom in town who led beautiful musicals, like HMS Pinafore. It was a good outlet for her to dance and sing and learn choreography and to express herself and be social around other kids. However, this director had her favorites for the best parts, and Yaya wasn't one of them.

And then there was Leo. He was an obese man, as was his wife, and they would arrive casually with giant, frozen blended Frappuccinos, larger than their forearms, for rehearsals. He directed 'Snow White & The Seven Dwarfs', in which Yaya happily auditioned for and played the evil Queen.

21

Yaya has a theory that when there is a strong dark feminine character, she backs down, however when there isn't she steps up, like the Queen.

Next she took on acting in Leo's play, 'Runaways,' where Yaya had her first solo, singing on stage with coffee grinds pressed into her jeans, and ketchup smudged into her tattered white suit shirt to try to appear as homeless.

Leila and Tom, Yaya's parents, have a friend named Sharon. Sharon drinks Diet Coke every morning. No coffee. No bullshit. She does what she wants and has made a decision to not procreate. She lives in cool urban Oakland, so if she feels like buying a fancy scarf for herself or picking up a freshly baked croissant, she can with ease, and on foot.

Yaya decides she never wants to have kids or get married either, if Sharon can do it, she can do it too. *Why would you bring a child into this loveless world?*

She never found much love and compassion in her own family unit, so she idealized the idea of being single and living alone, with privacy.

CHAPTER THREE

Yaya Discovers Her Body

Dance like everyone's watching.

The Dance teacher called her, 'Day.' She had never been given a nickname before. *How fun!* She has an amenable personality-style and has a preference for things that are pleasing. The teacher shows Yaya that it is okay to be yourself, laugh, have fun and play and dance!

Yaya says to herself *Right, right, I can just be myself.* She is not so convinced, and the thought becomes more fleeting the moment she gets in the wood-paneled cherry minivan by her Mom to be picked up. She was about thirty- five minutes late this time. They had been dancing. "What kind?" Mom asks. "You know... freestyle," said Yaya, "However it feels good to move." Her Mom's optimistic look turned more into a side lip of contempt at the lack of structure in their paid after school program.

Thirty years later, Yaya would become a celebrated freestyle dancer in the NYC underground conscious dance community.

However, Yaya's newfound discovery of joy in dance was quickly squashed when she awkwardly gets paired with the tallest boy in the class, for the school country line dance. She was already at her maximum womanhood height of, five feet and five inches.

It was 5th grade and prepubescence was on for Yaya. Her body was maturing and she begged her Mom for a real bra, like she saw in the 'Now and Then' movie, not just a flimsy trainer bra for babies. She was developing breasts and wanted to appropriately cover them in the way that seemed best to do. Her Mom thought she was too young for these sorts of things, despite her blossoming breasts.

Yaya's Mom's Mom, her Mormor (grandma in Danish) was a psychic and a palm reader. She would read tea leaves and offer tarot card readings, and had a funky second hand store with gems and dolls in British Columbia, Canada. However, Yaya's parents weren't believers.

She was not a nice old granny, but she was theirs and they loved her, and more importantly were intrigued by her.

One- day after-school, when Mormor was visiting in California, she read Yaya's friend Lydia's palm. Lydia was Yaya's young neighborhood friend. The two of them would play in the nearby creek or watch TV together.

Lydia's parents had been through divorce and she had a step-Dad and two brothers. Mormor had known nothing about Yaya's neighbor friend from before, but in reading her palm, she told all. It was extremely impressive, and Yaya was completely mesmerized by her Mormor's clairvoyant ability.

* * *

In the sixth grade, Yaya chose to wear short black jean shorts every single day, even with weather - for the entire school year. As she had long arms and a short torso 'the fingertip rule' somehow always found her at the lunch detention table with a gum scraper. She would be stopped at break, in between classes, her shorts measured, and then asked to change into her yellow and blue school uniform PE shorts from the locker room.

She didn't really mind getting extra trips assigned to the women's locker room, there she got to see the prohibited female body. Also, she didn't have a ton of friends, or a lot to do at lunch so being forced to sit at the detention table gave her a place to be. Plus, she thought it was a bit cool to be at the 'bad kid' lunch table.

Her door is closed. A few faint groans escape from her lips, as she hides under the purple twin sheet and the cotton spotted duvet covers, at the sensation being created with her fingers touching her yoni in an innocent act of masturbation in the dark room. The door jams open with an arm and she quiets down.

Yaya's Dad insists that for the sake of the home heating system and conserving energy, that Yaya's door remain permanently open. She peeks her eyes out from under the covers, her fingers dripping with her own wetness. She is hoping he can't smell what she can smell, from seven feet away as he stands by the foot of the bed.

On her 13th birthday, Yaya watches three drops of blood drip into the porcelain toilet of the middle school bathroom- and she lets out a squeal of exclaim. Yaya is thrilled, scared, nervous and proud to have made it to this initiation.

Yaya gets a giant white sticky pad from the nurse's office and gets a late pass to class. When she gets home from this significantly important day, which is both her first day as a teenager and her rite of passage into womanhood, her Mom is ready with a white paperback book with caricatures about the puberty process. She gives Yaya the book, says nothing, smiles and leaves her bedroom. Yaya reads it and cries.

Yaya knew that their mother/daughter relationship was strained, but this really sealed the deal for her. *How dare her Mom just hand her a cartoon book on this very important day?* She felt less understood than even before.

* * *

It's raining and they are at Cindy's house. They had been practicing their skit for core class (English and History combined), which involved two guitars, which neither of them knew how to play. They were just strumming and singing, with hopes of getting a few 'tickets to ride', which were actual tickets that could be used to buy stuff at the candy store or in a twice a year class run auction.

Cindy asks her older sister for a cigarette and they get one. *Score!* Yaya and Cindy swear to never tell where they got it from, as they sneak out the side door and huddle under the rain gutter to light it up with a match. They make the outdoor adventure seem more realistic to her parents by proceeding to jump around in the street in the puddles, which then becomes really fun. The girls are now hysterically laughing and playing in the street, and some other neighbor kids want to join them too. They then try to Febreze themselves fully from smelling like wet dripping smoke, just in time for Yaya's Dad to pick her up on his way home from work.

The Toucan Sam Print program had just been installed on their computer and Yaya was playing around with the formatting. She had just added up her weekly chore money (and money from working at the candy store at school on recess), to register for a Babysitting and First Aid class at the SRCC (San Ramon Community Center).

After participating in the babysitting training, she printed out four fliers, four-up, in color and then cut them into sixteen squares. The fliers had her name and her family home phone number. She confidently stepped out the front door onto the sunny sidewalk to place them in the neighbor's mailboxes. She started with the 'Twin's house' at the end of the block and worked her way up to the closest homes. A few hours later the Twin's Mom called to book a babysitting gig, *yes*, she was available! Yaya's Mom was not happy to find out about all of this, she thought her two daughters still needed a sitter.

The SRCC invites Yaya to come on a Youth Camping Trip and Ropes Course. She is excited about meeting new people and gets her friend, Amanda Carter, to come along. They take the bus to the hills and start to chill out on picnic tables and eat watermelon, when news spreads that one of the boys is there for Grand Theft Auto! Apparently a few of them had felony charges.

The girls had never heard these terms tossed around like this. Turns out, it was a special camping trip to integrate the juvenile hall kids with regular teens, Amanda and Yaya being the only girls, and the only non-delinquents!

This added a layer of excitement to the ropes course. They slept in a tent with the female chaperone while the men slept on the tarps, under the stars, with the far greater crowd of boys.

Back at school, Yaya gets told-on for not helping enough in the group project. In her mind, she did the whole thing! Perhaps the underlying criticism was that she was too bossy, she wanted it done perfectly and wouldn't let the other kids help. Her controlling perfectionism was starting to show! She popped a few Hot Tamales in her mouth and chewed as the teachers gave her a talking to, thanks to Penelope who had told-on her.

A few nights later, Yaya's Mom had a few neighborhood ladies over in the formal dining room for crafting and adult beverages. Yaya feels invisible and wants more than ever to be seen and cared for by her Mom. She experiments with some dangerous chemicals, hydrogen peroxide, by drinking down half the bottle in the blue tiled bathroom. Her cries for help fall to deaf ears when her Mom is further annoyed at her versus offering to help.

Yaya ends up vomiting by herself in the bathroom, confirming all current biases that her Mom is evil and that she is alone in the world.

A few days later, after school Yaya tells her Mom, "That sucks" after debating her homework schedule. Her Mom draws in her breath like a reverse whistle, grabs Yaya by the ear with her crispy flaky fingers and pulls her to the bathroom to forcefully wash her mouth out with bar soap. (She had developed a finger fungus, apparently from washing the dishes with very hot water).

Later on "That sucks" would be one of her Mom's favorite expressions. *Oh the hypocrisy!* Yaya was extremely sensitive to hypocritical actions from others. She would come to learn, much later, that this was because of her own self-betrayal.

After school, Yaya would go exercise the horses with Lydia and her family. The girls would ride Arabian horses almost every evening in Blackhawk. On the way home in the big truck, Yaya overhears Lydia's Dad talking about a friend that starves herself during the week and eats whatever she wants on the weekends. He said she "Looks pretty hot!" Never mind that this is an inappropriate comment, Yaya valued his opinion and thought this could be a useful strategy.

Yaya takes note and applies this to her life. After years of battling her own body with exercise, even as a child, she now knew of a new approach to try. She was desperate to be skinny like the girls on MTV, and her friend Lydia.

At Lydia's, they drink calorie-free Fresca in the afternoons, and Yaya hides delicious things under her bed all week, saving them up for early on Saturday morning when she will let herself indulge.

After starving herself most of the week and then binging on the weekend, she had developed a binge-purge cycle without even realizing it. Her body naturally rejected and she vomited the extra amounts of food she would consume on the weekends that she would hide under the bed. Sweets and cakes and candies, and some savory snacks as well.

On 8th grade graduation night, she weighed fifty pounds less than her usual size. Yaya splurged on calories that evening, as an exception, as it was a weekday, consuming a Friday night polenta graduation meal in celebration with Mom. Dad was out of town, *again*, doing business overseas.

Around the same time, Yaya discovers PETA and posts their posters all around her very colorful room, next to Kermit the frog. She watches a few videos and starts to believe some of their philosophies around the free-range movement. Yaya declares to her family that she will only be eating free-range chicken from now on, and otherwise no other meat.

Yaya's Mom prepares a lovely peaches and pork meal and tells the family it's free-range chicken. Yaya's brewing hatred toward her Mom continues to build, as she discovers the lie, halfway through the meal.

Yaya finds respite in the church youth group on weeknights, plus it's a fun and family-approved outlet to escape the struggles of life at home. Millie is one of the cool girls at youth group, one year Yaya's senior. She calls Yaya "Sox" because she always wears her socks pulled all the way up, a soccer player vibe. They play Frisbee golf and other sporty type games, including goldfish swallowing.

Yaya gets her wisdom teeth pulled and ends up waking up every few hours, post-surgery to take more Vicodin. After a day or two, she is out of her painkiller supply and her parents refuse to refill her prescription.

As usual, Yaya takes matters into her own hands and rides her bike to visit Millie at TCBY, the frozen yogurt shop, in San Ramon, which was a ten-mile bike ride. Her inner child usually gets what she wants, although not necessarily always what she needs.

Apparently, Millie had a couple of painkillers to spare from when she had her own molar surgery. Yaya ended up helping out behind the yogurt counter for a few hours, while Milo (Yaya's nickname for Millie) was short staffed. They both gossip about their youth pastor who has been checking out porn on the work computer at church!

The porn-watching youth pastor is asked to leave and the new youth pastor comes to town with his wife. They organize a new mission trip for the youth group to head to San Felipe, Mexico. Yaya raises funds and gets to go!

In Mexico, Yaya is on the roof tarring team, a happy place for her to be. She sees and really feels for the first time- that money doesn't buy happiness. Her family life was so focused on the opposite, all work and money, no joy. The area they are in is extremely poor and many of the kids are the shining example of what happy kids look like.

They played games, sang songs and hung out with the local kids as much as possible. It rocked Yaya's world and shaped her perspective.

On day five, all the women's periods sync up and they are all on their moon cycle. This would be the first of many times this would happen for Yaya. They climb the nearby mountain and enjoy lovely home cooked meals and the pleasant company.

The night they return, Yaya reaches a new low. Like a rubber band, expansion is usually met by contraction.

She is in the shower and doesn't see the point in continuing to live. *Why stay in the world when there is such poverty and injustice, and a felt lack of love at home?* She tries committing suicide by drowning herself in the shower. The existential moment passes and she gets out of the blue bathroom, unsuccessful at her attempt, but she always remembers that feeling of hopelessness marked by that day. Luckily, it was the 90s and information about suicide was hard to come by.

Yaya borrowed her Dad's yellow Discman as she ran the loop, a one mile circuit in the neighborhood where the Humphreys would walk, jog or run. He usually only used it on ski trips, so it was available during the mornings when she wanted to do some cardio.

She was still obsessed with her body image. She had a tape of Disco Funk that she recorded from the radio. It pumped her up and gave her energy to keep jogging. Sometimes she would bring Winston, if she had the patience to go at his slower pace.

* * *

It's the summer of 8th grade and the girls are up to no good. Yaya has flown to Raleigh, North Carolina to visit her long lost friend Cindy from their sneaky cigarette smoking days. They are ready to play Truth or Dare and experience their first kisses with some neighbor boys on the muggy, buggy sunsets of the Carolina water's edge.

They also go to the mall a few times. They are with one of Cindy's local friends and on a mission to shoplift. The three of them try things on and end up leaving with most of it. In Claire's at the mall, they get sloppy and no one buys anything and they set off the alarm.

All three girls get pulled into questioning by mall security and are asked to be picked up by their parents. Cindy's Mom and Dad are not amused. They pull Yaya and Cindy aside to the dining room table to discuss their bad behavior one-on-one. The girls vow to be good people and they show remorse. Cindy's parents punish them and fortunately promise not to tell Yaya's parents.

Cindy's family takes them out on the boat one stinking hot afternoon. On the way back into the harbor, Yaya prances off the front accidentally and hits her neck on the side of the boat and slips into the water. Cindy's Mom is worried that she has a concussion and feeds her some sugar.

"What they don't know won't hurt them," says Cindy's Mom regarding Yaya's boat fall and the shoplifting escapade, in choosing to not share this information with Yaya's parents.

Meanwhile, during this two-week trip of pizza, soda and southern grits, Yaya has gained over thirty pounds. After watching a Hallmark movie, she no longer binges and purges. She flies home looking unrecognizably bigger.

CHAPTER FOUR

Yaya Learns Ways to Escape

Double the pleasure, but is it double the fun?

Dad, Yaya, and Andrea were blading and Mom was jogging not far behind them. Yaya turned the corner sharply and braced down on her roller blades' back break. She skidded out and landed palm first on the gray pebbled cement rimming the Contra Costa Reservoir.

Yaya was a crumpled heap strewn about on the sidewalk near the cattails. "Well, get up!" her Mom ordered. Dad said, "Okay, let's take a look here," a bit more gently.

Andrea was up ahead, stopped and turned around, with her hands on her hips. Yaya had never broken a bone before, but somehow without this previous knowledge, the sharp tingling pain signaled to her whole system: *broken bone*.

They finished going around the loop of the reservoir trail back to the car. Yaya was still in a lot of pain and asked about going to the doctor. Mom snapped, "We aren't going anywhere until we go home for some lunch." As if to say, everything else -- including a potential fracture -- can wait. Food was always her priority.

They didn't go to the ER until later that night, at least six hours after the incident. Yaya did, in fact, break her wrist, and they were going to have to put a metal pin in it.

It was the beginning of ninth grade and Yaya was chunky, dorky, and had very few friends. She had rehearsed walking from her locker to the various classrooms based on her freshman year class schedule.

She wore a new light blue lacey tee and khaki pants, as well as a hot pink cast on her right wrist for her back-to-school wardrobe.

At mid-morning break a group of girls hug and joke around, eating fruit and wearing matching black Monte Vista Softball hoodies. She recognized one of them from her soccer days. Yaya walks up to her and re-introduces herself. Yaya gets introduced to the whole group with ease, and meets Sofia, who also has a cast on her arm, hers is just plain white. The two of them bond immediately over their casts, and become fast friends. The girls whip out Sharpies and start tagging both casts with joyous vigor.

* * *

Yaya and friends pile into the red convertible and head to downtown Danville to get Anna a meatless burger at Burger King. They pullover into the parking lot next door and Francis takes out a small dark glass pipe and a dime bag. Yaya's eyes get bigger.

"Anyone want to smoke some pot?" cheerily asks Francis. They all nod their heads, yes. She packs some green from the tiny Ziplock into the bowl and passes it around. They each light the end and pull-in until they are coughing and laughing and the car is full of smoke. They were all fifteen years old, and Francis was sixteen, and she had just got her driver's license and car. Yaya remembers her parents saying that red cars were more dangerous than other cars. She knows they just didn't want Yaya hanging around Francis, either.

They finish smoking the contents of the tiny bag. "Can we get more?" Yaya asks. Francis says that they can.

So they pull out of the parking lot and open the windows just a crack to let the smoke billow out, and a few minutes later they hear sirens behind them. *Oh shit. Of course we're getting in trouble,* thinks Yaya.

The girls pull over, after letting a bit more of the smoke dissipate out the car window and someone lights up a cigarette to help cover the dank odor. The cop checks the license and registration and lets the girls go. They promptly continue on to pick up more ganja (marijuana).

Yaya's Mom didn't get home until later every Wednesday, so Yaya and her girlfriends took advantage of this after school, parent-free-time and decorated the top deck of the playhouse with bright pink carpet, a radio, trippy lights and a garbage pail. They could sit up there and be hidden to smoke pot or their clove cigarettes and talk about the underground bay area raves they wanted to attend. One particular Wednesday, Leila got home sooner than they expected. Yaya heard her whistling loudly by Andrea's bedroom window, signaling that it was time for Francis to go home.

Sofia, her 'cast buddy,' lived in Round Hill, a nearby neighborhood, with her parents and two older brothers. Sofia and Yaya were fast friends, especially since they were both brunettes that dressed like tomboys, joked around, liked to eat candy, and have a good time.

During their high school years, Sofia, Francis and Yaya took a college road trip to Long Beach State University to visit Millie, she was a year older than them and already in college. As shenanigans usually happened when they were together, they ended up going to a male strip club and an all-night rave in Los Angeles.

Through all this, Yaya always got straight A's, maintained her place in honor roll and in leadership, and was rocking it with her SAT scores. Still, her parents thought she could score higher on her SATs, so they signed her up for a preparation course after school.

This meant she could be out on certain nights during the school week, which meant sucking up every ounce of freedom she could get. This also meant getting a little 'help' from her friends, who went along with the double life of fucking around while keeping the 'good girl' image for the parents. Anna, the newest part of Yaya's crew was part of the choir, too, and signed up for the same SAT prep course. Meanwhile, Sofia joined them for the ASL class on weeknights at the local community college.

Their 'operations' were simple and sweet. They dosed a little LSD one day in choir and quickly found themselves hysterically laughing, and tipping out of their chairs. This gave them an excuse to leave the room and chill out on the nearby path, the Iron Horse Trail.

They would sit together on the warm cement and look at the sun, letting their thoughts meander. They would eventually go to SAT class -- just a little bit higher than usual. They would also use their SAT studying as an excuse to go out again after dinner, doing anything *but* study.

The important thing to keeping all of this up was making sure that Yaya made it home for dinner. This was the gold standard of participation in the Humphrey household. She could even manage a conversation, while frying on acid, and looking her Dad in the eyes. She learned to play the part her parents wanted to see, to get what she wanted. Her operations became more covert. She internalized the idea: If you have nothing to hide in your attitude then you don't appear shady.

* * *

After getting her nose pierced illegally on her 16th birthday on Telegraph Ave. in Berkeley, Yaya's parents forbid her to go to Oakland or Berkeley at all. So of course, this meant that her and her friends would rush there after school just in time to drop some acid, smoke some pot, do a few whippets, and even watch a movie before speeding back to the suburban bay area.

One afternoon she pushes it and goes with her friends to watch 'The Cell', a science fiction psychological horror film. She made it home and got into an immediate fight with her Mom, which ended with Yaya screaming, "I Hate You, Mom!" with her Dad sarcastically joking in the background that it might make for a good tattoo.

Yaya's Dad had enlisted her to take an aptitude test online to see what kind of subject or major she might like to study in college. The result of this two-hour online test: Public Relations. *That fits,* thought Yaya.

Public relations relies on emotional intelligence, multi-tasking and persuasion to get what you want. Later, Yaya would be capable of planning a PR media tour from her Blackberry, all while in the line at the grocery store

With her tumultuous relationship with her parents, Yaya wanted to go far away. The University of Oregon seemed like a good option, a whole state away.

Yaya's Dad vehemently opposed this plan and insisted on her going to a state school in California, as it would be almost 200x less expensive. The final two choices came between UC Berkeley and San Diego State University (SDSU). SDSU won out: it was about a nine hour drive away, and they had an amazing campus and a great PR program.

Yaya starts playing around with online dating and matches with Dave, chatting with him for months. She was eighteen years old and this was her first online date from Match.com. They finally agree to have a date and meet in Walnut Creek at Yogurt Park. He is tall and freckled, a pro athlete. Immediately, he wants to hold hands with her as they walk around. They get a fro-yo and chat. He wants to rub his hands closer to her but Yaya is not feeling it. She politely excuses herself and hopes to never see him again.

He later marries one of the women in her circle of bay area friends.

In her senior year of high school, Yaya expertly navigates her double life. In front of her Dad, she prepares and practices her speech for running for 'Spirit Chair', eventually wowing other students with her performance. After her speech, while walking the hallways between classes, a boy came behind her and told Yaya she had balls.

She would occasionally skip lunch to join her friends and smoke some cloves, talking about their high school life, high-quality, suburban problems.

* * *

She looks up at the player in front her, the sun peeking around him. "Are you okay?" he asks. She looks down to a swirl of red and falls over even more onto the soil, having fallen from thrusting her body forward and catching his flags in flag football. *Oh shit,* she thinks. She has her hands outstretched as if they were cupping water from a fountain and is holding a red capture-the -flag waistband and is bleeding from her nose onto her fingers, and it's dripping down her hands.

Meanwhile, Andrea decides to strike up a mud wrestling match down by the lake.

Yaya cleans up and goes to Anna's tent for some pain meds. They 'hot box' the tent with weed smoke and Anna gives her some kind of prescription painkiller from her bag of goodies. Yaya visits the youth pastor, a football playing athlete from the Midwest. He predicts that she is going to have two black eyes and a broken nose in a few days. She tells him she wants to stay.

During Truth or Dare, Yaya shares some slutty information about herself that the youth pastor's wife finds too inappropriate. A few other girls also share some juicy dirt. The youth pastor's wife blackmails them to come to Bible study once a week at their house, and then she won't tell their parents. They end up doing sexual recovery Bible study for a few months.

In high school, she was grounded a lot, but was allowed to go to two concerts a month. This October, the Bridge School Benefit Concert was one of them with a stunning lineup featuring: Stone Temple Pilots, Crosby Stills and Nash, The Red Hot Chilli Peppers, and Neil Young at the Shoreline Amphitheater. It was raining and the concert was still on, rain or shine. They had grass section seats, which was pretty much why they went, to be able to lay out a big blanket and smoke weed and dance and sway at their leisure.

They were a bit unprepared for the rivers that would come soaking through their tarp setup as the rain persisted. They arrived plenty early to dose their LSD and whatever other substances were the vibe of the night, but Yaya was getting cold and wet before the concert had even begun. She struck a deal with their neighbors who were searching for a Chapstick. "Trade me a garbage bag for a slightly used Chapstick?" She popped her head through the thin, black plastic, creating a makeshift raincoat over her clothes. *Problem solved.*

* * *

Yaya had been babysitting the next door neighbors one night when she got a call from her sister. "Hey," Andrea whispered. "Mom and Dad just watched some 60 Minutes special about raving and they searched your room," warned Andrea. "You are going to be in a *lot* of trouble."

Instead of keeping her home, this warning sent Yaya out raving for one last hurrah before facing major punishment. Her parents found whippets, drug paraphernalia, 'candy' bracelets that glowed in black light for raves, alcohol, and worst of all, her diary. She was part of the bay area underground raving dance scene.

Yaya's parents simultaneously threaten that they're considering moving the family to Perth, Australia for the remains of her senior year. So, Yaya improvised Plan B behind their backs, enlisting the help of the neighbors. She had it all figured out: she can go to a local boarding school, and live with the neighboring family during academic breaks. In the end, the Humphreys stayed in California for a few more years, after all.

Soon after, she is taking a stroll with Francis down Telegraph Avenue in downtown Berkeley after school. They are on their way to Amoeba Records, hoping to maybe catch a slice at Blondie's Pizza. They pass by a handsome curly brown-haired chap in baggy jeans and a polo shirt who starts 'spitting game' (slang for hitting on her) at Yaya. She likes it. The three of them decide to go to the roof of the nearby parking lot to smoke a blunt together and do some whippets.

They get chatting and he tells her his name is Vin and that he is Celtic and Hispanic. He asks for her number before they head out and she happily gives it to him, with a kiss!

A year has passed since the last Spirit Chair election and Yaya is running again, this time unopposed. She wins and is thrilled to wear the Musty the Mustang Horse mascot costume to the Friday night football games. However, the inside of the horse is sweaty and dusty and musty! Yaya immediately comes up with an ice cream sundae fundraiser plan to raise money for a replacement costume.

The giant, extra-long sundae in rain gutters turns out to be quite a messy disaster, but she gets leadership to approve the funds regardless, and get the new outfit. Andrea, her younger sis becomes the incoming Spirit Chair the following year making it a Humphrey family tradition. The Spirit Chair plans theme costume days on campus.

The leadership class President hosts a full-on party and sleepover at her home, which Yaya is allowed to attend, as it's a school or church activity. Yaya gets drunk for the first time on Natural 'Natty' Ice Beer, and cuts her foot on some glass. She wakes up, head first in pillows in the backyard, "tagged" with markers all over her face and body.

Yaya knew she couldn't go home in her current state. Her parents would flip. She calls Francis for an emergency pick-up. Luckily, Francis had graduated early, and was able to drive her back to her empty house. Yaya lays out on Francis' driveway like a piece of bacon and gets hosed off and scrubbed down to get all the sharpie-writing off of her skin.

Yaya and Andrea, full-fledged allies at this point, decide to craft their own little party when their parents went to visit a friend's far away apricot farm. Andrea invited her twelve girlfriends over, Yaya invited hers, and they hosted a slip-n-slide day party in the backyard. The girls figured they had at least eight hours of freedom to play, drink, and get high while their parents were away.

Vin and Yaya are wildly in love and using terms 'boyfriend' and 'girlfriend' in no time. She would take the Bart train to MacArthur stop in Oakland after school weekly to go meet up with him and his boys. They would chill at someone's house, or have sex in his room at his parent's house. Vin's Dad worked for the same oil company as Yaya's dad, which she milked to her favor as much as possible in getting in good graces with her parents.

One night Yaya's parents went away for the night and got the girls tickets in the city (San Francisco) to see *Rent* as a special night out. Vin joined them on Bart on the way home, and the two lovebirds had a chocolate ice cream adventure that never quite washed out of the carpet. She successfully avoided getting in trouble on that particular occasion, however Mom was suspicious about why the hallway was extra sticky after that weekend.

For Senior Ball, Vin was her date. Yaya had gotten a navy and pearl vintage dress at the thrift store, which Anna's Mom was fixing for her to fit properly. It was strapless and fabulous. The girls all took photos at their friend's house with their dates.

Vin was mad late so Yaya started posing with Carrie Wise's Dad. He loved the attention and she loved not standing solo, when everyone else was with their date. Just before the limos were about to pull out, Vin showed up, dressed in a tux and red-eyed, ready to go.

They took some MDMA that night. Yaya was in leadership class and feeling over the moon in gratitude in this blissed-out state, so she was hugging and thanking the principal and vice principal, pupils dilated beyond belief. They had a fun Senior Ball dancing up a storm and going back to Sofia's to keep partying and eventually crashing. Yaya and Vin had sex on Sofia's couch, and she never heard the end of it.

After high school Sofia decided she would like to be called by her real name, Sophiane. Yaya was resistant to the change, however later she would grasp one of the principles of Kwanzaa, to call a person the name they want to be called, and honor her friend's choice.

They load up the minivan and Yaya and her Dad pull out of the driveway, waving goodbye to Winston, Mom, and Andrea. They spent the whole day on the road, heading south. They make it to the parking lot of the freshman dorms at SDSU and put the hazards on while they unload sheets, personal items, and a computer into the elevator, and into the tiny jail-sized dorm room.

After Yaya hooks up with her roommate's friend, the two of them aren't having the best cohabitation situation. A few weeks in, Yaya gets a random call asking if she wants to move into the new dorm, her first priority pick. The following weekend she takes a rolling cart of stuff over to the brand new dorms and says hello to her new seven roommates in their all-girl suite, complete with the seven boys across the hall.

They had a mini kitchen and a communal living room and bathroom on the ground floor. Yaya started fluffing up the sheets to accommodate her Powerpuff Girl comforter and was introduced to Jane, who she would be sharing a room with. Jane had just said goodbye to the other roommate who they had nicknamed,

'Fat Steph.' The new roommates all eyeballed Yaya up and down, carefully wondering if she was friend or foe. They end up getting drunk that night on the booze Jane had stored under her bed in a trunk with locks, and became good friends.

Yaya and her fellow dorm sisters became regulars at the nearby Theta Chi fraternity house. Rapper, Andre Nickatina, was performing at the frat house that night. They were expecting a bigger crowd than normal, and there was a twenty dollar cover charge per person to get in.

The girls swarmed the bouncer, offering him fries and a swig of their flask. Eventually, he let the four of them in with this trade. The girls marvelously find themselves in the back green room, without any effort, not too much later, smoking blunts with Andre himself. It was an epic night that was definitely one for the would go down in the books.

Another night, there was an after-party back at the dorm after a party bus visit to Tijuana, the Mexican border town, and someone's guest had let the water frog out of his bowl and he was jumping around the suite. The next day when they groggily rose and Yaya started making her famous grilled cheese sandwiches for everyone, (made in the toaster and on their Meal Plan supplies), she found poor froggy, croaked on the living room couch.

One of the roommates got up and was in the mood for a group shower, so they all put on their bikinis and showered together in the oversized disabled shower they had in their bathroom.

On September 11th, Yaya is hustling her hungover body across campus to make it on time to her 8am Honors Communications 101 class. She opens the door, sweat running down the sides of her face and sees that the class is watching what looked like a movie. *Thank God*, she thought, and took a seat in the back.

It was the kind of day where everyone remembers exactly where they were, and what they were doing. To this day, Yaya even remembers exactly how her flip flops glittered in the sun on the pavement on the way to class. She remembers realizing that what looked to be *King Kong* or *Godzilla* on the screen turned out to be the real live news, and the buildings crashing down were the Twin Towers in New York. All classes are called off for the rest of the day.

* * *

This first year of university, Yaya meets a friend who interned in India, and right away Yaya wants to know more. She joins the international business club called AIESEC. She meets new friends and gets matched with a paid work abroad internship in Istanbul, Turkey.

It was a fabulous win all around.

She buys her plane tickets and packs her bags, leaving the rest in storage in San Diego for the summer. Just two days before she is supposed to fly to Istanbul, she finds out that her job has been canceled. Yaya's Dad advises her to go to Turkey anyway for at least two weeks, and if it doesn't work out she can always come back. She takes her Dad's sound travel advice and goes for it.

She lives at the Bilgi dormitory in Istanbul, and gets an interview at Turkcell, Turkey's only company on the NYSE (New York Stock Exchange). She gets the job at their Treasury department, working on the intranet and encouraging their team to speak conversational English.

Nineteen-year-old Yaya is running around the streets of Istanbul, drinking local Efes beer and smoking narghile, also known as hookah. It's 2002, the World Cup is on -- a beautiful time to be in the sexy, cosmopolitan city of Istanbul.

Turkey is winning, Turkcell is a sponsor, so soccer is beyond fun to watch. Plus, she is there with 60 students from all around the world.

They take group bus vacations to Ephesus and Cappadocia, and they visit ancient ruins and experience Turkish nights with belly dancing and Raku (an anise/licorice tasting alcoholic beverage). On one occasion, Yaya almost misses the bus back as she gets completely intrigued by the circular basement where royalty kept their pigeon collection. It was mind-blowing that an animal, like the pigeon, who was despised in many parts of the world, especially London, UK where she grew up, was so sacred here.

In Cappadocia, she was supposed to go on a hot air balloon ride at sunrise. However, she got a bit too wasted at the Turkish night on wine and Raku and she thought she had lost her purse. It was safely in her room; she just hadn't brought it to dinner. So in the morning the crew going hot air ballooning didn't wake her up, as they assumed she wouldn't be able to pay for it, without her purse. She sadly missed out on this epic adventure.

Back at work, at Turkcell, she is given lunch tickets to use daily at nearby restaurants. Late at night on Istiklal Caddesi, the main street in downtown Istanbul, Yaya would find dolmas, ice cream, burgers, and other drunk munchies to feast on.

To Pamukkale, she traveled solo. She would go to this Turkish Wonder of the World by day only to be disappointed by the guard railings blocking access to touch the shiny white stone and crisp turquoise waters. By night, she was invited by the son of her hostel, to visit the thermal waters, privately on his motorcycle. She knew that this tour had a hidden agenda but she didn't care. She moved her one ring to her wedding finger, as protection, and said yes with wild abandon.

He wanted to grope her foreign full breasts, as they waded in the normally forbidden pools. She refused and held her ground and he delivered her back safely home to the hostel. She was a risk taker and into adrenaline and the experience at the potential expense of safety. Later, Andrea and Yaya would joke that they prioritized "safety, third."

Back in Istanbul, Yaya is sharing a room with seven Turkish women in bunk beds and having a lot of fun playing popular music and chatting. Across the hall is a private room with an Egyptian woman who smokes a lot of thin fancy cigarettes and drinks a lot of black tea. This is Mona.

Mona and Yaya eventually bonded one night in a long, deep chat. They started taking each other's photos on group AIESEC trips and wanting to be bus seatmates.

Ece was Turkish, and was sharing a room with Yaya, and her English was impeccable. The three of them, Ece, Yaya and Mona would hangout and party and go to nightclubs and even a beach rave.

Ece warned the two of them not to smoke any weed or hash, or the Turkish police would chop off their hands! That was terror enough for Yaya to take her longest break from stoner life, ever. She spent those three months completely sober from THC (the main active ingredient of cannabis).

Later on, as she matured she realized that what Ece told them was just an old wives' tale, but it was motivating enough to hold back from smoking the hash until getting back to the USA.

The semester of school ends for the Turkish girls and the three of them, Mona, Yaya and Ece move into the boy's dorm. Since Mona and Yaya are foreign this is allowed, and they make a special exception for Ece to stay with her friends for the summer. *Rock on!*

There was an entire floor of Chinese guys who would cook a lot and were studying to be hairdressers. Yaya definitely got her haircut by them one night, even though there was no common language between them. She was able to find joy in simple things.

Yaya meets a cute German boy who she invited over to pre-party at the boy's dorm - where the rules were much less stringent than they had been in the girl's dorm.

They were on their way to a whiskey sponsored, Human Foosball party. Let's just say that is the last time Yaya ever drinks Scotch whiskey, as they each strapped into the giant Velcro pieces of the Foosball game, to be minions on the field, dragged and pushed around on an apparatus holding them up and in-sync with the other players on their team. It was rowdy to say the least.

* * *

The summer of sophomore year was much less interesting. She had been living with a surfer dude who would rather throw plates away and buy new ones over washing them, in a two- bedroom apartment close to the gym where she worked in San Diego. She got a job up in Carlsbad as an assistant to a mortgage broker, she would literally make cold calls all day, and get one new prospect out of dialing 100. This trained her well to speak confidently when making PR calls to the media.

She ended up not getting paid and had to sue the company in court and won. She was used to getting her way.

Junior year, Yaya decided to study abroad in Vancouver at SFU (Simon Fraser University). She found the coursework much harder than her studies at SDSU. She had a few more roommates and got a job as a server at a Dutch pancake restaurant. She could take the bus to downtown Vancouver and go party, or check out the 'coffee shops' where it was legal to smoke weed.

She met a wook (a hippie type) from Oregon who was in the dorms next to her. They would listen to Radiohead together and sometimes make-out. He was also a burner (someone who attends Burning Man).

She also hosted a radio show of world music called, 'Jambalaya' on the college radio station. She went to Toga parties and joined the Ski Club to enjoy the local Whistler mountain. Plus, she was only an hour away from her Mormor and Morfar on Victoria Island. On one visit, her Mormor recited a dream to her, which was an exact scene out of Yaya's real campus life in British Columbia. Her Mormor had magical, mystical powers.

Yaya comes back to SDSU to finish out the Spring semester before heading abroad again for the summer. Vin, her high school boyfriend, drives back with her from Vancouver to California and they realize just how far apart they've grown.

After meeting the Egyptian princess, Mona, in Istanbul, Yaya signs up for the Salaam Project, an AIESEC international work exchange program with Morocco, Tunisia and Egypt - with hopes of going to Egypt to visit her friend. Instead, Yaya gets matched with a job teaching English in Casablanca, Morocco. She accepts.

Yaya and Junior, a tall Haitian man from the Midwest, became roommates and worked together at Action Jeunesse, an NGO in Casablanca. Junior was in charge of sponsorships, while Yaya was the English teacher, for the community of people whose families worked for the train.

A train car was her classroom and she painted the inside with fruits and shapes and colors, and common basic English language words. She made her own curriculum and her students ranged in ages from 5 to 25. They spoke Dirija, a blend of French and Arabic, so she was able to pull the French out of the cobwebs of her brain, from high school, and speak somewhat coherently.

Junior and Yaya and their friends would smoke hash out of a hookah at their flat. They would visit the souk (a bazaar) and buy alcohol from the black market, after hours. They would go on adventures, her favorite was to the Gnaoua Music Festival in Essaouira, where she met Ziggy Marley on the beach.

After Morocco, Yaya had one more year of study. Jane and Yaya were living together in a little back house in a cute neighborhood near downtown San Diego. In the front house lived a gay female couple with two little kids.

After graduating college, Yaya and Jane's families were in town to celebrate. The front lawn was sprinkled with their Moms and Dad, siblings and past roommates and friends. All their friends from the dorms were there, and they had a nice spread of food and drinks.

As the sun went down, the guests started to depart. Yaya and Jane decided to walk down the block to their favorite local bars to keep the party going. They were in the middle of crossing the street, a little tipsy and Yaya locked eyes with a bald-headed man walking straight towards her with bright blue eyes and a collared shirt. His name was Zane.

He looked to feel the same way about her as she felt about him, totally enthralled, so they exchanged numbers. Yaya told him they were going to the chess bar next door and he should come. Both of their friends were on a mission to go in other directions. Later that night, she busted in the door to their home and rushed to check her corded telephone for the answering machine. He had left her a message! He was inviting her to go kayaking on the bay in Pacific Beach with him and his wolf-dog the next day. She was so excited and called him back to say "yes."

CHAPTER FIVE

Yaya Learns Her Lesson Twice

You have to sit up and listen when the universe says, "Not this time."

Yaya starts to be more aware of synchronicity, flow and timing as she navigates her world as an independent woman. She's been re-reading The Alchemist, by Paulo Coelho, and each time, she receives a new understanding about 'alchemy.' She notices it around her daily, even with something as simple as her walks that seemed to be timed just right to the green of the pedestrian light every time she reaches the corner.

Lately, she has been walking to and from the Pacific Beach area to be with Zane, an MC and hip hop rapper whose claim to fame was that he once opened a show for Red Man at Cornell University. They've been dating for almost a year.

Zane was also into real estate and sold Pre-Paid Legal memberships, always looking for the next get-rich-quick hustle.

His routine was getting together with at least five guys for 'Old Man's Night' every Wednesday, to smoke a lot of weed and write song lyrics. Yaya would be a mainstay with Zane during these Wednesday events.

On that particular night, Yaya doesn't really feel like going, and would rather stay home and catch up on some needed laundry and housework. Zane called her a few times pleading for her to come by. She lived just ten minutes away, but she was tired and wanted to crash at her own place. Zane was not having it. After an especially rowdy night, he jumps in his Black Honda SUV and speeds to her place, which ends up with him getting pulled over for speeding and arrested for a DUI.

The next day Yaya gets the phone call from Zane from prison, she goes down to pick him up and drop him off at his place, deciding to break up with him right then and there. It had been over for her for a while, and she took this incident as serendipity. This was the sign she had been waiting for. It was time to break it off.

Other things started shifting for Yaya after that. Her Dad gets assigned to Thailand for work, and her parents suddenly decide that it's a convenient time to put Winston, the family dog, to sleep. Yaya finds this decision appalling and invites Winston to live with her instead. She moves to San Diego's North County to be closer to work, and enjoys a view and more spaciousness, and her new four-legged roommate.

With Winston suddenly a part of her bachelorette lifestyle, Yaya learns that she can't be out for more than eight hours at a time, and she needs to tend to potty breaks for her beloved senior smushed-faced pug. On the upside, all the things her parents were leaving behind, like the barbecue grill and lawnmower, now belong to Yaya to enjoy in her roomy surf town home.

Yaya starts to show her knack for Public Relations with her work at Great White Wines, highlighting the company's conservation efforts for Great White Sharks. As the media outreach specialist, Yaya strikes a deal to have the wine as the featured beverage for a week-long cage diving trip spanning San Diego to Isla Guadalupe. As a reward, Yaya gets a spot in the cage diving trip. Even though Yaya had been a licensed PADI scuba diver since her freshman days, it wasn't until those dives that she truly experienced the power of a Great White. After an aggressive chumming session, she couldn't help thinking that it could've gotten through the cage if it really wanted to.

Yaya finds a slightly different career at Muttropolis, a dog and cat boutique in Southern California with plans of expanding to fifty-five stores. They were looking for a Web Content Coordinator at first, while Yaya is interested in a PR position. They end up splitting the difference with Yaya and hiring her as the PR and Web Associate. Grace Rippa, legendary for being the former Marketing Director of a national franchise, becomes Yaya's mentor at Muttropolis.

Newly single and ready to mingle, Yaya is serial dating like crazy, at one-point juggling dates with a whacked-out fisherman with missing teeth, her former college professor, and a long curly-haired, heavy metal-loving, tech dude.

Yaya learns a lot about being a dog owner from her time at Muttropolis. She gets turned onto raw food for Winston as recommended by the store manager, Caitlin. Winston is going blind and deaf, getting anxious easily whenever he senses Yaya wasn't in the room with him anymore. His yowling is a big distraction at work, but fortunately, it was only a matter of giving more treats to Winston, so he would pipe down.

Yaya continues to work her way up the corporate ladder at Muttropolis, taking on more responsibilities and negotiating 18% raises for herself every time she is up for a review.

She wears her success as a suit of emotional armor.

After years of discussion and toying with the idea of entrepreneurship, Yaya finally takes the plunge and starts her own business. Of all people, it was Joey, the tech dude she was dating, who encouraged her to make it official, offering to hook her up with one of his clients. So Yaya marches down to the Treasury

Department and fills out a DBA (Doing Business As) form. They ask her for her alias. Yaya ends up using the usual 'alias' formula: your first pet's name combined with the first street you grew up on. She registers her business as Bridget (her pet rat Bridget the Fidget) Whitegate (the first street she grew up on in California).

She regrets this a few days later and calls the Treasury Department in a panic. Fortunately, she could still change one of the names in favor of the business she was in. And so, Whitegate PR was born.

Little did Yaya know, another thing would be born from her decision to take the leap into business.

Yaya wipes the sleep out of her eyes and pulls the second brown shiny cowboy boot over her left foot. Her boss, Grace, is calling. She answers groggily. It's 5am and she is on her way to meet Grace downtown at ABC for a TV segment about how to choose the best dog bed. Yaya's purple pickup truck is filled with all the props and samples and Grace was slated to do the live segment.

Grace says "Hi, we are being evacuated with the San Diego Fires right now. I need you to do the TV segment today, okay?"

"Okay," says Yaya. Her and Winston pile into the truck and head to the station with a bit more excitement than usual in their step. This is the first of many TV segments Yaya will do in her career about choosing the best pet products.

* * *

Andrea just got back from a semester in Peru and they were drinking Pisco sours. It was April and Yaya was cooking and preparing for a big party for April 20th, one of her favorite days of the year. Andrea wanted to meet Joey, so the three of them went to a concert down at Humphrey's by the bay. A bit of a sarcastic booze-hound, Joey was on his best behavior that night and they got along okay.

The rest of the week Yaya stayed in, although friends from up north were down to visit. She was living with a few roommates in Ocean Beach in an apartment which was connected to a taco shop drive-thru. You could see people ordering burritos through the kitchen window.

She was busy making weed butter and various infused dishes, the one of significance would be her THC lasagna. By the time the 420 party rolled around, Yaya was so exhausted from baking and cooking all week she spent most of the night locked in her room with Joey, messing around and eventually sleeping. He also preferred her all to himself.

* * *

Yaya parks in the valet parking and meets up with Joey for some après-work shots. They are there for a Meet-Up group that he organized. It's one of his favorite drinking holes. They get spicy chicken wings and enjoy various sipping tequilas over time.

Joey starts flirting with a woman sitting with them and Yaya gets jealous. The two of them have opened their relationship (after they both got caught cheating), but somehow, right in front of her seems unfair. In a drunken rage, Yaya marches out front, demands her keys from the valet boys and speeds off to Pacific Beach, planning to meet up with her friends.

She has had too much to drink and on top of it she is texting and driving. The plan was never to drive, she was going to leave the car there overnight and they were going to walk back to her place. She is texting her friends and making plans, and bam, hits the center divider with her truck.

There are no airbags in her periwinkle Toyota Tacoma, so she whiplashes forward and her lip hits the steering wheel. Now, she is frozen in terror of getting in trouble, complete with a bleeding lip. She decides to flee. She crosses the highway and makes her way to the shoulder where she walks a long way, still in a daze.

The ambulance finds her, patches up her lip and makes her wait until the cops come to take her back to her abandoned vehicle. They go back and make her do a sobriety test, which she clearly fails. *Those things would be hard enough sober.*

She gets taken down to the women's prison and her truck gets towed. During the cold night in the cell, Yaya and the other women are offered a tray of hot food. None of them want it. One lady takes all the trays and lays down, resting them on top of her, making them into a blanket. Yaya finally gets out in the morning and Joey comes and picks her up.

She gets Joey to take her to the tow yard, where she has to donate her totaled vehicle and remove any last personal belongings like the doughnut-shaped dog bed in the back and her sunglasses.

She has an appointment that day at the Humane Society to put Winston to sleep. He wasn't having fun anymore in his old age.

She is sad and embarrassed, and feels like a total loser. She has to go put her dog to sleep and she just lost her first and only vehicle.

Apparently Yaya didn't learn the lesson about DUI's during Zane's drunken night in recent year's past. This time, instead of running from Joey, she cuddles up with him on the couch, to feel warm and safe, in a time when all else feels lost.

That July, in the afternoon heat, holding an adult beverage, Yaya is complaining to her friend Ron that she had to get out of San Diego. He refreshingly looked at Yaya and said, "You have been saying this for years, why don't you go?"

She was extremely grateful for that crystal clear moment. She had trapped herself in this superficial so-cal scene, like groundhog day, of the never ending party girl lifestyle. This one comment sets all plans into motion.

She gives Grace her notice at work and starts applying for jobs in SF. She breaks it off with Joey once again.

She ends up going on not one, but seven follow up interviews for one tech PR Firm in San Francisco, and thinks she's getting the job, but she doesn't. With all these interviews she was sure she would get an offer.

Sophiane threw her a moving home to the Bay Area party at her house. *The guests erupted into a riveting acapella version of the Little Mermaid* at one point, and some cousins played video games in the den.

She also attends a bottomless brunch with their home girl (from the dorms) and they go to the How Weird Festival, where everyone is strange beyond belief, and Yaya gets mugged. Yaya ends up with no ID and no wallet, and in the ER. She pulls together enough information to be able to fly back to San Diego but she is barely scraping by.

While she was up in NorCal interviewing, she also got her toes painted, a pedicure, and they slightly cut her foot, which caused a crazy infection, resulting in a full body rash. The doctors think it's a fungus and she starts getting treated for that.

She is at work at her desk at the Muttropolis Headquarters, typing away, and it's catnip day. That means the warehouse side of the building is unpacking thousands of pounds of catnip, when the doctor's call her fuchsia pink, razor flip cell phone and let her know she has been misdiagnosed! They tell her she may have a staph infection and she should go to the hospital immediately.

She hits a new low of self-pity, wondering how she will get there, now that she has totaled her car and can't drive. She has almost finished one year of MADD (Moms against Drunk driving) and DUI classes with the city of San Diego, Saturday mornings at 8am.

She starts to quiver and tear up. One of the partners at Muttropolis is passing through the room and says, "Dana are you okay?" which opens her up to a full-blown cry.

First of all, she has a headache from the catnip, and now she's been told she has a major infection, so she is subsequently balling at her desk. *Can't she just catch a break?* Grace walks in not too long after, sees her streaming tears, and offers her a ride to the hospital.

At the holiday Christmas party for Muttropolis, Yaya ends up being the only single person at the party and she feels so alone. She gets paired at a weird threesome table, thanks to the assigned seating, with the store manager Caitlin and her husband, drinking the night away and eventually dancing with her arms around the speaker at the after party at the Belly Up. Caitlin wasn't that well liked at the company and there had been a whole internal clothing policy developed to combat her specific need to wear Ugg's.

Ever since Winston was a puppy, her Dad instilled a fear in her that a big owl would come down and eat him for supper if they didn't watch him closely to do his "doo" in the yard. They had limitless cocktails available at the holiday Christmas party, and Yaya was having her fair share. The CFO of the company was wearing an owl pin, which Yaya decided to interact with, based on this childhood fear-based story, about six drinks deep.

That night Rosemary, her birthday twin (with about twenty years in between), drove her car to Yaya's house and had her husband follow, so everyone got home safely. Yaya felt like such a loser, having to be cared for by the members of her work team.

The next day, bright and early, Grace called Yaya's office number and said "How's it going party girl?" *Whew* thought Yaya. At least Grace was going to be cool about it.

* * *

It's February 14th, and Yaya is at a speed dating event at Bondi, an Australian pub downtown. She is still desperately trying to find love in all the wrong places.

About five minutes into the event, she makes eye contact with Joey. Oh boy, here we go again. She is about four drinks deep and marches right over and sits on his lap. They start making out and she goes home with him. Something familiar. What can you say? She's still a love addict.

At work the next day, Joey drops her off at Muttropolis, around 10am, her now usual stroll into work time. Most of the others arrive at 8am or 9am, but she stays late. *It's a Marketing schedule,* she says to herself to justify it. Plus, Grace always works out in the morning for a few hours and comes in around noon.

She finds the coffee pot full and nicely brewed, thank God. The hangover is thumping loudly in her front forehead. She opens the fridge, no milk. She opens the freezer. There is a big gallon of vanilla ice cream leftover from a birthday party not too long before. She adds a nice big scoop of creamy white into her coffee cup. This is the beginning of a beloved morning ritual at the office.

While she is home for a few days recovering from the staph infection in her foot, she applies for one job in New York with Working Women and gets the interview! She interviews on the phone for the Marketing Manager position and gets offered the job. They pay for her to fly to NYC to meet Natalie Anniston, the CEO, and to meet the team. She has no idea what to pack, so she brings everything.

It's August in Manhattan and she knows not what to expect. She packs suits and sweaters and all kinds of accessories and shoes.

She has one friend in NYC, Walid, a Tunisian from AIESEC and the Salaam Project, and he is living in Astoria, Queens for just a few more weeks before leaving for Kenya, and he agrees to let her stay there with him.

She arrives at LaGuardia Airport and goes straight to Walid's apartment. She is about four hours late, as she nonchalantly missed two flights that day, busy chatting.

She finds the key buried in the window sill, per his detailed instructions, and lets herself in. She drops off her big bag and takes a second taxi to Brooklyn to join him and some friends at an underground party.

She is on a desolate block with just driveways and metal garages, all pulled down. She wonders if this might be the part in the story where the taxi driver tries to rape her, but alas, they see a door open and a party ensuing inside. She pays and pops out and happily joins the party.

She is standing at the top of the stairs when a short, brown, cheerful woman smiles and compliments her dress. This is Marisol. Marisol is friends with Walid and they all hangout and chat and cheers the rest of the night.

It turns out that with her fifty pounds of luggage, she has no pairs of matching socks. She has to borrow Walid's wooly man's sock to go under her boots for her in-person dinner interview with Natalie.

While she is there for two days she decides she better start scouting out a place to live. She looks at one apartment in Manhattan in Midtown, it's a roommate situation and it's within her budget. The place they call the kitchen has a sink, a mini fridge and a hot plate - for three people! The living room has been converted with a loosely hanging sheet into the third bedroom. It's generally unclean and hasn't had a deep scrub in decades.

So she changes her strategy and lands in a brand new building off Ave M in Flatbush, Brooklyn, plus it's furnished... *score!*

She gets the job!

Borrowed from Sex and the City, Yaya has a 'Toss or Take' party before she leaves. *Which clothing will she no longer need?*

On the way from San Diego to New York, Yaya stops at a wedding in Dana Point to celebrate her friend's union of vows. Yaya and

Sophiane are road-tripping north and quickly get changed in the car on the way to the marriage ceremony.

Afterwards at the awkward cocktail reception, they meet Jocelyn, a wild Cisco employee and party girl, currently living in New York City. She has brown curly hair and an outfit to die for. She is hanging with Auntie Lola, her godmother and the Wise's family friend.

The wedding is fun and they drink too much and dance too much, and then a small crew sneaks off to go smoke some pot. Yaya doesn't want to invite Jocelyn to the after party and mess things up with her potentially new friend. She has a history of getting too crazy and ruining everything!

The next day at brunch, she tries not to disclose how much fun they had at the hot tub after party, while the girls exchange numbers. Yaya had a new friend.

CHAPTER SIX

Yaya Escapes to New York

New York City is not a city, it's a universe.

Day two in New York City, it was the Tuesday after Labor Day, 2008. Yaya bounced out of bed, thrilled at being in a city whose backbone was public transportation. Her nightmare and dread from her DUI experience was behind her, and she was determined to move on.

It might seem like pushing it when she had applied for just one job in New York. But something inside her knew it was the right one. And it was. Yaya had a new lease in life, a new job, and wasted no time, finding herself in the Big Apple within two weeks.

Now her phone alarm rang. She wanted to snag the bathroom before her roommate did. No way was she going to be late on her first day of work in New York City!

Everything seemed bright and clear. She brushed her teeth and bobbed back a few steps on the thick hardwood floor into her bedroom.

She had hustled through the airport with two extra-large suitcases on the airplane from California then shipped the remaining dozen boxes of her life's possessions in the mail.

Family heirloom lamps, her art, party costumes, Moroccan teapots and other prized items, had all been left in San Diego for second-hand shoppers to delight, devour and discover.

She glanced out the window above the twisted stairway. To her satisfaction sunny rays were pouring in. *It was going to be a good day,* she sighed, smiling. She pulled an iron-less blouse over her head and lifted her smart work trousers around her protruding hips.

Getting ready in the morning never really took a long time. She smushed some powder and blush on her high cheekbones (she had been told that made her seem trustworthy) with a drug-store fluffy makeup brush. She applied quick strikes of browns and beiges to her eye crease, followed by dabs of black mascara from the everyday pink and lime green tube she pulled out of a shiny plastic pouch. She lifted some thick-soled brown Dr. Martens over her unmatched white sport socks.

Weighed-down purse over her shoulder, she walked two blocks along Brooklyn streets with a pep in her step, going past the Dunkin Donuts (which was non-existent in California at the time), to the subway entrance Avenue M.

She quickly swiped her cheery yellow MetroCard through the metal slot. *Yes,* it worked, she thought and pushed through the spinning metal pegs. Time to board the crowded train. She felt like a proper New Yorker, staking out a place for her hand on the metal pole for the commute ahead.

She rocked as the train lurched forward in unanticipated movement. "34th Street, Penn Station," she heard in a deep muffled voice over the speaker, barely audible.

Oh, that's my stop, she thought, double-checking the screenshot image of the subway map on her phone. Her office was in the heart of the fashion district. Yaya was almost running as her hop-walk-bounce led her south toward 27th street, weaving through the swarm of people on the sidewalk.

Triple-checking the time, she entered her building. *Not bad,* she thought. The jam-packed elevator stopped on the 8th floor where a dingy sign read: Working Women. Yaya holds her breath as she opens the glass door into the office.

Natalie, with her short-blond-bob and thick, squared-off jaw glanced up briefly, barely acknowledging Yaya. Not exactly a warm welcome on her first day.

Yaya quickly finds her desk chair and takes a seat next to the woman she's replacing. They only have two days to train and pass over all the knowledge of working this position. She starts opening spreadsheets and Yaya takes notes.

They go fast and furious until a mid-morning coffee break. She can definitely get used to this type of schedule. At Muttropolis, coffee breaks meant walking into the makeshift kitchen and making your own pot of coffee. Here, it meant leaving with colleagues to the outside world and having your beverage served. She was drinking it all in.

Once Natalie leaves the building for her afternoon meeting, the office culture turns into gossip hour among the six women in the cozy 300 square foot office.

It was drizzling as she left the office. She steps over a puddle in between the sidewalk and the street just as a large gray rat with a very long tail crawls over her rain boots. While completely grossed out with this New York moment, she was also feeling magically-connected to this large strange energetic city, her new home.

Another New York moment comes in forty minutes, when Yaya starts to realize that her stop, Ave M, is not listed on the upcoming stops. *Uh oh,* she thought.

She sees a Costco in the distance out the train window, and gets out and goes for it, walking a few sketchy blocks in the dusk. The familiar layout and brand was comforting, and gave her some space to regroup.

She went in, bought herself a pizza-wrap calzone-thing and sat at the red indoor picnic table. To her delight, the couple who came to sit next to Yaya seemed accommodating, and they started chatting. They turned out to be Jehovah's Witness who do translation work for the *Watchtower*, a monthly magazine.

Losing her way turned into this random encounter with people she wouldn't have normally talked to, much less shared life stories with. They end up driving her back to her apartment, none the worse for wear. Yaya was discovering the generosity and kindness beneath the tough exterior of the city.

* * *

Her perfectly-manicured, short, French-tipped nails, snatched the shiny Diet Coke can off the pine wooden butcher block table. It was the third one she'd had this evening.

"How many confirmed workers do you have lined-up for tomorrow?" Natalie barked.

"Twelve," Yaya calmly responded, "So we will have at least ten who show up." Natalie's husband's eyebrows lifted with curiosity over the crisp edge of his New York Times.

"While we are here in the mall, go buy yourself a new dress shirt," Natalie ordered as she handed Yaya a gift card to Ann Taylor.

"Okay, thank you," she said, surprised by her generosity.

"What about my eye?" Yaya asked, pointing to her red, oozing left eye socket. "Do you think I can work publicly like this tomorrow?"

Yaya was in the throes of pink eye, something she told Natalie before the work trip. The only reason she pushed through was because Natalie told her to come anyway, and not cancel for "something so trivial."

Irritated, Natalie gulped down the rest of her Diet Coke, smashing the can down heavily and clawing at her cell phone. "Of course, you must," she uttered. "I'll have my brother, order a prescription for pink eye for you."

She breathed out a mixed sigh of relief for the medication, and frustration that she had to work in this contagious and uncomfortable condition in front of hundreds of thousands of women. Yaya slinked down further in her chair.

Meanwhile, the server appeared with their suppers. Yaya happily bit into a piping hot fresh New England-style fish and chips, clamoring for this brief moment of comfort. She then moved on to check her company Blackberry, to search for a FedEx or Kinkos location nearby. She was anticipating another late night rendezvous at the print shop to get some last minute documents for Natalie.

Her body craved rest after being on the road for so many weeks, but instead she knew it was going to be another light night of sleep, with Natalie's ongoing barrage of requests. It was their tenth city in the Northeast in just eight weeks, hosting huge career fairs for women.

"How is everything tasting?" The blond preppy server boy asked.

"Hot and delicious" Yaya smiled, eager to please.

"I'll take another Diet Coke," ordered Natalie. As they left the dinner Natalie reminded Yaya to "get a new shirt."

At the time, she was appreciative about the gift, and in hindsight she could see how it was wrapped up in a bow of disapproval and criticism for how she was currently dressing.

Yaya goes back to the hotel room after finding a black-collared, smart dress shirt to wear at Ann Taylor. Adina, her new intern from Romania, will be meeting her at the hotel soon.

When Adina came in for the internship interview, Yaya asked her, "Tell me about yourself?" Adina spent the next hour spilling her life story. Yaya got up, walked to Natalie and said, "We need her."

And that was that, she got the job. She was older than Yaya and had a Master's Degree.

They stayed up late in Adina's hotel room, chatting into the wee morning about life, love, and work. The event the next day went off without too many hitches. Natalie gave her keynote speech to empower women to negotiate, although all of her salaries were non-negotiable.

* * *

Yaya births a new dream, which propels her into the nightmare of the next decade, so she can wake up to a true reality.

When Emily and Sophiane are visiting Yaya in New York City, they visit Emily's mom's friends who are a cute older couple, who have lived as neighbors for thirty-five years of their romantic relationship.

Emily and Sophiane were working at the Toy Fair. The girls get ready to go out for the night, using every mirror in the house to dab on their makeup. They are starting the night at a diner on the Upper East Side to meet Emily's mom's friends. They are in their 80s and the cutest couple that could be, holding hands and politely waiting for one another to finish their sentences.

The girls ask the story of how they met and how long they have been together. "35 years," says the woman. "About 20 years ago, we gave each other the keys to each other's apartments." They have lived a few blocks away from each other for all these years. "When we want to see each other, it's an easy walk over. When we want space, we have it." Yaya's jaw dropped. She had never heard about such an arrangement, and it definitely appealed to her. Yaya decides upon hearing this that she wants a partner that is her neighbor too.

The girls changed the topic to Thailand, as they had just got back from visiting Yaya's parents in Bangkok, and checking out some

66

full moon parties in the beach areas. Yaya had just accepted the new job at Working Women, and sacrificed missing this family trip to Thailand with her three high school girlfriends.

That weekend, Yaya left her Blackberry at the office on her desk not wanting to be bothered with work emails during her friend's visit. After this "stunt," she was let go.

It was the first time Yaya had been in debt. She had gotten an email about becoming a secret shopper for a local store, *sounds great*, she could use the extra cash she thought. Against her better judgment she ended up sending money via Western Union, to some unknown place, with the promise that she would get triple in return. The same day, Yaya's roommate throws her homemade pot of vegetable soup down the drain, and she gets let go from Working Women after just eight weeks, which means she doesn't get the moving bonus of $3,000 that Natalie promised her upon relocating from San Diego.

Yaya is unsure what to do on such a day. She remembers stories of friends from years past going to the bar on the days they got fired. Somehow that doesn't feel like it's calling her.

Yaya decides to go full time with her business - Whitegate PR and makes one phone call to Cleo. Cleo is an author of over twenty pet books. They met over "mutt meatballs" at Muttropolis. She asks Cleo very plainly if she knows anyone who might need some PR, and Cleo hires her on the spot to handle her e-newsletter, and also introduces her to another client!

Meanwhile, she gets an email from the one client she had on the side, thanks to nepotism with Joey, and they want to hire her for more hours too! She falls asleep with a smile on her face knowing that she now has three clients, less afraid of paying next month's rent than she was that morning.

Yaya wakes up with a jolt and goes for a walk to get a coffee. It's Saturday! She walks. And walks. And walks and walks. For miles.

She passes Dunkin Donuts after Dunkin, all closed. She thought she had moved to the city that never sleeps!

Finally, she found a bodega that was open and had some drip coffee. Not exactly what she was going for, but she liked that they added the cream and sugar for her. It was the Sabbath, and she was living in the heart of Kosher Brooklyn. On the way home, she found a little desk sitting outside the junior high school. Score! A desk. The new work from home situation just got a little easier.

She decided there was no need to live in deep Brooklyn anymore with two frustrating roommates. It was time to bite the bullet and live by herself. She had lived with thirty-nine roommates in her life, and enough was enough. She was able to break her lease early thanks to an understanding landlord. She then got to question which borough she wanted to be in. Queens? Brooklyn?

After visiting the one apartment in Manhattan, which had no kitchen, just a hot plate and a sheet drawing up walls between the living room and the bedroom, Yaya ruled out the city. It was too crowded, too expensive, and old.

It was now between Williamsburg or Astoria, the most western parts of Brooklyn and Queens. From what she could tell, she could live in a studio in Williamsburg, or a one bedroom in Astoria for about the same price.

Devora, the elderly Bulgarian real estate agent she met via Craigslist, sold her hard on Astoria. She drove Yaya in her car from the realty office to the old school Italian coffee spot, to the bakery, and got them sweets, a real tour de Astoria. At the bright apartment she wanted, the landlord preferred a single girl from California in the unit versus a family, and gave her a couple hundred bucks off the rent, and so they had a deal.

Joey invited Yaya to spend Thanksgiving with him and his family in Arkansas. They spent the first night in Nashville on the way in, drinking and walking around, getting "bebidas para llevar" (drinks to go). Joey's family was Spanish and very musically inclined.

In Arkansas, they went hunting for clay pigeons and enjoyed riding around the property on 4x4s. They were in a dry county and would travel to the next town's Walmart to get booze to enjoy with their fresh rabbit tacos. This was the last trip that Joey would enjoy Yaya's company. She finally got the courage to break things off with him once and for all; they had been in a ping-pong relationship for years.

Yaya is now an entrepreneur and feels the weight of the world slowly creeping up on her shoulders. She is fully responsible for her own rent, income, bills, body and health.

She had been playing soccer in Central Park on the West Side with an international crowd every weekend for a few months. One weekend she hurt her nose, and she slipped in a pot hole and twisted her ankle the following weekend. As she walked up the stairs of her 45th street apartment in Astoria, she vowed to herself to not play soccer anymore, and instead play safer sports, such as no-contact, running in a straight line. And just like that, after her ankle healed, she picked up running.

Devora introduced Yaya to the local Bulgarian bar owner, Ivan. He ran a small lounge on the end of the street of Devora's office, about a ten minutes' walk from Yaya's apartment, called Deja Vu. Yaya loved to get dressed up in sequins, glitter, and sneakers to dance the night away to green laser lights, smoke machines, and the live violin paired with the DJ.

She did a trade with Ivan to market his bar, and in exchange she got free drinks. She would sip on her pear vodka mixed with cranberry, night after night. These were still her party girl days, in her 20s. On the weekends, Yaya would hit the clubs and house parties, and enjoy fancy limo rides with Jocelyn and her work friends, but Thursday nights were almost always at Deja Vu.

She was out for the first time since really ending it with Joey, when a small Egyptian hottie was demanding her attention. His name is Horus, The Bike shop Guy. He had brown features, tan skin, a dress shirt on, dimples, and a soul patch. He's about five foot and seven inches and likes to feed her marijuana cigarettes.

* * *

She was riding her bike where Broadway meets Steinway in Astoria on her way to visit a PR client. She just passed the liquor store when boom, the taxi car door wrenched open and into her. She flew onto the ground, and magically was fully intact, no bruises, no cuts, nothing. She brushed herself off and rode to the next stop on her ride, a bar. As she was parking her bike at the bar, she was hit by a car. She walked in and was full of exasperation, and shared her two recent incidents loudly with the bar. The bartender says, "You know, they say, bad things come in threes."

She picked up some fliers and put the plastic bag on her handlebars to ride just a few blocks on the sidewalk to Deja Vu. She is creeping slowly along, on her bike, outside the laundromat around sunset and the bag of fliers wedge in between the spokes on the front tire, propelling her off the bike and flying forward, landing on her head.

Luckily, she always wore a bike helmet. She landed on her elbow and it is now twisted the other way. Someone at the laundromat calls 911, and just minutes later Gabriela, her friend from her triathlon training, comes by, peering over her with concern. They had a whole night planned ahead of biking and parties, all gone to waste.

Gabriela stays with Yaya in the ambulance to the hospital. They have to relocate her elbow and give her some heavy pain meds in advance of the repositioning. An apprentice pops her elbow back into place in the most excruciating moment of her life. After this procedure is finished, they wait. And wait. And wait. Yaya is dying to get out of the hospital and Gabriela is patiently waiting with her.

They finally get dismissed from the hospital around midnight. All they want to do is get high. Yaya calls up Horus, The Bike shop Guy, as they are about ten blocks from his apartment. As usual, he is home. He was on disability from getting hit by a garbage truck, and spent a lot of time on pain meds at home. He agreed that they could all come by.

Gabriela phoned her husband Ricardo, she called him "Flacko," which means small man in Spanish, and asked him to meet at Horus's for a smoke. Gabriela and Flacko hangout for a few hours before they need to get home to their daughters and their dogs, and they say goodbye.

Horus and Yaya try having sex with her cast on and they find a few positions that work, before passing out for the night. In the morning they rise and get ready to take his dog Ra out for a pee.

The morning routine. Wash face, brush teeth, put clothes and shoes on, and make breakfast. Horus, The Bike shop Guy wasn't expecting company so he takes a few leftovers and mixes them into one bowl, stirs them into oblivion, and then pops it in the microwave. Yaya takes a few hesitant bites and Horus eagerly finishes his weird food creation. He then goes to open the front door. It won't budge.

He messes with the locks and uses his key, nothing. He calls the super, the super comes and is banging on the door. They are both pushing on it. It's sealed shut.

Eventually, Horus climbs out the window and down the fire escape to go get some food so they may have a late lunch, however, Ra still hasn't made it out to pee. After hours of being locked inside, the sun sets and the building super has managed to unhinge the door from the outside, so they may finally get out.

* * *

It was a Sunday Night. Halloween. They were gathering energy to go out together for the first time that weekend. It was one of her favorite holidays. Horus, The Bike shop Guy was Egyptian and decided to dress up as a pharaoh. *How original.*

First the collar, then the leash. Down the hall, into the scummy dark elevator - a few decades old. He was pulling, anxious to get out for the first time that day. His bladder control was remarkable; he knew that the end of 'holding it' was now near. His black shiny coat raised on guard as he heard a jingle around the bend. The neighbor's dog was returning from the back yard.

The air was crisp, leaves strewn all around the vacant tarmac basketball court. It seemed as if no one had played any ball here in years. Ra immediately peed, this time dismissing the usual sniff-and-search for the prime spot. Horus brought a ball to toss, the original lime green had faded into a mossy yellow, the fabric puffing up around the rubbery edges. He bounced it off the metal chain link fence.

Ra lunged towards it, strong paws skipping on the dewy leaves, catching it in his big wet jaw. He's ready for more play and exercise, but lacks the training or the genes to know to naturally retrieve and return the ball. Horus skirts to the side towards him, a defensive soccer move, jutting his knee out trying to block the dog in good fun. He calls Ra by name in a deep raised bark, as his face scrunches together in a moment of displeasure.

Symmetrical eyes are surrounded by deep grooves from his brows to his forehead from years of critical self-judgment. Out of the left corner of his big lipped mouth, he mutters something about the damn dumb dog. She takes a turn, grabbing the scuzzy ball and pretending to launch it at the back fence lining the street side of the big yard. Ra jumps in a false start, noticing mid leap that the ball is not released yet from her grip.

His tail wildly springs back and forth smacking against his side body as he approaches her, snout ajar. This time, she lets it go. Horus shuffles around as his slip-on flip flops drag on the ground making a *shhhh* sound. Ra gets a few more rounds of toss before they need to

72

return inside for the getting ready to-go process. Ra has a history of chewing up household items, usually electronic in nature, so Horus, The Bike shop Guy arranges a haphazard gate situation, attempting to block access. They slam closed the big metal door, and from inside Ra can hear the bolt turn into a locked position.

They head to the city to the club. Horus, The Bike shop Guy used to be a promoter here, and the two of them would get in for free. They go up the stairs and hangout, dance on the couches and chill around.

Eventually, Horus, The Bike shop Guy angrily buys himself a shot. He had been expecting that Yaya would be buying him drinks. It's a Sunday night, and they are both out of it and decide to take the bus back home.

Once they get back to Horus' place, he launches into a rage-filled tirade about how awful she is. In efforts to catch some shuteye, she tries to give him a blow job so they can both just go to sleep. However, she is really sleepy and apparently is falling asleep on the job, which enrages him even further. Very early in the morning, she quietly packs up all her belongings, never to come back to see him again.

After what felt like the longest degrading night of her life, Yaya hops on the R train to the city, to launch a one-month-long pet adoption Pop-up store, the first of its kind, in the city.

She has two days to set up. There are six vendors coming to drop off their wares. She has Ikea cabinets to assemble and boxes to unfold. She is tired and heartbroken and has to merchandise a Pop-up store for the first, (and definitely last) time in her life.

A few of the companies she had rallied onboard had shipped stuff. She was unpacking it and taking inventory and sorting it. A few of the vendors were local and they would be dropping merchandise off. She spends a full day in the Pop-up store with a box cutter, on her knees trying to make tails of all these pet products.

The following day she is a bit less disheveled, figuring out the POS (point of sale) system and arranging balloons for the launch party, when the rude dude from the participating dog poop bag company comes in. She had been calling him all morning reminding him to drop off his stuff so he could be included.

The poop bag guy is clearly angry. He starts storming around the 200 square foot area complaining that he should have a better section, etc. She appeases him somewhat, and he ends up leaving. All the ducks and catnip are all in a row!

For the most part, they are ready to open the doors to the public the next day. The concept for the Pop-up adoption shop is that every day during the month of November there will be different adoptable pets in the window. She has lined up a different participating rescue group for each day.

She wakes up with vigor, brews a to-go coffee and heads down to the new store! When she originally signed the contract she was promised two interns, she was starting to wonder when they might show up.

She unlocks the door and sets up shop. The lady with the adoptable kitties for the window arrives with way less hands than kitties, and needs Yaya to help. In typical cat-adoption-lady fashion, the oversized woman with greasy hair and baggy wrinkled cotton worn clothing says, "Here, take this one. Be careful, she might have worms."

Yaya holds the kitten in her palm trying not to let it wriggle away or touch too much of her body. Not only did this woman bring way too many animals, the agreement was they were to have a maximum of five adoptable pets in the window, and they were not supposed to have contagious diseases!

It was the longest month of her life. Working day-in and day-out, weekends too, no rest for the weary. She ran events, processed transactions, and dealt with customers and the animal rescue people.

The following month, on a December day in NYC, Yaya was promoting a pet brand at a winter adoption event booth for a city-wide shelter group. Santa was there, famous local spokespeople, and over 100 cat adoption groups were at the Chelsea venue.

Kittens and cats were getting applications to be adopted and all was going pretty smoothly, until an old man with a baseball cap on walked in with a big brown paper shopping bag. He said he wanted to relinquish his fish. A few authorities freaked out, and said that they cannot accept aquatics, and Yaya asked what was going on. So the old man told her that he had won the fish, who he named Monster, at the St. Gennaro festival. He's had him for three years, and he just can't take care of him anymore. She liked his story, so she decided to adopt Monster.

Her friend was picking her up later, and Monster, the goldfish, rode in his bowl, in a big brown paper bag from Chelsea to Astoria in the front seat of a new car.

She had him for two more years before he passed. She buried him under a bush in her building's yard.

* * *

After a night of volunteering at a poker charity event in the city, the photographer gives her a ride to Deja Vu for some after-partying. She is dancing her usual way through the bar and a few drinks deep when she stops and says a prayer: *Can she please just meet someone to love?*

In this moment of manifestation-desperation-creation, her dream comes true.

Within moments, a tall, dark and handsome shaved-headed man in a dapper hat says hello. They get talking and she asks what he does? He responds that he works for Moroccan royalty as a Bellman. *Wow!* thinks Yaya. She did a research paper on the King of Morocco when she studied briefly at SFU and knows all about him.

It must be a kismet.

They flirt, chat, and dance, and have a few more drinks and smoke a cigarette. He ends up walking her home and sleeping over. They hookup, and the next morning she wakes up to find him gone and a note with his watch, "Nice to meet you, Adil (and his phone number)." *Now, she had to see him again to return the watch.*

She walked to the kitchen and opened the fridge. Conveniently, her blue purse was in there! "Last night was a doozy," she says to herself, under her breath with a smile, grateful to find her clutch.

Slowly but surely, Adil moves his belongings into Yaya's Astoria apartment. She starts by offering him her gym clothes, baggy shorts and shirts to wear so they can work out together. Then, she starts to give him space in her dresser drawer. Despite her many attempts to ask him where he lived, she never got an answer. He would pick her up at home in his black Escalade after work and they would go party downtown with his Moroccan buddies, until the wee hours of the morning.

Adil activates a badass part of Yaya that she hasn't seen in a while.

They go on a date to Socrates Park in Astoria one night, walking there just before sunset. The park closes while they are enjoying some beers on the rocks down by the East River, the park attendant hadn't seen them.

In order to get out of the locked fence, they decide to scale it and climb out. This fence is about forty feet tall, and Yaya keeps up with Adil and jumps down with ease.

Adil's friends owned a horse ranch. Yaya got on a horse, with the intention to do a mellow trail ride with a bunch of the guys, and her horse took off. She ended up grabbing on for dear life onto the horse's neck, as it raced out of the trail ride line and to the front of the pack. If she had let go, she would have been trampled and severely injured or died. She stayed on, and eventually the horse slowed down and one of the trainers got him under control to stop.

Afterwards, they were chilling and drinking beers and barbecuing at the ranch, when Adil got a call from a woman. They chatted and spoke in English for about an hour. Yaya was getting increasingly jealous with each minute, feeling left out and bored, since usually the guys conversed in Arabic.

They finally call it a night, heading back to her apartment and sitting on the couch getting ready to watch Netflix and chill, when Yaya finds an empty cocaine baggy on the side table next to her. Now, she had seen the boys doing bumps here and there at the club, she had given up coke years before, and she actually didn't mind the drugs, however she did mind the secrecy. She was already pissed at Adil, and exploded into a fight with him. She goes to bed and leaves him to fend for himself on the couch.

Yaya breaks up with Adil and goes to a pet conference in Las Vegas, where she takes the media on tours of her clients' booths all day. They joke around that she walks over ten miles a day, but her feet aren't laughing.

Here she hangs with her dog trainer friend. They cackle, gamble, and eat at the Paris casino's buffet. They bring the dog trainer's dog to the House of Blues to dance with Pat Benatar. They actually sneak the dog into the concert and dance in the front row! Benatar gives the dog a face rub, and they party-on afterwards in Mandalay Bay. Drinking, working, and hanging with her pet buddies cheers Yaya up, at least temporarily.

She goes back home to Astoria. There are lingering reminders of Adil all over the apartment. She misses him. He calls her and invites her to her favorite local Indian food place to "just talk". They end up walking home together, having epic make-up-sex, and getting back together, likely all according to plan.

* * *

Yaya is asked to officiate the wedding between Adina, her intern from Working Women and her fiancé, a Persian man from the Bay Area. Yaya happily flies to San Francisco, honored to marry the happy couple.

First, she does the Alcatraz swim with her friend Francis. They wake up and walk down to the marina in the early morning with their bright swim caps. They get their wrist bands and race chips, and hop on a boat to sail out to Alcatraz with about one hundred other swimmers. The lineup into their numbered heats and jump in, on command, one by one into the shark-infested, frigid water.

Yaya zips up her borrowed wet-suit, stuffs one last bit of hair under her cap and pencil dives into the water. Tucking her chin in and powering through the strokes, arm after arm in a vigorous front crawl. Every three of four strokes of freestyle, she turns her head up to the right to breathe, and gulps a big gasp of air.

After the race, they enjoy bagels and laughter at the sunny finish line. Now she has to get ready for the wedding. She packs up her things and heads to Oakland to get dressed in her new soft pink ruffled gown.

At the venue, she goes to the bar to get a glass of red wine for her friend, the bride. The bartender gives her attitude and says, "First of all, the bar is not open, and second of all, I am not giving red wine to a bride who may spill it on her white dress before the ceremony." Yaya had to stand her ground, the bride was wearing dark green and she had paid for it. That seemed to work, and Yaya appeared back in the green room to meet the bride to be with a nice big glass of Shiraz.

She was not drinking yet herself, as she wanted the ceremony to go flawlessly well. The couple read their own vows and promised to make lunches for each other. It was all very cute.

Later on Yaya met up with the grooms' friends and was doing bong hits in the van on the street, and started to have a crush on his cousin. They ended up exchanging numbers and 'hanging out' quite a few times that trip.

* * *

On October 22, 2012, Hurricane Sandy blew into the NYC area. Yaya was sporting a hot pink wig, and hosting a Halloween Dog Costume party called, 'Pups on the Runway' at a dog hotel in the city. Adil was back in the picture and was new to Halloween, and he was happily decked out in a cowboy costume. He had beautiful olive skin and nice muscles, and was wearing a leather cowboy vest and a cowboy hat, borrowed from Yaya. She had asked him to bartend for tips.

The New York City pet socialite crowd was getting fierce for placing 1st, 2nd or 3rd in the costume competition. These women, and gay men were usually friendly, but this night they were bringing their full bitchiness. They all wanted to place and win the mediocre prize baskets she had pulled together of various dog items. The squabbling contestants deter Yaya from hosting this pet fashion party again.

* * *

She was poised to run the NYC marathon. The New York Road Runners (NYRR) has a program called, 'Twelve Plus Two', where if you run at least twelve races the year prior with NYRR and volunteer for two, you can qualify for the following year's marathon.

With Hurricane Sandy causing major horrific damage to so much of NY and NJ, the race was canceled just a few days before. She was standing in line at the Javits Center, to pick up her race badge, sandwiched by foreigners, who had flown in from France and other countries to race, when they announced the cancellation. She was trained and ready. It was a disappointment, however, with the major loss that her fellow New Yorkers were experiencing- it was trivial.

A few groups of runners ran the course regardless, and Adil and Yaya ran twenty-one miles that day. She wanted to test out some new shorts she had bought at the Javits center concessions, but she remembered the runner's mantra "nothing new on race day." Afterwards, they went up to the Bronx for "power fish soup," a thick fishy broth that was complete with all kinds of seafood and rice.

There was no power. No water. People were charging their phones at 7-Elevens and getting water from the hydrants. Trees had blown down and continued to crash down on people, cars, and homes for almost two weeks. Astoria is relatively high ground and they were safe at home, binge watching a lot of series on Netflix.

Many friends lost everything. Cars drifted away. In Rockaway, the damage was the most disturbing. The entire boardwalk was dismantled, and homes were submerged.

Her marathon race placement got moved to 2013.

* * *

A woman named Beth from Long Island, who referred to herself as the pitching queen, had reached out to Yaya with a nice note about how she rescued her pups and had been in PR forever. She wanted to meet Yaya for lunch at her favorite Thai restaurant in Chelsea. Yaya wasn't looking to hire or partner with anyone at that time, she was about five years into running her business full-time, but she was so compelled by Beth's successes she knew she had to take a leap of faith and work with this woman. They had an amazing three hour drinking lunch, in the fabulous Thai place, where the walls are made of pink carpet and the wine glasses are always full. It reminded her of her childhood double decker playhouse.

Beth and Yaya worked together for years. Beth had been booking clients on TV for decades and started to do the same for their Whitegate PR clients, and then for Yaya. The first TV segment Beth booked for Yaya was in Fresno, the armpit of California.

Yaya was visiting her high school friends. Anna and Yaya take a road trip to Fresno with Anna's feral cat, named Mother Fucking Jones, to film the live TV segment. This cat once vomited up a condom in Yaya's San Diego apartment after a party. This cat, and her hippie mama, know no limits.

Beth convinced the host of the show on "We are Fresno Live" to have Yaya as a guest with the cat, to talk about 4th of July pet safety tips for pets.

They peel into the station in Anna's swampy blue Honda Accord, running a bit late. They yank the cat carrier out of the car and bring the poor cat into the studio. They have just been driving for about three hours. Yaya touches up her make-up and they go into the production room.

Yaya displays all the gear on the table and the awkward sound guy comes out and asks to drop a microphone on her lapel. She takes a seat and they are about to go live. The cat is chilling in the cat carrier amidst the table full of products. The TV host almost introduces Yaya as "The Plant Lady," and catches herself and names her, "The Pet Lady."

Oh, that's good, thinks Yaya. The Pet Lady. She liked it. The name stuck and Yaya got the trademark and the website (thepetlady.net) and started to be introduced this way on television, all the time.

Meanwhile, the cat jumps off the table and has left the segment. Yaya recovers well and keeps talking as the cat springs up her leg, digging her claws into her pantyhosed thighs, piercing the fabric and the skin, while Yaya is expected to keep smiling - live on camera. The cat continues to crawl up, claw by claw until she is in Yaya's lap. She manages to hold it together for the final minute of the segment talking about sound phobia and helping your pets with the scary fireworks. The two amiga's (friends in Spanish) pack everything back up quickly and duck out of there, with the traumatized feline, to get some Vietnamese soup at the nearby Pho place. They are super hungry. Being on camera takes a surprising amount of energy.

Anna enjoys wearing patchouli oil, and her car and purse can usually be described as 'swampy'. You might find a used razor, empty pack of cigarettes, a bottle cap, or a half used wet nap in either location. However, she's brilliant, and loves animals.

CHAPTER SEVEN

For Yaya, Things Go Up, and Things Go Down

You want to see craziness in a person, just call them crazy.

It was New Year's Eve. Her holiday friend (the friend that she spent holidays with), was single and wanted to hangout. Yaya was still in a relationship or a situation-ship with the controlling Moroccan man, Adil. Yaya and her holiday friend, decided the three of them would go to one of those all-you-can-drink places in Manhattan. Plus, her friend was DJing.

After dancing and sweating a lot in the stuffy upstairs bar and ringing in midnight with streamers, confetti, and horns, they stayed a while longer. At all you can drink places, Yaya would get overwhelmed with choices, so she usually had at least three drinks going on. At least at that point in her life, in her late-twenties, that is how she rolled.

In college she created a homemade shirt with one of her favorite quotes, 'I like three drinks better.' Anyway, she had a beer, a wine, a water, and some kind of strange cocktail all under way, all at once. The crowd was thinning as people scooped up their sequined partners (of the new and old variety), and headed home to crash out or get lucky.

Her holiday friend and Adil both wanted to leave, but Yaya was the party girl, and she was having fun, or determined to make it a good New Year and therefore a good year. She was a bit superstitious in this way. Plus, she was somehow always the last girl at the party.

So they hugged her holiday friend goodbye as she embarked to her apartment in Hell's Kitchen, just a short walk away. Adil was quickly getting more frustrated with her as he also wanted to leave.

They had spent weeknights and weekends over the last year partying with his friends every night of the week until much later in the evening, often after 4am, but for some reason this particular night he was inspired to leave. She couldn't understand it.

Yaya's DJ friend had just ordered some fries, and she wanted to help her out with those. Yaya remembered the DJ kept asking if she was okay? Even in her drunkenness Yaya remembers thinking, *I look great, I feel great, I am here with my friend and my boyfriend, what could not be okay?*

When Adil and Yaya finally left, they walked out of the bar, down the steep brick stairs, out onto the big gray, empty Manhattan sidewalks. They turned the corner to Fifth Avenue, and they had a bit of a discussion, an argument if you will. He pushed Yaya, headfirst, with her face, right into the big brick wall.

Screaming, bloody, crying. It was the first time and last time he would be physical with her.

They walked up to the Bellevue Hospital on 23rd street, not too far away. She woke up there manic, drunk, pissed off, sad and toothless. Her front left tooth had been knocked out. And the front right tooth was severely chipped.

The following two years would involve bone grafts, implants, surgery, various temporary veneers, a crown, hours of appointments laying in the dentist chair, and tens of thousands of dollars.

The following morning, the first day of the year, Adil convinced her that she had a drinking problem and that she should stop drinking. It may have been true, and it was another form of control.

Yaya's 30th birthday was in two weeks and she decided that for her 30th year she would be 'California sober', and refrain from alcohol. She would rally, party, and go out, just like before, just without the alcohol. In order to stay awake she would consume copious amounts of sugar, cookies, brownies and fake soda.

She was invited to guest lecture at FIT (Fashion Institute of Technology) in the pet branding class. The two women who ran the program wanted to retire and invited her to start teaching the class. The authorities at the university called her and asked about her education experience. Did she have a Master's degree? The answer was no, and she had no intention of getting one, so they thanked her and hung up. She thought it was over.

A few months later, FIT calls back and offers that she teaches the Fall semester, based on her life experience. Yaya no longer needed to have a Master's degree to teach there! She built out the syllabus and got to join the elite group of people who called themselves, 'Professor.' Her ego really liked that.

She started teaching as an adjunct professor in the Pet Product Design & Marketing Department, two classes: 'Who's Who in the Pet Industry' and 'Intro to Pet Product Marketing.'

* * *

It's the big day, her 30th birthday party. Yaya has declared to many of her friends that she is not having a wedding, so this is about as big-ass a party as it gets. She decided that marriage was 90% not for her at a pretty young age, unless of course diplomat immunity was on the table. She had friends fly in from North Carolina to California. She even hired her friend's band to perform.

She wakes up raring to go, like the first day of school, happy and excited and ready to plan and figure out the details. Yaya loves to wear the event producer hat.

Adil wakes up feeling sick. This is the first time this has happened in the two years they have been together. Cindy, her childhood friend, and her husband go out to find some lunch and bring back some soup for Adil. He eats it and manages to pull himself together just in time to depart for the party.

She is wearing pink and orange sequins and feeling jazzed for the party. Her friend pops by a bit early and shoves a big piece of infused chocolate weed brownie in her mouth. Usually she would want this, but tonight she has rented a space, has food and decorations and wants to be able to mingle and chat with her friends. She gets a little too high from that intense brownie bite and becomes a zombie, just walking around the party managing to say "hi" to people.

Eventually the Manhattan party space rental comes to an end, and Adil has been giving out the after-party address... incorrectly. They have plans to have an after-party at a sushi bar downtown and he 'accidentally' gives her friends an address to a different bar.

A few months later, she was down in Florida to attend another pet trade show. She was still in the middle of having massive dental work done on her front two teeth. She ended up doing a national TV segment as 'The Pet Lady,' while her front left tooth was made all out of composite, a temporary and not-so-good looking. "Oh you are having dental work done," said one of her favorite clients. The following week she went back in to get the veneer she needed.

* * *

It's April's Jazz fest and Adil and Yaya are in NOLA for Yaya's upcoming race, the half Ironman, also known as a 70.3km.

They enjoy street food and eventually make their way to the bike rental shop, off the beaten track. Despite her bike reservation, made months in advance, they are out of racing bikes and she gets a standard hybrid. *It's going to be a long bike ride,* she thinks. They eventually take a van taxi to the starting line to drop off the bike, just in time, within seconds of them closing down for the night.

For some reason this sets Adil into a rage, even though he is not racing, and when they finally get back to the room, it's after 9pm. They haven't had dinner. Yaya decides she is too exhausted and is just going to grab a banana in the gift shop and go to bed to get a good night's rest. Adil flies off the handle and demands that she orders him some pasta. He gets loud. He is being awful.

She calls the front desk and happily orders some food that he has to pick up, hoping she can lock him out of the room. He ends up eventually calming down and not falling for the 'leave the room for dinner trick' and they go to bed, torso to torso, arm in arm, dinner-less and even more tired.

The next day, she swims, she bikes, and she runs.

She gets to the last portion of the race, the thirteen mile run, tired and in the Louisiana heat and is ready to rest or walk. She asks someone what time the Abita beer and Popeye's Chicken will be going on until at the finish line, and someone pipes in - "I think 4pm." She starts running.

No way did she come all this way to end up getting to the end with no victory beer.

She runs and runs. She makes it to the grand finale after about eight total hours of laboring fitness and meets Adil in the park. He is happily there enjoying the festivities as if nothing had happened the night before.

Yaya realizes that the race after-party in the park goes on until after sunset, and there was no reason to rush. Oh well, it motivated her to keep on running. They have an Abita Purple Haze, and grab a van taxi to head back to the hotel for a much needed shower. With all the action she ends up leaving her wet suit on the curb, never to see it again.

Spring turned to Summer, and Yaya warned Adil that he would have to find his own place for a month while she was away in Europe doing a house swap. "Mmm, hmm" he nodded, in apparent agreement. It was coming down to the last day and Yaya was packed and ready to go.

The house is clean and nice and has towels laid out and instructions for the house swap guests. Adil was at work and she locked the door and headed out to catch the subway with her luggage.

Beth and Yaya, and her assistant Kelly at Whitegate PR, meet for a final Thai drinking lunch at their favorite place in the city. Yaya is about to embark on a one- month trip to Amsterdam, Turkey and Togo.

Before flying out of Newark, Adil busts into their private lunch, and grabs a small pouch with the keys within Yaya's big red leather purse. He takes off running down the street and she tries to stop him, so he throws a glass at her head, which she miraculously dodges. They call the cops and she chases him to try to plead with him for the keys back. Luckily, she still has all of her IDs needed for air travel in the next hour.

She calls a locksmith to change the locks on her apartment door.

Meanwhile, he breaks into her apartment, which had been carefully prepared for the house swap.

Yaya and her friend Sara safely make it inside the house they are swapping with, in Amsterdam. Meanwhile the nice Amsterdam couple come into Yaya's NY apartment to a door that is wide open, with garbage food remains and soda bottles laying strewn about. Rightly so, they don't feel safe.

Yaya pleads with Adil on the phone to no avail from Holland. Yaya ends up offering to pay for the Amsterdam couple's hotel in New York.

In Amsterdam they visit the Van Gogh museum and take canal rides and visit the coffee shops. They ride bikes and eat pomme frites.

Afterwards, Sara and Yaya head to Turkey for a week-long reunion trip with the crowd that Yaya interned with at AIESEC ten years before. They hang with Mona and Ece. They go to Vos Vos camping, a fun party beach club, and Yaya gets the bright idea to jump off the closed pier. She watched two couples doing it and wanted to try. So they climb to the end of the pier and she moves the bit of cautionary tape aside and jumps in!

Ooooph! Right to the bottom. The impact of her body weight comes firmly down on her foot and she immediately knows some serious damage has ensued.

On this trip, she was smoking a lot of cigarettes. She now sprained her ankle jumping off the pier into very shallow water on the Black Sea. She bought an Ace bandage and flew to Ghana to meet up with her sister in Togo.

In Ghana, they visited an old slave trade fort, which was also a fishing town. They boarded a small van full of very heavy Ghanaian women with big bags of dried fish, a few trees, and a few live chickens, in order to make it closer to Togo. They then transferred onto a bus where a woman poked her head in the bus window, offering bags of clean drinking water. She also kept repeating the phrase "Biscuits, wow," over and over, as if it would make her dry, bland biscuits for sale more appetizing and alluring. The girls found this very amusing.

Once they got to the Togolese border, they were invited to a small wooden hut, which they were told was the customs office. A few officers, one tiny library pencil, and about twenty minutes later, they were filling out 5x7 blank note cards with their contact details, to then be added to a plastic Rolodex, apparently a catalog of all their country's visitors. Yaya marveled at this national security policy. She had been to more secure grocery stores.

They then took a motorbike taxi from the Ghana/Togo border to the small village where Andrea was volunteering as a nurse. It was a missions' type place, which had a school and an infirmary. That night, Andrea was called to 'catch' two babies from some local Moms from the village, who were delivering.

The next day, Yaya put on her hot pink, lacy tank top and tight black Lululemon leggings, and headed down to help work. The woman running the facility told her she was being, "culturally insensitive," and would need to change before serving their guests. Yaya decided to change departments. *Who was this woman anyway?*

She started carrying bricks with the guys in the working crew. She was still limping on her foot, but she preferred the energy over here. They were going to build a gazebo, so the local patients had a shaded place to wait for the medical services.

In Togo, an entire church congregation prayed for her foot one Sunday morning, and her sister's Togolese boyfriend's Dad was a foot specialist and had put special cream on her ankle. It seemed to be healing.

When she returned, she had strict orders from the NYU doctor not to do anything. She was still a 'gym rat' at this time, and after much negotiation, her doctor agreed she could do the rowing machine. As she couldn't really train for the upcoming marathon race, she at least decided to stop doing harm, and that's when she really gave up smoking cigarettes.

A few weeks after Yaya returns from her trip, she finds Adil on her fire escape late at night crying. He is drunk and weeping in the rain, and begging her to please forgive him. This moment of vulnerability encourages her to say yes to letting him back in, one last time. Compassion was her super power, she just hadn't learned to give it to herself yet. They cuddle and their chakras familiarly line up, and she gets the best night of sleep she has had in a really long time.

Yaya finally gets to run the NYC marathon in 2013. She runs across the Verrazzano bridge from Staten Island to Brooklyn, and across the Pulaski Bridge into Queens. While running on the 59th Street bridge, which connects Queens to Manhattan, her favorite Aviici song, 'Wake Me Up' comes on, and it brings her to tears. She had seen him perform live at the Sziget Festival in Hungary.

The last few miles in Central Park she was so tired that she actually remembers running with her eyes closed. She had trained in that park for so many months and so many miles, her body knew it. She felt she had to turn off part of her body to get some rest, and she kept running, more so, so that it could be over sooner.

There were official race photos, an orange finisher poncho, a warming metallic blanket and of course a medal, all at the finish line. She ran it with the time of 4:44 - the time of angels. Let go and let God.

Her running buddy had invited her over for pork chops for a pre-race dinner the night before for fuel.

Gabriela and her family gathered at the finish line to meet Yaya, as well as her friend Alice and her small dog. They asked her, "Is your family flying in to congratulate you?"

No, not exactly. She kept it to herself, but what Yaya wanted to say was that her own family wasn't really into celebrating her. She ends up ordering some hot and sour soup, one of her favorite comfort foods, popping some Ibuprofen, and going to sleep.

Later, in one of Yaya's visits with her parents, the NYC Marathon comes up in conversation. Yaya pipes in, "Oh, I did that!"

Her Mom looks at her and says, "You did not," blatantly denying it in front of her girlfriends. Yaya was floored, feeling like the physical ground had actually been taken out from under her.

Other parents would have celebrated their children, she thought. Instead, her Mom seemed determined to embarrass her and knock her down in her moment of glory. For the first time, Yaya becomes aware of her Mom's tendency to gaslight her.

When she mentioned this to her high school friend Anna, Anna said she had thought Yaya's Mom had been a narcissist for years.

* * *

Yaya met Holly and Matt through networking, who introduced her to the real estate agent at Boulevard Gardens, where she is able to put an offer in on a one-bedroom apartment. She had been trying to get in touch with someone at this building for years. The three of them go on long walks together - often stopping at breweries to try out some local craft beer.

Holly and Matt, her trusty neighbors are also in a cult called the Masons. They invite her to become a female mason in OES - Order of the Eastern Star or the Daughters of Mokanna. Yaya's grandfather was a Freemason and she pledges and gets in. They do charity work and drinking brunches, and have weird formal meetings on 23rd street in funny red hats.

On a cold November night, she was catching some warmth and inspiration at a women's benefit shopping party in Columbus Circle. She meets a famous fit model over a glass of bubbly who was explaining to Yaya how she lives between Manhattan and Greenwich, CT and Florida and could no longer care for... a frog. Her daughter had moved off to university leaving her 6th grade science project at home. The frog, named Prince Charming, was now twelve years old and his life expectancy was eighteen.

The woman explained that he had lived his entire life on Poland Springs water, and that he ate frog pellets. She wasn't sure what to do with him for the holidays, as she was going to be leaving again for Florida. Yaya recently had made a life choice to start drinking filtered water, and was having Poland Springs delivered monthly to her apartment. She offered to take the frog off of the woman's hands, and invited him to come live with her in Queens.

So that was that! They made a date and Prince Charming was chauffeured from Greenwich to Manhattan where Yaya picked him up. They took his castle out of the tank, so as to not squish him and he came home with her in the subway.

Prince Charming, she called him P.C., happily lived in Yaya's kitchen. He was an African Dwarf Water Frog, and he liked a water temperature of about 72 degrees, and he sang every night. The sound was like someone is humming underwater.

Yaya's offer for the co-op apartment was approved, and after much paperwork, she closed on her birthday in the dismal conference room.

As one door opens with real estate, another door closes with Beth. She finds out her PR colleague Beth is lying to her and Yaya makes a big decision and lets Beth go, and levels-up her 'adulting.'

Yaya's parents fly to NY to help her move from her rental to her new purchase, about five blocks away from Astoria, to Astoria Heights, as she likes to call it. Leila and Yaya find some 70s wallpaper to go in the bathroom, with gold floral detail. She also wants to have an accent wall in the living room, bright orange, the color of the second chakra, representing happiness!

While they are mid-move, Yaya suggests they order-in for dinner. Her Mom, being an avid cook, has literally never done this before. Yaya calls and orders a couple of burgers from Bareburger, gives her credit card on the phone and her Mom is completely mesmerized when the order arrives. Yes, food delivery. Not only is her Mom a boomer, but she lives in rural Washington where these urban luxuries are sparse.

Whenever Adil and Yaya were happily together, which did last for a while, they enjoyed cooking. He had a Moroccan tajine, that he borrowed from someone, and they would make lamb and chicken, and Halal beef tajine with garlic and tomatoes, and cumin and harissa. She liked the Halal way, killing an animal with a prayer of gratitude with merciful swiftness seemed in integrity.

Although he was controlling and limited her time with others, she thought their time together was fun. They would chop carrots in the kitchen and mess around and smooch and dance and cook, and sop up the juicy couscous with chunks of white French bread dipped in with two fingers. Many of their meals were finger-licking good, as they ate the Moroccan way, with their right hand.

After moving into the new East Astoria apartment, she finally cut all ties officially with Adil.

Yaya attended an AIESEC alumni party in the city and is happily milling around chatting with the other folks. Adil randomly shows up to the private party and orders a Corona beer. Yaya is not expecting him and did not tell him where she would be, she had been avoiding and ignoring him after breaking it off with him. A friend senses something is up and comes over to her and places his hand gently on her mid back, "Is everything okay?"

"No," she said. "Please get the bouncer, he needs to leave," she says, gesturing to Adil.

Adil comes over and tells her that if she doesn't call him back, he will "put a bullet in her head." Right at that moment, the bouncer appears, and someone stands on a chair to make an announcement. All perfectly divine timing. Thankfully, he heads back downstairs and exits.

She stays, trying to enjoy the rest of the party yet a bit afraid of what is in her future. She flashes back to a moment when he told her, "Don't worry I will protect you." *Who did she need protection from besides him?* she thought.

The event dies down and an older woman asks to walk her home, which is perfect since Yaya doesn't want to be alone. They are heading in the same direction, south, as Yaya is meeting up with her friend Jamila for a drink.

Yaya tells Jamila all that has just ensued. Jamila is also Moroccan and has met Adil a few times. She tells Yaya, "You know you are not going home tonight right?"

"Oh!" swallowed Yaya. She had not considered that.

Jamila invites Yaya to spend the night. They head back to her Brooklyn apartment after eating kale salads and drinking some cocktails. Meeting up with Jamila is the ideal solution to this crazy night.

The weird texts start coming in from Adil. He is threatening her further and suggests that she is not safe in Brooklyn. She is paranoid that he may be tracking her somehow on her phone. She turns it off. Midway through the night someone comes and loudly pounds on the door. Yaya freezes. It was probably just a drunk neighbor, but it leaves her unnerved for a few more hours.

Jamila jumps up in the am with the New York sunrise and hops in the shower to go to work. Yaya takes her time after not really sleeping and hangs around with the roommates making breakfast and coffee, playing with their pet turtle and messing around with her new vaporizer, until finally dragging her ass down to the local police station back in Manhattan to the same precinct where the incident occurred, to file a report.

After waiting about ten solid minutes, a female cop with a ponytail and a short library pencil, listens to her story and takes some notes.

She asks if there were any incriminating voicemails and texts, there were. Yaya is assigned homework to get videos from the bar and from her apartment from the night before to corroborate her story. She also calls her friend from the alumni party and asks if he will provide a testimony. He will.

Adil was at her apartment all night banging on the door and trying to break in. Luckily he couldn't. There is footage of him in the elevator coming and going several times. The alarming piece here for Yaya is that he had never stepped foot in her new apartment and she is not sure how he could have found it.

She is able to secure a restraining order, but is still afraid to stay at her apartment. After about a week staying at Jamila's, she asks Yaya to please leave as she needs her private space back.

Thank you Jamila.

Yaya ends up staying with Alice for a few weeks after that on the Upper East Side. Thank you Alice.

Back at home, each night as Yaya's stoned head hits the pillow, she wonders, eyes wide open, *Will this be the night that Adil comes back? Will he try to break in again? If he rings the doorbell what will she do? Can he get in?*

These thoughts and questions race through her mind. She adds 911 to her speed dial, just in case. She gets hot and tosses and turns in the layers of sheets and blankets. She walks to the kitchen to make some Cal/Mag, a calcium magnesium powder that she mixes with water to help her sleep. She is afraid.

In the morning she rises, tired and groggy and makes a big stretch to reach the front and back white metal frames of the bed. She walks to the kitchen to brew some hot tea. She is off coffee for a while to help her nerves. She has to take the subway today to the city, so she adds some pet CBD from one of her clients into her mug to reduce the anxiety.

She dresses and prepares an over the shoulder bag and heads out, constantly checking over her shoulder behind her in case Adil is following her.

Renee, the Power to the Pussy artist, calls her. She has been going through a divorce and things are getting worse. "Hey, I have a favor to ask you. My roommate doesn't like my big pink chair, and I am wondering if you would like it for your apartment." "Sure!" says Yaya.

It's a giant hot pink throne, and it's totally fabulous. Plus, this means that Renee will be coming over more, which is a bonus, so she is not alone as much, even though Renee is often in a swampy-distant-melancholy mood. Renee brings the chair over later that evening with two young dudes. They chill and smoke a joint, for the four of them. Yaya prepares some chips to entice them to stay just a little bit longer.

They head out into the dark night, whispering sweet good nights to her as they bounce. That night, Adil comes.

He pounds on the door and jolts with the lock and rings the doorbell, demanding that he let her in. She calls the cops and the building's security very quietly from her bedroom on her cell phone, so he can't hear if she is inside or not.

The cops come and bang on the door. Yaya thought they should have a better system, since she was unsure who it was exactly. They had come in the front door and taken the stairs. Meanwhile, Adil had heard them and hopped in the elevator to the basement and fled. This was also caught on video.

They told her to take it easy and that no one would be able to break into the big solid fire door that she had. That gave her peace of mind.

She lay sleepless in bed again, trying to convince herself that she was safe. Fears weren't always rational.

The next day, Renee phoned with another proposition. Maybe she could stay with Yaya for a couple of weeks on her couch, in exchange for a framed piece from her Power to the Pussy art collection? Deal.

Yaya wanted the hot pink Chanel bottle art piece with a banana. Renee came over that night with a tiny suitcase with her belongings and a few light pink jackets for them to personalize and wear to the Women's March in DC, which was coming up.

They got high together and giggled, and took turns sitting in the hot pink throne and watched little bits of black smoke-like energy bits float around the apartment. Yaya did not like the look of them, they seemed like bad energy to her, and she immediately busted out the sage, to cleanse the space.

Renee and Yaya had always had an on-again, off-again friendship, as Yaya thought Renee was a bit selfish. She was not too happy about the bad vibes of energy that she assumed were coming off of Renee and her things, but she was grateful to have the company. That night she slept with one eye open, but it was sleep after all.

Renee goes through with the divorce and eventually moves out, leaving the art and the throne, just in time, while the women were still friendly with each other.

* * *

Yaya packs her mask and snorkel and all the swimsuits she has, bikinis and one piece Speedos, to get ready for a week long scuba dive trip to Bonaire. It's a Dutch island known for its scuba diving, donkeys, and flamingos. She is going with her college friend Rick from San Diego, who is a dive master, and his two friends from Northern California. They all fly in and arrive at the resort lobby to get their room assignments. Yaya is with Rick, and the other two friends are together right underneath them, and they are right next to the pool, great!

Yaya happily unpacks and explores the place, as she is always curious about using all the amenities. The girls go straight to the pool. First things first, Rick and Yaya are also on a mission to score some pot. *Who to ask?* They start with the waiter at the restaurant with dreadlocks. Bingo. He can get them some "green" on his break in a few hours.

This island is desolate. They walk to town to enjoy the famous local gelato, and to go over the salt beds to see the sunset pink flamingos in action in their natural habitat.

They are set to do two boat-dives each per day, with one additional shore dive per day, welcome at their leisure on lunch breaks.

Yaya has about thirty dives under her belt from various trips around the world, and she is excited to be dive buddies with Rick, as he has a lot of experience. They suit up and jump in! Rick likes to get into a cross legged yoga pose in the water and meditate and wait for all the others to get in. They keep each other in-sight at all times, luckily the water visibility is super clear. They see turtles, and ancient tiny seahorses, and lots of bright coral and fish.

A few days into the dive, Rick and Yaya had just finished dinner and smoking a joint, and were sitting around the bar having a drink when Yaya started convulsing and slipped out of her bar stool. She seemed to be having a seizure!

She was slipping down when Rick and another bar goer caught her in each arm and pulled her towards the nearby bushes to lay down. There was a doctor on the dive trip with them, who Rick went to locate. They came back quickly to see Yaya sitting and patiently waiting, seeing some stars, but generally better. The doc said she seemed fine, there was no need to go to the hospital, but maybe she should consider taking a break from diving the next day.

She had had some tooth pain earlier that day on the last dive, so she made plans to visit the dentist in Bonaire the following day to get things checked out, and to make sure she was all-good to continue diving. At the dentist, he checked out all her fillings and gave her a stamp of approval to dive the rest of the week.

On second thought, maybe it was more the weed than the diving. They had heard about this synthetic weed, maybe it was causing the reaction more than any toothache or diving, or maybe it was a combination. It may have just been too much for her nervous system. As her sister always told her, with Yaya, there were usually too many variables.

They dove, and dove, and dove, and dove. They even found a big bait ball to swim in a few times. This is a huge school of fish swimming quickly in a figure eight pattern to avoid getting eaten by sharks, big fish, seals and other predators. *Boy, did they have fun there.*

Towards the end of the week, the girls rented a car to go check out the donkey sanctuary.

They got to pull in and drive around to visit the rescued wild donkeys. They were aggressive, big creatures looking for snacks. Their big brown, smelly noses tried to investigate the car window and the inhabitants of the car.

* * *

Alice asks Yaya to join a shamanic medicine journey with her and Aaron, in three months, that coming December. (She had introduced Aaron and Alice to each other about a year before and they had developed a podcast together).

Yaya immediately said yes. She doesn't know any details and is a full appreciative yes to this.

Her soul knows this is a positive direction. The first week of December rolls around and she partakes in a brief 'dieta' (diet), limiting processed foods, meat, sex, and most other substances in preparation for the ceremony. She walks into the room and is immediately greeted by the other two dozen participants and the shaman, Ohad.

They settle in and Ohad asks the group if anyone has experienced Lucid Dreaming? Yaya raises her hand, and shakes her head, yes. Ohad responds, "Well, that is impossible, right?" Yaya furrows her brow and wonders why he brought it up if he was just going to deny its existence.

She remembers thinking she would like to meet his Dad. She is curious about this Israeli self-proclaimed shamanic healer.

She is reminded of a radio show she hosted in college at SDSU called, "Who controls what you know?"

Where does this guy get off telling her what she has and hasn't experienced? she thought. She would later learn that a master shaman understands life through their own experience, and always honors other's experiences.

When Yaya was a girl, her soccer buddy Carrie Wise and her twin sister attended a séance, where they claimed to connect with ghosts! Yaya never discredited their experience, and always honored that that was true for them. Although she had never witnessed ghost energy herself before, she had the capacity to believe it was true, and no reason to deny it.

They go around the circle of participants and set their intentions, sharing them out loud, and Ohad makes private notes about what he would be giving each participant, from his 40 plant based medicine options.

There were about twenty of them sitting in a circle, a few familiar faces like Alice and Aaron, and many other newcomers.

She wondered in anticipation, *Which of the various plant medicines she would get tonight?* He started most of them off with a natural heart opener known as 'sass' for sassafras.

After they each swallowed their plant based medicine and were a few hours into the experience, she walked up the stairs to see who was in the bedroom and met a cute little blond from the Midwest, who whispered in her ear, "You are enough."

It was the perfect thing for her to hear at that moment. Ohad was drinking a big mug of something hot and came to check in on her. "Can I have a sip?" she asked.

"Sure," he said, and he handed her his mug. "I'll be right back," and off he darted lightly into the kitchen. She sat in the middle of the carpet feeling content and gazing around.

He came back and said, "Drink this tea." It was something they called MA (Psilocybin Mushrooms and Ayahuasca) as a powder made into a hot tea. The active chemical in ayahuasca is DMT. She calmly drank the mysterious brown bitter liquid and slowly started to gyrate with time. She had a lot of energy. She stood up and moved her limbs around delicately. She felt ecstatic.

A tall, nice-looking man came to check on her and see if she wanted to go to the basement with him and play music. "Yes!" she said. He played 'Rocket Man' and other Elton John tunes on the piano while the two of them guessed the words and sang along. She sat on the cold cement floor with her knees up, locked in her elbow creases, very close to the drum kit.

They were guests at the home of a famous *Cirque du Soleil* performer.

The basement was full of instruments and sound-proofing insulation. They finished their concert of two and headed back up the cold gray stairs to join the others in the spacious living room. A curly haired gentleman had a hairbrush out and asked if he could brush her hair. *Perfect*, he could, as she loved that. He sat on the couch and she sat on the rug and he brushed and brushed her silky thick brown hair.

Around two in the morning, Ohad announced that he was leaving to go home if they were ready to snack and ground down.

Everyone was safe and feeling good and coming down from the medicine. It was now time for resting and grounding with some hearty vegetable soup and sleep.

In the morning they awoke to an even bigger feast. Ohad had stopped at his favorite kosher bagel place on the Upper West Side and brought a bounty of bagels for everyone to enjoy. They were soft and fresh and varied from pumpernickel to blueberry. There was fresh fruit that had been cut into cubes and hot coffee freshly brewed. They made plates and gathered back around in another circle for a closing sharing ceremony.

On Monday nights Ohad hosted integration, basically a chance for people to share and check in with how they are doing from the weekend journey, or past journeys. They met in Zev's small apt, in Harlem. There were pillows and a few mattresses they laid out for maximum lounging-comfort for the dozen attendees.

Yaya was wearing a dark green, long-sleeved dress that was fitted and stretched down to her mid-thigh. She had to leave shortly after, to be a guest on Celebrity Catwalk TV. Her eyes met Connie's. Connie had just come up to the city for a few days from New Jersey, they both expressed interest in dancing and made plans to dance later. *Yay, a new friend*, thought Yaya. After sharing at integration Yaya bounced to go take care of her TV segment. Afterwards, she texted her new friend Connie that she was too pooped to dance-party.

Yaya was invited to 'journey' at the farm a few weeks later. The Farm was Bartholomew's house, Ohad's Dad. He walked around with a cigarette or a joint in his mouth, and a big-laughing-welcoming cough. His farm had a few goats, a few chickens, a dog named Royal, and a big trampoline. Across the street from the main house where they circled, was a big plot of land with big dreamy plans to sew crops and make events.

She sat by the older women, Dr. Vicki and the healer she had just met. The three of them were having a pleasant discussion about holistic things in the city. Yaya was pretty focused and serious when it came to soul work, and she was certainly there to do 'the work.'

Ohad started the fire and dimmed the lights and asked a few people to light the tea light candles around the place. They sat in a circle, as they do, to start. Yaya was sitting cross-legged on the carpet.

About an hour after taking the medicine, Yaya turned around and asked if she could place her hands on the woman's right knee who was sitting in a plush chaise lounge behind her. The woman nodded. She held the kneecap gingerly, cupping it with both hands.

After the journey, she ended up falling asleep in the warm loft upstairs, cuddling with a few of the community members. The next morning, Bartholomew started making some Challah French toast, which roused them awake.

The woman whose knees she had held, came to her and said that the ache in her knee, which had been there for the past few weeks, along with all her leg and back pain, were now miraculously gone. *Wow,* Yaya contemplated on this revelation while chomping into a dripping hot-maple-syrup bite of egg-soaked, cooked Challah.

But Yaya had pain of her own to deal with. Her persistent stomach ulcer and left hip pain, which she usually blamed on running, were constantly acting up. She attended a networking meeting in Manhattan and refrained from drinking alcohol. Her networking friend Nancy, who has had ulcers in the past, takes Yaya to the Walgreens right there in Times Square to get some medication.

Back upstate later that weekend, on another journey, she meets Caleb. During the night hours of the journey, Caleb is crying and wailing. Eventually, Yaya cozies up with him and holds him as his wails gradually turn into a whimper, and eventually quieted down.

In the morning, Caleb returns the favor by giving Yaya some insight into her pain from the perspective of Ayurvedic practice.

104

They talk about Pitta energy, and how Yaya, who is fond of coffee, alcohol and hot sauce, may want to balance her fire or Pitta energy by balancing her consumption of these firey substances. They leave their tender embrace and join the others for a Buddhist meditation around the pool.

After the meditation, as everyone was getting ready to return home, Caleb couldn't seem to find his car keys.

Yaya feels her intuition leading her once again. She knows exactly where the keys are. *They are under the wooden deck in the back.* And when the owners of the house opened the space under the deck, they instantly found the keys.

These incidents seem to follow Yaya, and each time she shows her *knack* for finding things. Before her spiritual work, she would chalk it up to photographic memory. But photographic memory couldn't explain her finding things that she wouldn't have seen before, such as Caleb's keys.

As Yaya went deeper into her self-discovery and soul work, she realized that this *knack* she had was characteristic of her gypsy heritage. She learns that gypsies were known to spend a lot of time in the Middle Realms, and are known to be skilled at finding lost things.

A few weeks later, Yaya flies to San Francisco to enjoy a more traditional ceremony with her high school friend, Francis. Francis has been doing medicine work with ayahuasca for a while now, and the two longtime friends are excited to share this work with each other. Cesar is her Peruvian shaman. They drive to the home in San Jose where the ceremony is taking place. Yaya had taken an allergy pill that morning, and was having an internal debate on whether that was a smart move or not, knowing that they are on a one-week dieta. They pull into the driveway and unload their sleeping bags, pillows, and blankets.

They arrange their spots for the ceremony, a yoga mat, sleeping bag, pillow and a plastic wellness bucket. Oftentimes when drinking medicine (ayahuasca) there is a need to purge, or 'get well' as they called it. They were prepared.

The twelve of them sat in quiet anticipation. The Peruvian medicine man came and gave an introductory talk about the night. Then they went up to meet him one by one to take a small shot glass full of an orange, thick, bitter liquid from the jungle, a psychadelic made from vines and leaves. Once everyone had 'drank' he started playing various musical instruments and singing in tongues. The music was not supposed to be familiar. He invited them to come up and drink again.

At one point, Yaya got really hot and started pulling off her blankets and clothes. She made her way to the bathroom where she purged out of both ends and then came out and collapsed right on the floor. When she opened her eyes, Cesar and another person were holding her, perhaps they had caught her before she had completely hit the ground.

Some cried. Some laughed. Some tried to sleep. The man on the couch behind her just lay with a big smile on his face - while she suffered. The next day she was chatting with him about his experience, which was extremely gentle and positive and he decided to gift her his favorite book, 'Power vs Force.'

Back in New York, after a full day of an NLP (Neuro-Linguistic Programming) workshop with her journey brothers, more deep inner work, she uses the bathroom as a last stop before going outside, and sees she has her period! She had been on the Depo Vera birth control shot for about ten years, and had been off of the shot for one year. She hadn't had her period in eleven years! She was reclaiming her femininity and this was a step in the right direction.

She walked outside to see the sparkling bits of gentle snowflakes falling all around her as she bounced with joy into the first snow that year, happy and light as a kite.

CHAPTER EIGHT

Yaya Finds Her Voice

Be careful what you wish for.

They woke up at sunrise, after specifically sleeping early the night before. The girls hopped on their bikes, and rode out, away from the camps towards deep playa. They found a Canadian Goose made completely out of pennies and decided to stop to take a break and eat some magic mushrooms for breakfast.

The day before, Yaya had attended a tapping workshop with Francis led by a beautiful woman in an exquisite dress.

The sisters rode and laughed and enjoyed the warmth, gaining strength as the sun rose over the playa at Burning Man. Yaya pointed to a giant copper cow ship, "Let's follow that!" she exclaimed. The girls pivoted directions and started following the big shining art car with horns.

There was a swarm of people dressed in white, all coming to dance with this cow ship and the girls were excited. They parked the bikes and joined the sunrise dance session. At one point, they even got up on the drawbridge and were dancing right next to the tapping woman in the dress, from the earlier workshop session, and she was holding a real live hawk on her arm. It was markedly magical.

The cow ship moved and was going back to its camp, the girls were in their element and decided to stay onboard. Yaya had a

107

community green bike, which was free to use and meant that others could find it and use it too. Andrea had brought a bike. Andrea went hunting for it later and couldn't quite locate where the cow ship party had been. By leaving it out there parked and unprotected, it became a piece of MOOP (Matter Out of Place).

During the moment, out in deep playa, it can seem so clear that you know where you are, between the other pieces of art as reference. The trouble is that on the playa these art cars move and big installations go up and down.

The dusty, satisfied girls walked back to camp, for their actual breakfast, still feeling euphoric. Luckily, it was not their shift to prepare food that day.

They walked into the makeshift living room, made with PVC pipes and sheets and pillows and found Tyna smoking a blunt and decided to join her. Some others were starting to face paint. They could overhear in an Australian accent some laughter and chatter about scrambling the eggs. It was The Burn night, the night the 'man' would burn down. All forty of their camp members were planning on meeting up at sunset, dosing a bit of acid together, and walking over to see the man burn.

At dusk, one of the camp mates was hula-hooping with fire, and sent her flaming hoop on top of the shade structure. Luckily nothing happened. The young campers encouraged her to try again.

Yaya, the oldest one in the camp, couldn't handle continuing to watch this game so she walked away to pursue something else. The hula-hooper succeeded this time, miraculously not burning anything down.

Andrea was dressed in a skimpy tight bodice as Wonder Woman. Yaya suggested she wear a sweater or something on top as it would get cold that night, plus acid made it feel colder. "Don't tell me what to do," she screamed and stormed off.

They would spend that night away from each other, in a tiff, doing their own thing. Andrea visited high rise cuddle puddles in the sky, while Yaya was not quite open enough to enjoy that type of activity, and was gifted a white scarf made out of rabbit.

Francis made Yaya promise on the drive into The Burn that no matter what, she would not go on any see-saws. Francis' friend had fallen off and broke her legs the year before, and Francis did not want to see it happen to one more. Yaya took this vow seriously, and adhered to it while on and off the playa. During a trip to Moscow, she would have to politely decline a seemingly fun see-saw invitation.

Yaya had flown from a Chicago wedding, directly from a Tough Mudder Race in upstate New York, with her big borrowed green army battle bag, ready for The Burn. She often found herself booked back to back with events, without a lot of downtime.

Francis picked her up at the San Francisco airport and they joined the queue to enter Burning Man. The drive to Reno took about six hours, and the wait and drive into the burn was another eight hours. They took breaks driving and switched to pee, snack, and rest. Just getting in felt like part of the initiation.

Their camp offered candy. A tall man came in to get some candy while Yaya was volunteering on her shift at the candy shop. He suggested that he was going to kiss her on the count of three, and then he did and it was splendidly hot. She was seen by the smooch police, one of the camp mamas who was clapping for her on the sidelines.

Afterwards, she stopped by the kitchen to see what was going on. There was a crew of five having some snacks. Yaya tried her first gluten-free pretzels, they were super crunchy and salty, an explosion of texture in her mouth. She really liked them.

Meanwhile, in the road gathered a group of campers, watching a beautiful woman from their camp spinning on a human wheel. Yaya wished she could be brave enough to try it.

At Burning Man, there's an element of survival. In the middle of the whimsical and surreal wonders, even when surrounded by the multitudes, the experience can magnify the isolation within yourself. After all, we all come into this world alone.

Only the Dr. Seuss rhyme could describe it:

> *You are on your own, and you know what you know,*
> *and you are the guide who will decide where to go.*
> *You will come to a place where the streets are not marked.*
> *Do you dare to stay out, or do you dare to go in?*
> *It can be hard for a mind maker-upper, to make up her mind.*
> *I'm afraid sometimes you'll play lonely games too,*
> *games you can't win, because you play against you.*
> *All alone, whether you like it or not.*
> *Alone is something you will be quite a lot.*
> *You will get mixed up of course,*
> *with many strange birds as you go.*
> *Life's a great balancing act.1*

Back at home after Burning Man, Yaya hosted a women's circle for the New Moon. She was having fun with tent life and posted up the tent in the kitchen to make a yoni-steam-section. Her journey sister Connie, had recently been trained in yoni steaming, and they set it all up with heat and herbs and water, and trapped the steam in the tent.

The women's circle attracted about eighteen women. Yaya was practicing facilitating groups and cultivating her intuition. They sang and drank cacao, and they shared feelings and made noise with maracas and other small bells and instruments.

That night Yaya realized that the pink chair had to go. Even though she loved the aesthetic, she believed it carried some bad energy that she no longer wanted to have around. She was learning to shed the things that no longer serve.

1Shmoop Editorial Team, "Oh, the Places You'll Go!," Shmoop University, Inc., Last modified November 11, 2008, https://www.shmoop.com/oh-the-places-youll-go/.

Yaya gets a powerful reminder to just be herself

Be yourself, everyone else is already taken.

They walked through the door exactly as she predicted at 4:02 pm. Just in time for hugs and love from the Canadian journey sisters. The house was magical. Mirrors, shamanic symbols, charms, a dark basement. It was perfectly what she wanted and was worth the eight-hour drive through the spraying Niagara Falls. As the others jittered with nervousness, excitement, and small bursts of laughter, she found solace in herself.

Yaya found her spot, in the middle. Unapologetically in the middle. Absorbing the energy. Soaking it all in. Not knowing what to do with it all.

Her shaman teacher walked by. She wanted to share the energy with him. He says, "You don't have to do anything, just be yourself."

It feels good to share the energy. It becomes too much sometimes. Through connection and sharing she learns the power and boundary of herself. One of the women had been suffering from a headache. Yaya caught herself judging her headache being due to alack of hydration, etc. *It's okay,* she thought.

The older man caring for the woman with a headache had exited and she found an opening in the bay window. It felt like daytime energy, but the sun had recently set on the trees.

She found her voice. *Where does it go sometimes?*

It's crystal-clear. The way it was created, God's perfect likeness. She belts out loudly and purely, but not in an ego way, in a God-is-all-around-us, grateful-kind-of-way. She sings the lyrics "Know you are loved, rest in peace."

Because peace is for us, right now. Right here. To check-in, feel, notice, and remember, to bring with us from this moment on. To freeze time and check into the heart version of herself, a deep remembering.

At that moment, not doing anything, not trying, just allowing. Just giving in to the free flow. It's so beautiful. Let her sing.

She has given herself permission and then once it's granted it can never be taken away. It's a new 'click' to the right of 'getting it.' Like on the spin bike, one more level, now no level beneath will be comfortable again and she feels it in her bones. All the way to the luz bone, the only part of the body that can't be burned.

Is that where the shifts take place? She wonders.

No journey will ever be the same. Maybe that was her own form of being vulnerable. Shining those God sent gifts. She thanks the shaman for bringing his vulnerability, and then thinks that maybe she was simply ready to let it happen all along.

She knows things. It's just there. The secrets. She feels them. No words need to be uttered. However, other words do come. With the tantra guy, and the headache woman, and the messy love they've so desperately tried to create. She sees it so clearly. She is learning to read the energy.

She can get out of the window and into the world - back where the people are. Not because she was ever above them, but there was maybe an air of aloneness.

She's fancy. She sees. She knows.

Some like it hot.

The heat is on.

Yaya had just finished an energetic healing session with Aaron, and she pops out of the elevator into the street to go to the subway.

She gets about halfway down the block and runs into her friend Claudia, who asks her to join a hot yoga class right then.

She is always up for new experiences, so she walks into the stairwell, the smell blasting her with hot chlorine. Yaya has nothing to wear, but Claudia has a plan, she is a yoga teacher there and quickly outfits Yaya head to toe from the Lost and Found.

She discovers the magic of Bikram hot yoga. The series of twenty-six postures and two breathing techniques really speak to her. She sweats, she gets to be dommed (dominated), she is asked to stay present, she gets her heart rate up, and she gets to rest and meditate in savasana (the final resting pose). It's the full package in one hour. After watching the documentary about the man, Bikram, she prefers to call it, 'hot yoga.'

Ayahuasca knows what you can handle, and gives you what you need.

Tiny wax circular candles add a dim yellow light to the small, full rectangular room. A group of half dozen women cozy up next to each other in mismatched nylon sleeping bags and earthy hand-knit blankets. Tall men, short men, round men, and a three-year-old boy, snake their way into a wavy line formation around the women and chocolate-lab-colored furniture. Yaya was surprised that children were also participating.

Gray sage smoke twisted around the room, softening the clarity of the hard faces, patiently waiting in line. The Colombian man in a brown poncho kneels by a small wooden table, and offers a shot glass filled with an unripe tomato-orange colored liquid to the small child.

Behind the un-curtained sliding glass door, we see pine needles and shamrock green nature throughout the blue night.

She pulled herself away from the rambunctious wood fire and starry wet sky and heel-toed her damp bare feet back inside through the squeaky glass door as quietly as possible, in an attempt to minimize taking up too much space in the group of unfamiliar women.

A thought passed through her mind: *This might be it, no visions (from the medicine) tonight. Just keep breathing through it.* And just like that, the nausea turned on and she fell to her knees, now back in her spot inside, on the $40 Target-brand, blue sleeping bag.

A wave of thick swirling mauve, and bright white energy cascaded down in a very clear vision, like two kundalini snakes. She knew then that it was a sign that she needed to heal her femininity. Simple, with unmistakably profound clarity. She downloaded her message from the ayahuasca, which is considered grandmother plant medicine.

Yaya connects with her mermaid tribe

The next morning, to her exhilaration and surprise, she rose to chatter about a mermaid parade. She wiped the crusties out of her eyes, and unfurled the big black dusty plastic bag full of mermaid costumes. The bag was the size of three grown adults. The windowed room was full of hope and opportunity as teal and agate colored sequins ricocheted the light rays off the sea green wall.

She let the homey beige carpet support her comfortably as she folded in half to dive deeper into the bag. The lead mermaid wrangler reappeared wearing all violet and handed Yaya an appropriately sized gown. She dropped her grip on the edges of the bag and accepted the beautiful intricate costume in outstretched forearms.

She slipped it over her hips and underwear and reached just above the bum crease for the zipper, cinching the shape around her smooth torso and breasts. A different, shorter woman dressed as a Tiffany blue, shiny mermaid, placed a shell adorned crown on her thick brown hair. "Let's go," the purple mermaid sharply blurted, as the corners of her tight raspberry lips sighed up and down.

This mermaid parade was intended to raise awareness for ocean advocacy. They gathered in a church parking lot to collect mermaids, sea creatures, and signage, until they amassed approximately thirty sirens. Then one of the large, and in-charge women, started them off belting a chant to be repeated through town. They walked around on sidewalks and across streets, until they made it to the final destination where there was a play about the ocean put on by a local organization.

After the joyous mermaid parade, Yaya cautiously entered the elderly man's home into a musty room, which appeared to be an office. He was a healer and had worked a lot with plant medicine. The shelved walls were heavy with books and a small computer was the centerpiece of a desk covered in papers, clip boards and newspapers. The sticker in bold, black font stuck to the wall a few feet below eye-level jumped out to her, like a neon golf tee in a bag of white balls, which read in all caps: YOU ARE NOT SPECIAL.

Yaya froze, as if a high-speed, well-lit train was coming full force towards her in the deep part of the night. She had always thought that she was pretty special.

The gentle bearded grandpa said lovingly, "Come in here." As his tall frame slouched over the tiny gas stove. He was fussing with the boiling water. The sticker compelled her to read it once again before refocusing her gaze into the warm, worn kitchen and then on him.

They spoke about carrying trauma and baggage from our ancestors and he did a special "limpia," or soul cleaning on her.

Later on, during the second night of the ceremony, after the sun had set and the clear crisp night darkened the periphery, the wizard-man from the kitchen rose, fueled by the energy of the fire and the ceremony and bellowed, "Bless Yourselves!"

He was not the same frail wise man she had encountered in the kitchen earlier, but a large life-force sharing his power and insight with the intimate group of thirty, as he offered a handful of crushed leaves as an offering into the blazing fire.

Sparks rose and disintegrated into the air, creating an extra flicker of orange light.

She would end up participating in hundreds of traditional healing grandmother medicine ayahuasca ceremonies, similar to this one, over the next few years.

Her gypsy roots led her naturally to this kind of work. Something told her there was something lost that she needed to retrieve.

Yaya shifts from one mystery school to another, from medicine oriented shamanism to sex shamanism. She would joke that each one was her favorite cult.

"We are the fucking medicine," she thought.

Her medicine community friend, Pam, was living with their friend in Jersey City. She had just come back from a compelling retreat called ISTA. Pam couldn't tell them much about it, just that it was another powerful mystery school, without the medicine.

Pam did say that there was a tray with nature items, and she had picked the pine-cone. The other person that picked the pine-cone was her partner for the next activity.

Being with her in person, in her presence, Yaya wanted some of what Pam had going on. She could feel the difference in Pam.

Yaya registered for ISTA Level 1, the International School of Temple Arts, for sexual, shamanic and spiritual teachings, the following day. With energetic training like ISTA, Yaya believed that the magic and the lessons began the moment she registered.

At ISTA, Yaya learns to accept dark feedback, to form an integrated, realistic, and relatively stable image of herself that simultaneously includes both strengths and flaws.

First, she has a bit more self-reflection to do.

When the student is ready, the teacher appears.

She was still living in East Astoria, feeling scared in her apartment most nights and generally fearful walking to the subway. She would put on a brave face for others and for herself, but at the end of the day she would spend many sleepless nights worried about her safety.

She was in professional 'talk therapy,' and had a restraining order from the ex-stalker and was doing integration work in the community, and yet still she was seeking more healing.

She registered for Kamp Connect, a two- day program at a yoga studio in Brooklyn.

She remembers hustling the pace of her walk to faster than usual, as it was brisk and she was cold, and she didn't want to be late, as she traveled the few colorful blocks from the subway to the venue in south Brooklyn on a Saturday morning.

The day began with some loving eye-gazing, icebreakers, and connection games and activities. At the mid-morning snack-break an overzealous, chubby guy named Emilio came to chat with Yaya. He asked her, "You're Jessica, right?"

"No," she pointed, "That's Jessica."

Yaya knew exactly who he was talking about and she was flattered that he got them mixed up. Jessica and Yaya both had brunette hair, similar height – both girls of European descent in eccentric clothing. Yaya remembered when she entered, like a gale force wind.

Fully blinged-out and adorned from head to toe, dripping in jewelry and accessories, from tattoos to her signature yellow, thick framed eyeglasses, to her long shiny earrings, to wild sparkly flared-out pants, stylishly yet strangely put together. Yaya immediately walked over and introduced herself. She learned that Jessica was a Doctor.

Each hour was led by a different instructor. They had a wild dance with the Goddess Witch, and they shared tender moments in group chaos. Yaya disclosed in a whisper that she never wanted to have children, her deep mother-wound, which immediately got noticed by Jessica, as she craned her neck around to see who had spoken.

During the very last activity of the day in a tantric massage, Yaya and Jessica, The Doctor, were partnered. *Finally*, she thought. Yaya was curious about her and energetically felt the magnetic pull towards her. She would later understand this as the human magnet syndrome.

They used fun props like feathers and fruit, and were guided to engage all the senses for a pleasurable experience for both partners. Yaya fully melted and really enjoyed this massage exchange with Jessica. Afterwards, it was Saturday night and a few people were talking about going to the Arabian Nights restaurant nearby for a group dinner.

Yaya asked Jessica if she was going. She said she was. Then there was some talk of carpooling. Emilio asked Jessica if he could ride with her, and she said yes. Yaya asked to ride with her also, but Jessica, The Doctor, hesitated.

She felt rage! *How dare she say yes to grubby Emilio and no to me, especially after our new yummy post-massage connection*, she thought.

Yaya insisted. The three of them walked a few blocks to where her car was parked. It was a casual four-door that had been heavily used.

They walk into the restaurant. Yaya and Jessica ended up sitting next to each other at a long table of twenty, and ordered the same exact thing for dinner.

Jessica, The Doctor, was surgically precise in asking her some deeply targeted personal questions, which Yaya diligently answered. Then in a blink of an eye, she whisked off, mumbling something about a birthday party at the House of Yes. Before leaving, she left Yaya her email address so they could stay in touch.

Yaya was smitten. She had never met anyone like her before. It all seemed so exciting.

Yaya emailed her a few times inviting her to various things, events and dance parties. Jessica The Doctor, politely declined each and every time.

Eventually, she suggested that she do what her other friends do, and pick a time to come out to Rockaway for a sleepover and go for a magic-acid-induced-beach-walk. They settled on the Wednesday before Thanksgiving.

She met up with Holly and Matt, her cheerful neighbors at their local place with $6 IPAs and a vast selection of local craft beer, which they were all super into at the time. Two drinks turned into four, and Yaya finally crawled out of the bar to make it to the bus to Rockaway.

She arrived at Jessica's around 9pm or 10pm, super apologetic for being late. She was a little tipsy and agreed to be hypnotized. *How fun,* she thought. She hadn't 'played' hypnotism since elementary school with Lydia and their friends.

Jessica kept topping up Yaya with sweet red wine, and then they spent quite a bit of time in the Meditation Room, while the other couple stayed in sleeping bags in the makeshift living room, furnished with three mattresses.

It was only later that Yaya realized that Jessica, The Doctor, was programming Yaya for a 'power-of-suggestion' hypnosis.

The next day they had a glorious breakfast, before she had to sadly depart to head to Long island to spend Thanksgiving with her dear friend Alice and her family. The magic beach walk would have to wait.

Never trust a person who doesn't like animals.

Jessica, The Doctor, was afraid of dogs. "You just need to accept your own unpredictability," Yaya suggested.

"Ah, did you coin that phrase yourself?" Jessica asked wryly.

Yaya took it as a sign, and thought it was some kind of divine intervention: this awesome new friend, with her fear of dogs, has energetically connected with her, The Pet Lady!

She was lost and searching for a purpose. Jessica's problem gave Yaya a temporary purpose. A false sense of purpose, but a purpose nonetheless. She wanted to fix her so badly, and help her overcome her fear of dogs.

Through this divine experiment, she did learn her purpose, it just wasn't what she expected. This lesson had much more to teach her.

Gradually and systematically, over the next few months, without realizing it, Yaya fell under the seduction of The Doctor, the bisexual, mentally unstable narcissist and hypnotist from Georgia.

It was New Year's Eve, and the girls decided to spend the evening together. It was only their second time hanging out. They started out at Jessica's place with a sushi boat for two for dinner, followed by selecting outfits to go out dancing. Jessica disapproved of what Yaya had brought to wear and loaned her something she deemed was "more suitable."

They were in the nightclub's bathroom, and Jessica, The Doctor, had just given her her very first bump of K (ketamine). Yaya walked down the stairs from the bathroom, holding it together, and moving her hips in a circular motion to steady herself. They ran into a smiley redhead who told Yaya, "You are beautiful," and gave her a sticker and a business card. The world was still swirling so she danced it out.

Yaya comes to terms with her habit of avoidance

Yaya is dancing onstage at the House of Yes, her favorite Bushwick dance club venue, like she is known to do. Mainly enjoying the wood floor, spaciousness, and the energetic vibe up there. She prefers it up here, to being close to all the foreign millennials, who found out about the special club on TripAdvisor and are drinking and taking plenty of video as a bucket-list thing.

Yaya is dancing next to a guy with a plaid shirt and a beard who starts mirroring her movements. They dance, and dance, and dance, for what feels like hours. Finally, they embrace in a hug and decide to get to know each other and talk a bit in the outdoor section.

His name is Buck. "Do you smoke weed?" asked Yaya.

"Yeah, do you have any?" he asked. She laughed. She did not have any on her.

They danced a bit more, ran into Jessica, The Doctor, and decided to go back to his place to continue making out. Jessica, The Doctor, seemed surprised by the whole thing. Yaya was confused by this reaction, she thought Jessica, The Doctor, was all about the little-black-book and hooking up with as many people as possible. She wanted Jessica, The Doctor, to be proud of her. She cared deeply for her approval.

Yaya and Buck got back to his place and met his dog, a cute mixed-breed, who was excited and friendly. They dated for a few weeks, which looked like getting-high, and taking the dog for walks, and having sleepovers. Touch was her love language, and she craved bodies touching in sleep, cuddling, and spooning.

Sometimes they would grab a drink at an open mic night here and there, where he was performing as a comic.

After her birthday, he asked her to go for a walk and she thought she knew where the conversation was going, so she bailed and went for a jog by herself instead. They stopped seeing each other. She was still not good at endings and preferred to try to avoid the hard things.

* * *

Yaya had her hair curled and was dressed in heels, loading an Uber in Florida with all her props from the TV segment she just finished, when her Aunt Audrey called her cell.

Grandma Humphrey had died. She stopped for a brief second from what she was doing and decided now was not the time to process this. She had to go back to the trade show and drop off all these things and start working the media tours.

On one of the tours, she took around her running buddy, who now worked for a pet media company. She asked Yaya, "Are you okay?"

"Well, no, my grandma died."

Her friend responded "Sheesh, well you are doing a really good job compartmentalizing things right now." Yaya realized that she was right. She had put the thought of her grandmother's death in a corner of her mind, and temporarily locked it away for later. A familiar tactic she used to procrastinate dealing with uncomfortable feelings.

After three hard days of running around the show, the size of sixty-six football fields, and drinking way too much free wine, she flew straight to California to attend a wedding and ski with her high school friends for a couple of days, followed by going straight to Charleston for a windy boat cruise. By the time she arrived in South Carolina she was a mess - physically, emotionally, and spiritually.

At the VIP boat cruise in Charleston for the 40th anniversary race of the Cooper River Bridge Run, they met the organizers and the artists and all the big wigs involved in the show. Mar had invited Jada and Yaya to come to host a pet fashion show at the race, and Yaya had invited her friend Veronica as her plus one. They ate shrimps and cheese and had cocktails galore aboard the windy ship, cruising the Charleston Bay.

She slowly twisted from her crunched side, to her back, as she groggily opened her eyes in a muggy Holiday Inn. As she reached for her phone to turn off the alarm, she noticed a throbbing pain in her left shoulder and neck. She looked over at her friend, Veronica. She was stealthily sneaking in some early morning work emails, on her iPad, under the covers.

Yaya wanted to check out the race expo next door. As she waited in line at the crowded expo to pick up her race number and walked through the lanes of athletic shoes and gear, she was beyond pleased to see that Aleve was a sponsor.

She got her badge and race backpack for the next day and bought some sneakers, which came with a free hyena stuffed animal. She found some self-massagers to try out on the painful upper shoulder area, and an eager salesman with a 'Tens' machine let her wear the device as she walked around. Plus, a nice sales guy offered to rub her back with cooling gel.

She was wracking her brain, trying to determine what she had done to cause this annoying issue.

Maybe it was too much drinking and dancing at her friend's wedding on Saturday night?

Was it whiplash reappearing from her DUI car accident in her 20s?

It must have been sleeping on her side… or did she somehow tweak her body on her skis and not remember?

There were too many variables. She reconvened with Veronica and her crew in the afternoon, and they estimated that it must have been from the cold wind whipping on her neck on the top deck

YAYA FINDS HER VOICE

of the boat cruise the night before. She was skeptical. She knew that the wind always seemed to cause her Mom to complain of a stiff neck. Maybe she was just getting older. Still, she had only just turned thirty-four years old.

That evening, they were invited for cocktails at a famous reality star's home from Southern Charm. They met her butler, her five dogs, including her beautiful pug dog, and she gave them a tour of her estate, complete with a Monet in the living room. She had taught art history and one of her husband's had run the Met for a while. It was a real treat. They all pinched themselves while enjoying deliciously made drinks in her foyer.

By Friday, the pain had seemed to double in intensity. They were preparing for the pet fashion show at the race luncheon with adoptable dogs, (the whole reason for the trip), and she was able to push through the feelings of pain in the upper left side of her body with the busyness of the day.

After the pet fashion show, at one point her friend played piano while she sang, and they put on a nice impromptu variety show for the other hotel guests.

The next day, she woke up early, buzzing with excitement and anticipation, it was now race day. As she undressed out of her PJs and dressed into her sports bra and tank, it was absolutely excruciating to lift her arm through her clothing. She contemplated not going, and again she decided to push through.

She walked out of the hotel lobby, across the dark parking lot to the yellow school buses that were moving people to the start of the race. She quickly consumed the Aleve provided in her race backpack. The sun hadn't yet risen.

Lots of runners were clamoring onto the buses. She was alone.

She found her way to her race number corral, eyes pacing the crowd from bag to bag, for any extra Aleve in other participant's backpacks. *Aha!* She saw another woman, sitting on the pavement, who seemed to be chilling with her clear plastic backpack, complete with the Aleve inside.

Yaya approached her and asked her to give her the pills. The woman calmly asked, "What's wrong, Honey?" Yaya almost burst out in tears right then and there. She kept it together and explained that her shoulder and back were hurting. The woman asked Yaya to join her on the hard ground, as she was a massage therapist and would be delighted to give her a rub.

She thanked God and sat down. The woman gently touched the area, after giving her the Aleve, making her feel comforted and safe. The woman's friends arrived and Yaya felt like she had been intruding, so she graciously thanked her and went back to her spot in the crowd, as they all waited for the countdown for the race to begin.

They were off! She loved the excitement of race day, she picked up on the energy of the other racers and the cheering crowds. Usually she liked to follow the expression, "nothing new on race day," but she had bought some new neon yellow and purple 360 brand sneakers at the expo the day before, and she was wearing them.

The race started on the Mt. Pleasant side of the bridge in Charleston, and the bridge was long. Every fifty yards or so they were joined by live music and DJs on the race route.

As she climbed the bridge, she felt the pain, and used the energy of the music to push harder, run faster, and finish sooner. It was just a 10k but she was feeling the intensity in her body around five kilometers. She just kept placing one foot in front of the other.

At the finish line, she was pleased to see that with not much training she had achieved her Personal Record. The post-race event was complete with more live music and tons of entertainment, freebies, and snacks. She was dancing really wild and reconnected with her crew! Pure bliss.

They had been invited to a hosted breakfast, where there was a massage therapist! *Yippie!* She signed up immediately and Yaya received the last massage of the morning! As she explained what was going on with her, the massage therapist carefully suggested that Yaya was on her way to experiencing a frozen shoulder. She gently rubbed and pulled her limp body, improving the bodily sensations greatly.

Yaya proceeded to have a few more complimentary adult beverages, after her massage. They made their way to yet another after-party, complete with a clambake, and delicious southern delights. She continued drinking. Eventually they made it back to the room. The alcohol surprisingly wasn't alleviating the pain, but it was a nice distraction for her mind.

Yaya woke up at 4am with an acute pain in her back. It was an intense, jarring, screaming-loud, back pain. It was a sharp, insane level of pain - unlike anything she had ever known before.

She got up and started walking around, she wasn't sure what to do. She was worried and upset, and in excruciating pain. She paced around the room for a minute, trying not to disturb Veronica, who was in the Queen bed parallel to hers, soundly asleep.

She wasn't sure what to do, when she remembered there was an ice machine on their floor. She grabbed a white stiff shower towel from the bathroom, walked down the hall and loaded it with as much ice as she could carry and waddled back to the room in her bathrobe. Leaving the door ajar with the top gold lock, so as not to mess with finding the key. She dumped all the ice on the bed, lay on it and went back to sleep. She woke up a few hours later, cold and frozen into place. It was hurting a lot.

She couldn't handle it! She felt like screaming and crying all at once. She finally resolved that going to brunch with a group of people was better than staying in her hotel room alone, because maybe one of them would have a muscle relaxer?

She was convinced that would help. After arriving thirty minutes late in an Uber, and dripping water down her back with melted ice packs, they made it to brunch, and alas, she scored a Xanax from one of the breakfast goers in the crew.

She took half of the muscle relaxer and saved the other half for the evening, *just in case!* One more night to go, before heading back home to NYC, where she could elicit the professional help of her doctor. It couldn't come fast enough.

The next day she woke up in more pain, more than she even thought possible. She was reaching new levels of pain thresholds that she had never imagined humanly possible. Yaya believed in sexual healing, so that night her 'booty call', her Brazilian Tinder friend came over... sex was one of the only things that made her forget about the pain, even if temporarily. It was the best relief she could get.

He noticed that she was in pain and as a martial arts and jiu-jitsu practitioner he showed her some helpful moves and stretches. He stayed over and the next morning, he called them an Uber and escorted Yaya to his favorite chiropractor in the neighborhood.

The chiropractor cracked her neck, gave her a thorough cupping treatment, and referred her to the pain doctor down the block. Coincidentally, the pain doctor's phone number had magically already been saved in her iPhone database. Yaya has no idea how it got there, and again took this as a sign that it would be a good idea to see him.

The pain doctor gave Yaya a steroid shot in her neck and ordered she get an MRI. He suggested she not return to the chiropractor until they got the MRI results.

The chiropractic adjustment helped temporarily, even if it created a placebo effect, and then the shot in her neck just thirty minutes later, seemed to tighten it up again.

She had to wait a week until her MRI appointment. In the meantime, she was laying on her couch, agonizing, not sleeping, unable to work, and consuming quite a bit of cannabis.

The pain doc also recommended that she go to Physical Therapy. *Excellent.* She knew the place she wanted to go, she had dislocated her elbow a few years earlier in a bike accident and wanted to go to the same place.

She walked in the physical therapy place and was able to see the physical therapist who "loved working on necks." She trusted her completely at this moment. *If she loves necks, I want her to love mine,* thought Yaya.

She started with the heating pad, which feels like black velvet enveloping all around her, followed by a giant professional grade electrical pulse machine and some mandatory stretches. She also gave her a few stretches to do as homework – basically looking up and down and side to side, slowly to strengthen the area and get range of motion back. It reminded her of a very slow-motion version of head dance from the movie, *Night at the Roxbury.*

She was going to physical therapy two to three times per week, while on a parallel path, making visits to the pain doctor. The MRI was extremely stressful.

She arrived at the MRI place, to wait her turn to get sucked into the full-body machine. Yaya lay on the hard, cold machine, and had to remain unmoving for the next thirty to forty-five minutes, while they scanned the area. There was peaceful music in the background playing, while the MRI machine was making loud, screeching, and jolting sounds.

Yaya has a yoga and meditation practice. This MRI experience took all of her breathing techniques and tools to stay not moving in this space for this lengthy period of time. She was unsure how the other, maybe not-so-conscious or well-equipped patients in the waiting room, were going to get through this?

She felt compassion for the older woman who was chain smoking outside, waiting for her turn, and the heavy guy in the lobby. The MRI really rocked her world. It was challenging. She had an epiphany that day: *Maybe all humans are the same. We are all given the same pain and suffering and intensity through different lessons, yet strength to pull through challenging moments.*

After countless calls to the clinic to try to get them to hand over her results without having to visit the doctor again, and pay another co-pay, she reluctantly returned to the pain doctor to get the MRI results.

It's been a few weeks now, and she is at wits end, desperate to find a cure. She had been self-medicating with marijuana, which only slightly relieved her suffering. She found that alcohol only made the area throb more, so drinking was not on her list of options. She hadn't slept in weeks.

She was diagnosed with osteo-arthritis, a herniated disc, a bulging disc, *and* tennis elbow. She was pretty high and sitting in the patient's chair, and the doctor looked at her and said, "We found a significant amount of THC in your urine."

Yeah, I bet you did, she thought. She has spent the last month laying on the couch trying to relieve the agony by smoking weed and having sex.

The next words out of his mouth took Yaya completely by surprise.

"How would you like to have a Medical Marijuana card?" he said.

She pinched herself to see if she might be in a daydream. She looked at him guiltily and uttered a very meager, "Yes."

He said, "Great! Let's fill out the paperwork. What would you like?"

"Gummies, pre-rolls, topical cream, cookies..." she started listing, like a kid in a candy store.

"Woah, slow down," the pain doctor laughed, "We only have three things: THC pills, CBD or THC oil, or a vape pen." *That works, too*, she thought.

When the Medical Marijuana card arrived in the mail, she headed over to the Herbal Health Center to pick up her goodies. She walked up to the front vestibule and met the helpful pharmacist who walked her through the options.

She decided on two vape pens: one with a high CBD to THC ratio, and one opposite, as well as some CBD oil. She was looking forward to relief with the CBD without the psychotropic effects of weed, so that she would be functional enough to work.

As an entrepreneur, she worked on her own schedule from home, but there were projects building up that she needed to get done with a clear head.

That weekend Yaya flew to Calgary, the land of her birth, for a guided psilocybin journey. She felt she was in a safe space there with trusted space holders. They had their fill of the hot tub, hikes around the snowy property, and a playful resident Bernese Mountain dog.

Later that night, in a deep moment of surrender while in the bathroom, she was given a message from Great Spirit. Leaning on the towel rack, Yaya cried to the skies. A message formed in her mind: *turn your pain into beauty*. As someone who channeled her inner alchemist, this reflection resonated and reduced her pain from a level fifteen to about a nine on a ten-point scale. She could definitely still feel it, but it was now more manageable. The ceremony helped her to let go.

Her friend and his wife had invited her over for Passover at his parent's house in Long Island, weeks before, and as a shiksa, she was very excited and looking forward to celebrating this holiday for the first time. She had been told by a dear Jewish friend that fruit was a nice thing to bring to the occasion.

She had picked up a couple of mangoes when they stopped at the grocery store for special Kosher pickles, but her arm was so weak she could not even carry the bag. Her friend saw her twinge of pain and carried the bag of mangoes for her.

Once they got to the house, the environment was very argumentative with constant fighting between the parents and their kids and spouses. This increased the pain and throbbing in Yaya's neck.

She started to see where people got the expression, "pain in the neck."

The following weekend was spent with one of her clients on a book tour with a very packed schedule. The author was a cat expert, and Yaya was going to spend a lot of time traveling with her. It turns out that like Yaya, the author had also been suffering from back pain. Her strong recommendation was to "run, not walk" to an acupuncturist.

She set an appointment, but had to wait another week to give enough time between her cupping massage and the acupuncture session. She was piling on the treatments.

Thankfully, it seemed to temporarily alleviate the issue. The acupuncturist suggested that she should come back for at least two more sessions. He also thought her muscles were 'wet' and prescribed a Chinese herb to 'dry' them out. She felt a little better. Plus, it was now Spring, the season of hope.

She came back for a second acupuncture visit after a work trip to Bologna, Italy. She had her own version of *Eat, Pray, Love* there. The acupuncturist thought that the vacation abroad seemed to relax her. From his observations of her body, he suggested that she should try not to equate her self-worth and value with extreme intensity.

During the session, the needles were a bit bigger, and felt more painful than the last time. It also seemed to initiate more intense throbbing.

On her third appointment, she had come in to the office early to catch up with her friend Aaron. While waiting for him to finish a call, she occupied herself by checking out his office knick knacks. Among his books on healing and consciousness, Yaya found, 'Healing Back Pain' by Dr. John Sarno, and started reading it.

Two chapters go by, as she waits for Aaron and the acupuncturist.

In the book, Dr. Sarno suggests a pattern of pain and specific ailments that may be tied to repressed emotions in the body. Suddenly, it all started to make sense.

Her grandmother had passed a few days before the pain had hit back in March, but she was too busy with work, life, and travel plans to really deal with the information. She was really good at compartmentalizing. Sarno explains in the book that commonly people with 'type T personality' have ulcers, hip pain, and back pain. Type T people are stimulated by risk-taking, stimulation-seeking, and thrill-seeking.

This is scarily too close to home, as it parallels Yaya's story. When her ex-boyfriend Adil returned to her life as a stalker, she had a persistent stomach Ulcer. She had also been suffering ongoing left hip pain, which she usually blamed on running. It had ceased in November, after a special healing, and now in the Spring, she thought, maybe it had moved up to her left back, neck, shoulder, and arm.

After this last acupuncture appointment, her friend Aaron said, "Oh, that book is in the "free" pile. We've been trying to clean out the office." She happily takes the book, and considers it as a positive sign of synchronicity.

She is supposed to go meet Renee, the Power to the Pussy artist friend, for drinks in the east village. Again, alcohol does NOT help, it actually makes the pain more severe. They meet, drink, and head to the art show that Renee is featured in. The whole time Yaya is thinking that she wants to get back to reading the book. At this time in her life, she is still strongly identifying as a party girl more than a bookworm, so this is odd behavior for her.

Yaya decides to leave early, she says goodbye to her friend and gets on the subway. *Perfect!* Now she can read. She takes the 6 train, hoping to connect at 59th street and Lexington to transfer to the yellow R train, which takes her back to Astoria. She is completely engrossed in the book and ends up far north on the 6 train, all the way in the Bronx.

Pouring through the pages, devouring the content, she finally finds her way home, hours later, and can't wait to look up Dr. Sarno.

He talks about his work at NYU (New York University) and Yaya is thinking, *great, maybe he is based in NYC and I can make an appointment tomorrow?* She gets home and googles him, finding out that his clinic is on 23rd street. She scrolls down, and sees disappointing news: Dr. Sarno had died twenty years ago.

She finds a few other doctors that use his technique. Dr. Sarno explains the Type T personality as a people pleaser who cares about other people liking them, matched with a bit of perfectionism. Repressing emotions like anger, fear, and sadness is often the root of the pain.

The next morning, she has self-scheduled to go on a forty-four mile bike ride from Astoria to Rockaway (and back) with a few friends for a beach day to visit Jessica.

She reads in Dr. John Sarno's book, that probably most doctors have said, "Take it easy, don't exercise, etc." However, that will only make you more depressed and sad because you are not getting the serotonin and other benefits from movement. His advice is to continue life as normal without fear!

Yaya decides to go for the bike ride, and not be scared, to "Go for it all."

At the beach, Jessica, The Doctor, separated Yaya from her friends and took her upstairs to her apartment to offer her a bump of K and have a long chat.

After the bike ride, by Sunday morning her pain was nearly gone. By accepting that the pain was not physical -it helps relieve it!

It's now Memorial weekend. She finished Sarno's book. Now what? She jumps over to Amazon to her Audible account and sees what else she can download on a similar topic. Boom! Think Away Your Pain – By David Schechter, M.D. It's a continuation of the theme and she decides to pursue therapy. Not physical therapy, because the pain is not from something physical, but talk therapy.

Yaya asks around and settles on a regular therapist covered by her insurance network. The therapist is offering CBT or EMDR.

They started with the EMDR treatment, which is basically thinking back to traumatic experiences, and going through them with some resources and a vibrating device that you hold in both hands, with the vibrations switching back and forth from left to right. This technique is originally from Dr. Shapiro, and is believed to work on the nervous system by having both sides of your body process emotions and eliminate black and white thinking.

So began (or continued) her healing journey. She also opted in for a gluten-free lifestyle, and her cooking started to contain turmeric, black pepper and coconut oil, in efforts to reduce inflammation in her body.

This also meant no more beer. It took her a few months to really figure out what gluten was in, and not in. Plus, she was spending more time with Jessica, The Doctor, and therefore attending more yoga in Rockaway, which seemed to be helping.

* * *

Sophiane and Yaya had decided to take their Moms to New Orleans for the Essence Fest. It was the summer of 2017. It was hot, and their boutique hotel had a small pool in the middle of the courtyard.

They would venture out to listen to jazz and brunch by day, and return for cocktail hour by the pool in the early evening. They were invited to a real NOLA parade by a local krewe with a brass band through the outskirts of town, from a woman in the thrift store they were shopping at. They ate and drank and were merry.

One night there was a huge line outside the House of Blues for a ticketed event they were having. Leila casually walked to the front of the line, passed the bouncer, and right into the club. Yaya followed close behind, shaking her head. "Mom!" she exclaimed. "You must have a ticket to get in here right now."

"Well, I just want to take a look," said Leila. They were now both standing in the middle of the House of Blues with no tickets or wristbands.

They left and found a funky jazz bar playing live music and danced the night away. Yaya was starting to see where she got her hip-shaking moves and her rebellious spirit, "the apple doesn't fall too far from the tree," and as they say, "Like mother, like daughter."

Yaya had been collecting new clothes to impress Jessica, The Doctor. She wore a new white linen dress, complete with a bright embroidered parrot on the front. She had been invited to Rockaway, to Jessica's penthouse for a body-painting party. Basically, the artist was body-painting Jessica to practice for a showcase that weekend, and another friend was also coming over.

The four of them sniffed bumps of K, smoked joints, and listened to music. Jessica has a crafting corner, which the girls discover and bust out a box full of large plastic gems.

They dump out all the gems and make a giant constellation of crystals on the floor in the meditation room. It's beautiful, intricate, and sparkling, and takes all their focus.

At one point Jessica asks Yaya if she wants the red pill or the blue pill, like out of the *Matrix* movie. Yaya says purple. "Oh, she doesn't know," says Jessica laughing. The artist, Jessica and Yaya end up having a three-way-kiss and Jessica invites Yaya to sleep in her room's bed with her. Yaya declines, wondering if it's fair to leave the others by themselves in the living room. She was still prioritizing others before herself.

* * *

Pouring rain is pounding on the windshield. They find parking in the gushy mud and wait for the downpour to subside a bit. Yaya prays for the weather to clear and within a few minutes they catch a break from the rain. Yaya and Jessica each grab their bags and place them on a tarp and drag the whole load directly to their New Jersey beach camping spot, which has already been setup by their friend the body-painting artist.

They share a giant bell tent with inflatable couches with him. They add a few accessories to their outfits and head out into the Gratitude Festival for the first night of the party. They are walking towards one of the main stages, when Yaya sees Jessica's friends from a distance, completely melting from too much acid. Jessica decides to stop and talk to them while Yaya goes off to explore on her own. It's the first time they are apart at the festival.

Yaya is dressed to belly dance and has lost quite a bit of weight since meeting Jessica, The Doctor about six months before. The diet of K, plus dancing on the weekends, and the Vagal nerve being overly activated, must have had something to do with the disappearing twenty-five pounds.

She lets the blue sparkly beads flap back and forth on her front pelvis with swift control as she sways her hips to the Arabic-inspired music.

She is dancing onstage and locks eyes with a tall thin man wearing all festival black. He gets closer to her with each song, eventually coming to dance with her. They start making out as he pulls her hips closer to his and they grind and move in synchronicity with the music. He is Middle Eastern and loves her shape. She can feel it. It's hot.

They walk on the beach, back to the camp where they meet Jessica on the dance floor. She already knows him and likes him, which is a relief for Yaya. He is interested in taking things to the next step and they go back to the bell tent. There is an extra tent in the back that they go into to "hook up" in.

Yaya has condoms, but she is paranoid that they are going to get walked in on. It happens. She is always paranoid about getting in trouble, especially since this isn't her tent. The artist comes back while the man in black is inside her and asks for his sleeping bag, which they quietly and quickly slide out the zipper door to him. They keep thrusting. It's magical and on fire. She stuffs her face in the pillow to dampen the whimpers and screams she is letting out with each orgasm, growing with intensity as he plunges his throbbing hard cock into her.

* * *

Jessica and Yaya fly to Reno together and took The Burner Express Bus into the burn, no traffic, no lines, it was really express. This year, Jessica, the Doctor and Yaya, and her cute little ornery blonde friend, and a random Dutch guy were sharing an RV together. Jessica had arranged for the RV to be on the playa when they arrived at their camp.

Jessica and Yaya get the big bed and the other two share the pull out couch. It was a small space for the four of them, but they made it work. They are all RV virgins so half way through the week they are out of water in the toilet and can't get the lights to turn on. Their neighbor, Will, sees that they might be having some RV trouble and comes by to help. (It turns out he is the brother of Caitlin, the store manager from Muttropolis and he lives in the Bay Area.)

Will and Yaya make out a bit on the dance floor. Jessica insists that the three of them, Yaya, Jessica and Will all spend the evening together. Will is a long-time Burner and has never had a night out exploring.

Later as the three of them are walking, Will is trying to "play some game" on Jessica, and she denies him. He tries to hit on Yaya and she also rejects him. He asks if the two women are together, and neither girl responds. Each secretly asks him later, *"What did she say?"*

The next day is really hot. One hundred degrees in the desert-kind-of hot.

Yaya asked the cute blonde to flag down the RV sewage guy so that they can get their RV drained. Their blond roommate gets half naked and chases the gray water truck down the street to get cooled off. She comes back empty handed.

Yaya remembers that if you want something done right you have to do it yourself, and goes and gets the RV cleaning truck guy herself. Finally, they were able to wash their hands again, all it took was $40 cash and some momentum. Jessica peered in and mumbled, "I thought that might happen."

That night, the blonde roommate, Jessica, and Yaya go out on the bikes together. Jessica rides a trike with a big basket, as she never learned to ride a bike as a child. They are out in deep playa, trying to stay together, and Jessica yells out, "Babe," and Yaya instinctively turns to look and responds.

The next day, Jessica has plans to go on a date with a woman, and she tells Yaya that she should come. The three of them start off together until they lose the date in the crowd and end up dancing at Camp Question Mark, their favorite sound camp, until past sunrise.

That night they wore flip flops. They came back to camp around 9am to sleep until 3pm and their feet were a dusty disaster. Jessica offers to vinegar off Yaya's feet because she doesn't want them in bed as is. She obliges.

The two of them Neutrogena-wipe their faces down, brush their teeth and hop into bed with the AC on. Jessica asks Yaya to cuddle her, she wants to be the small spoon. Yaya tries and wants to but finds that she just can't, she is afraid to touch her. She gets stuck in her head and just lays there like a lox.

Back in Queens, they have their first threesome together with Pepe, a friend they met at The Burn, planned and hosted by Jessica. Yaya shows initiative and goes at it with him, but he can't really handle it. These two brunettes are really turning it on for him. He goes limp and the play party ends rather quickly after starting off with a lot of heat and promise.

Soon after, Yaya flies to Arizona to finally attend ISTA Level 1. She stays at her friend Mary's house in Phoenix for a few days before heading out to Oracle, AZ for the retreat. While in Phoenix they check out a college football game, have some nice meals and Yaya is active on Tinder, while Mary and her husband are at work during the day.

Yaya meets up with Luis, a Tinder dude who is recently married and ethically non-monogamous. Yaya is a bit of a size Queen. He uses a Lelo vibrator on her in conjunction with fucking, and they have the most mind-blowing orgasm together, going to the milky way and back. They decided to stay in touch. It seemed as though the tantra training started early.

It's time to go to ISTA, and Yaya has arranged a ride share to the ranch. It's about an hour drive from Phoenix and they pass by the Biosphere 2. Yaya insists they stop and check it out. It's like the 1990's movie, "*Bio dome*," with a full living Eco-system completely enclosed and self-sufficient with an ocean and a desert and all the natural elements found here on earth, recreated.

They pull into the ranch and see a small group gathered. Yaya hops out of the car and is immediately triggered by a small Indian woman who wants to know the room assignments before everyone else. The organizer announces that she will be with Yaya. She winces. *Of course.* She knows it's all going to be potent medicine for her.

By the end of the week the two of them had pushed their twin bed frames into each other so they could have one big bed and were cuddling. They even self-pleasured together. At this mystery school they learned a lot, they shed some layers of conditioning and went through many rituals.

One of the first practices was Latihan- a sensual, sacred movement practice. Yaya loved it and wanted to play Latihan more.

One activity that blew her mind was when they talked about Shells; the shells we wear based on expectations from life and the people in it. For example, Yaya was going to be born in Cameroon, Africa, where her parents were living. They thought she was going to be a boy and they were going to name her Michael. Then Leila jumped on a plane and had her in Calgary at the same hospital she was born at. From birth, Yaya wore a shell of 'baby boy', followed by a shell of being 'a nice girl', 'a tough girl', 'a tomboy', 'a brave girl', 'an older sister', 'a good girl', 'a straight-As girl', a 'band playing girl', 'a theater girl', 'an independent thinker', – and the list goes on.

Learning to shed these shells and layers of self can help us get back to the stinky onion layer of who we actually are before all these labels got put upon us.

Yaya is buddied with Lara, a trans-woman, who is also one of the assistants. The shells discussion breaks Yaya down to tears and she confesses to Lara that she is attracted to women and may be a lesbian. It's confusing to her identity after all these years of being with men. Lara understands and calms her gently, before leading a loud, raging heavy metal music, therapeutic head-banging meditation session.

Yaya flies back to New York City feeling empowered, and goes to visit Jessica right away, on a school night. The two of them barely say hello before Yaya gets her shoes off and the two of them are making out and heading to Jessica's bedroom.

Jessica gets her finger inside Yaya and starts pulling her clit gently forward with a repetitive cum hither motion that makes Yaya feel ecstatic. They jump on the bed and face each other and play and smooch and hug for hours. Eventually, Yaya goes down on her, and for it being the first time ever with a woman, she thinks it goes rather smoothly.

A woman had gone down on her once before, about ten years earlier after a wild trivia night for one of her author clients, but that was all of her experience with the female body.

On the weekend, Yaya wears her 70's designer hippie pants, and a jewel encrusted bralette to the techno party. Yaya gets there a few hours before Jessica, takes some ecstasy and dances in the very front by the speakers. Yaya gets too hot and takes her pants off, she is wearing cute little white dance shorts underneath. Jessica finally arrives at the party, more than fashionably late, and hangs out chatting with the body painters.

She asks Yaya to hold a cup of brush water for her body-painting friend. Yaya gets bored with this task and brattily sets it down on the floor, although keeping her eye on it. Jessica summons the cup and Yaya briskly picks it up, delivering it to her. *Did she pass the test?*

Yaya was still afraid of being at home alone and was spending more and more time with Jessica. Jessica rarely visited her there. Jessica had a fancy security alarm system that she convinced Yaya to get; it was a monthly subscription for a long contract. Yaya went for it.

The following weekend Yaya and Jessica skip the parties and register for a three-day silent meditation retreat in Rockaway.

The two of them are in a bit of a tiff, having no label and no conversations about their status, which further confuses Yaya.

They bring their to-go cups of coffee, arrive about seventeen minutes late, as per usual with Jessica, and sit on cushions towards the back with the rest of the sangha, listening to Bhante and his teaching of the morning. Next they go into walking meditations, a sitting meditation, and then lunch time of simple rice and cooked vegetables to be eaten quietly in the yard.

After lunch, they are all assigned on various teams to take care of retreat house work, and Yaya walks to the bathroom to grab the broom to sweep the stairs. Bhante corners her and tells her firmly that Jessica The Doctor, "is a good person."

Having this respected leader come to say that to her affects her mood. That night, they break the silence back at Jessica's, as they are in the commuter meditation program. Jessica asks Yaya what she wants. Does she want the label of Girlfriend?

Yaya is in internal turmoil and fog, she can't decide. She eventually squeaks out an uncomfortable, "yes," and they sleep soundly wrapped up in each other before going back to the meditation house for one more day of silence on Sunday.

Yaya had noticed that the front screen on the window of the meditation house was busted, possibly from the Buddhist house cat, so she brought Jessica's hair blow dryer to use a patch and patch it up.

Yaya calls her Mom. "Hey Mom, you know my new friend Jessica?" Yaya asks.

"Yeah, the Doctor?" Leila says.

"Yes, her! Well she is my new girlfriend."

"Mm hmm" replies Leila, like she just told her that she had toast for breakfast. Yaya was extremely nervous about coming-out to

142

her redneck parents- and it couldn't have been more casual. Her Mom was very accepting of it, as if she had been waiting for it, and quickly moved the conversation along to other topics.

The new happy queer couple head out hand in hand, as dancing Queens for yet another Burner party at a club in Brooklyn. When they get to the front, Jessica shows her NYC ID. The bouncer says, "Nope, not here. I need to see your real ID."

Yaya pounces in, "Hey, that is a legal ID!"

Jessica calmly looks at both of them and says, "I have it in the car, I will be right back."

Yaya, not sure how to act as girlfriend, accompanies her back to the car to get her driver's license. Yaya inappropriately getting involved in Jessica's ID situation could be a clue or a signal to her of her own codependency, but it's too early for her to see this, she is still living in the toxic fog.

A few weeks later, Yaya makes plans to have dinner with Sara. Sara lives right by the synagogue where Jessica sometimes likes to spend Shabbat, and she figured this would be an opportune time for them to meet.

At dinner, Yaya comes out to Sara. Sara gets angry and defensive and loudly exclaims, "What? You told me you weren't a lesbian!"

Yaya is taken aback. She thought it would be easier to tell her friends about Jessica, but apparently not!

She was not expecting this reaction, nor does she remember the time that Sara is referencing. After dinner, instead of having them meet, Yaya walks Sara to her place to cool off and she goes to find Jessica's car parked nearby. She is done partying with the rabbi and the two of them head back to Jessica's place in Rockaway.

They love waking up together and fooling around, usually Yaya going down on her, and making coffee, listening to music, and having a picnic breakfast. Jessica has no dining furniture, so they usually lay a plaid blanket down on the carpet and have a brunch laid out on the floor.

Yaya always makes breakfast while Jessica gets ready, this process can take upwards of three hours. Yaya is learning about patience.

While on their beach walk that day, holding hands and smiling in the midday sun, they have taken some acid and are enjoying the carefree moment in the sand. Jessica introduces the concept of sex parties. Yaya is immediately intrigued and wants to learn more. Apparently, Jessica goes most Thursday nights to a sex club in Manhattan. It's right across the street from where Yaya teaches at FIT. Jessica, acts coy like she doesn't want to tell her too much. They decide to go together in the upcoming week.

Yaya climbs up the four sets of stairs in the winding yellow lit staircase until she reaches the top, where she enters and joins a line for the coats. Jessica, comes in a few people behind her and joins Yaya in line. They get to the front of the line and the coat check woman recognizes Jessica and gives her double cheeked air kisses. She explains it's Yaya's first time and they both get handed their own locker key.

Yaya is wearing a matching red lingerie top and panties under her street clothes, which she carefully peels away in the dressing area and shoves in her locker with her purse and shoes. Jessica, goes to check out the snack room, which has some crumbled cheese and a weird little bowl of purple grapes, next to the hand sanitizer, while Yaya goes straight into the 'play-room.'

She finds a guy, or a guy finds her and they get to the squeaky plastic covered mattress and start playing. He removes her panties while kissing her neck and reaches to grab a magnum from the side tables with supplies. He gracefully pulls the wrapper off and slides it on his big black hard cock before entering her, without missing a beat, he has caressed her nipples and butt cheeks and kissed her belly, all in one sexy motion. Yaya overhears Jessica, talking to another person in the room. "It looks like my girlfriend is a fish in water here."

Jessica also plays with a few men that night and at one point they form a little orgy on the back mat. Afterwards, they get dressed and are ready to leave when the owner calls Jessica, into the back room. Apparently they are friends.

* * *

It's the morning after a fabulous hotel takeover sex party at the Holiday Inn in NJ and the girls are eating pancakes and drinking coffee at the diner next door, reminiscing about the fun action from the night before.

At one point, Jessica and Yaya were facing each other on all fours, getting fucked from behind (with protection of course) and holding hands, with a huge crowd of about thirty men watching them. It was possibly the hottest moment of Yaya's life. She stored that flashback in the spank bank for future reference. The girls felt like Queens of the slut ball.

Yaya was spending increasingly more time at Jessica's place. Tuesday and Thursday nights for lifestyle play parties, often Wednesdays for meditation and pretty much every weekend. Yaya would sleepover Friday after dancing all night with Jessica and return home sometime midday on Monday after making breakfast and coffee, and doing the dishes. They lived for the 4Ds in raving; sleep deprivation, drugs, dancing, and drums.

CHAPTER NINE

Yaya Falls for It

Her feet were firmly planted in her high-heel converse on the wooden pallets below. The heel was built like a tennis ball, absorbing the constant bounce of her body. She has closed her eyes momentarily to let the four-way sound surround and penetrate her. She loves to feel the sound and ride the sound waves, and turn the music energy into dance energy.

She lifts her head and meets the angel, her higher self. A beautiful Victoria Secret model angel version of herself with brown curls and wearing all white appears above her. Yaya smiles. This vision, while perhaps a dissociated perspective, brings her much joy. She thinks: *She met her higher-self angel.*

There are about forty dudes in hoodies, some sitting in chairs, some dancing either on the wooden pallets, or on the cement floor of the warehouse. The music is minimal bass, which really gets the girl's bodies' moving. They make it to the 'stamina crew', the point of the night where the music stops and they turn the lights on and take a photo of whoever is left, usually a group of eight or so around 5am.

Yaya prides herself on making it to the stamina crew. Survivors of narcissistic abuse are excellent at enduring.

Yaya had purchased a hot coffee from their little store where you can buy beer, ramen, or seltzer, so she was still wired for dancing.

Yaya's high school friend Sophiane was with them this night, visiting from California. The three of them drive back to Jessica's place and The Doctor surprises Yaya with a class pass to yoga and a towel as a Christmas/Hanukkah/Birthday present!

Yaya thinks nothing of this gift being presented in front of Sophiane, in mid-November. Jessica always said she was shitty at gift giving and birthdays and so she wanted to make sure she got her something.

Yaya is feeling happy and skinny and has a regular yoga practice, and this gift just reinforces it. Christian, one of her favorite clients had told her recently, "You seem really happy, whatever you are doing, keep doing it!" Yaya had still been buying yoga classes one by one from Chaya, at Yin and Yang Yoga Studio in Rockaway.

The next night, Jessica, is going to another sex party in NJ. Yaya is on her period and Sophiane is engaged, and the girls are not planning on going, so Jessica really puts the pressure on for them to join her.

Yaya decides in the end to go to the sex party with Jessica and leave Sophiane home alone. This is the beginning of Yaya betraying her longtime friend Sophiane to prove her loyalty to their relationship. Yaya justifies this action in her head, due to a previous night with Sophiane and her fiancé, in their past, when they wanted to drop her off at a club to dance solo while they went back to the hotel to pack.

Yaya walks into the play party wearing weird fall pants, with leaves all over them, with sexy lingerie underneath. Jessica, has given her a small purple cup to insert into her pussy to still be able to have sex for an hour or two- while on her period. She awkwardly squeezes it together and tries to insert it, feeling anxious about the whole thing.

She takes off her pants and leaves them in the hotel bathroom and comes out trying to psych herself up, to be ready to fuck.

Jessica and her are offered a weed gummy and accept, it's only 5 milligrams. *This might help her relax.*

Towards the end, she is having sex, doggy-style in the other room from Jessica, when some blood starts getting on the sheets. *Oh, party's over,* thinks Yaya, not wanting to tap-out before her girlfriend.

She goes home with Jessica, to cuddle with her and wakes up early to take the bus back to East Astoria, so that Sophiane and her can go ice skating in Central Park.

The owner of the Manhattan sex club passes away. Jessica puts on her black corduroy one-piece to attend the funeral. Yaya finds her black dress in her bin of clothing in Jessica's guest bathroom, and gets ready to go with her.

"I am not always happy, you know!" Jessica warns Yaya. Yaya didn't think anyone was always happy.

Yaya thinks it's the right thing to do, to attend the funeral and support her partner during this time of loss. They had visited him in Rockaway, just a few nights before and shared a joint on his porch. He had died from cancer.

The girls take an Uber to the funeral and one of the young boys from the sex club drives them back to Jessica's after the burial.

* * *

Yaya is leaning over the granite counter tops at the rental home in Oregon watching her Mom scoop a mixture of raw turkey and egg into freggedella balls to fry, these are her classic Danish meatballs.

Yaya's Dad walks in and makes a comment about her leggings. Yaya is wearing brightly colored spandex.

It's Christmas time and the Humphrey four are away together to spend the holidays in a rural town by the beach. Usually a comment about this would erupt into a full blown fight with F bombs, as

Tom is always sarcastically poking fun at everyone and in their family dynamic, and Yaya is the scapegoat.

Yaya decides to own it for a change and agrees with her Dad that she is always wearing spandex leggings and doesn't get defensive about her weight or about the comment at all. This is a landmark twist in reaction to a Yaya-and-Tom-conversation. Yaya is clearly maturing and growing.

Yaya always makes it back from holidays with the Humphrey's just in time for New Year's Eve. There is no way she is going to ring in the New Year with her family watching the ball drop on TV.

Instead, Jessica and Yaya have tickets to visit Ecuador for three weeks, encompassing New Year's Eve and Yaya's birthday! Ecuador's motto is 'Ama la Vida' or 'love life,' and they plan on doing just that.

They fly to the capital, Quito, and spend a few quaint days in the mountains, taking their friend Alana (code word for acid), hiking to the waterfalls and visiting the mariposarios, the butterfly gardens. When the girls walk into the butterfly den, thousands of brightly colored monarchs and blue and yellow and brown butterflies fly all around them. They can take photos and even feed them a sugary juice on their fingers. They watch them mate and fly together for hours. These creatures live for such a short amount of time and they are all about joy!

The girls eat the best fried plaintains on the planet with fresh guacamole, and generally fall in love with the cuisine, the country, and the cacao. The place they are staying has a pool, offers massages, and grows their own coffee beans on site!

After a few days in the calm and tranquility of the mountains, they hop on a bus to go to bustling Guayaquil. They spend a few days in a cute yellow Airbnb, with breakfast and a terrace looking out on the promenade.

Yaya makes sure that she can prepare hot water with lemon and honey for Jessica, and for herself, each morning before breakfast. Yaya still hoped that sacrificing her life for her partner would magically transform her.

They take long walks through town, stopping to shop or try some interesting street snacks. Eventually they meet up with David, Andrea's first boyfriend's little brother, as he has some local weed for them. (Andrea lived in Ecuador for a few months in college, where she met her boyfriend.) Jessica, Yaya, and David go to a funny little macaroon shop to get hot cocoa so he can roll one up in the bathroom for them to all smoke.

Two nights later on New Year's Eve, Yaya and Jessica find themselves searching for a club to dance to in Guayaquil, only to realize they should have taken David's offer to hang with the family, as many Ecuadorians stay-in with family on this night.

They had been to the burning of the Año Nuevo Dolls earlier, and had seen fireworks and the widows dressed in drag, but that all subsided around 7pm. After taking multiple cabs and searching all over town, they end up at a lesbian bar, which is more than excited to have them.

They head upstairs and a guy on the microphone gets their names and throughout the night, over the loud music, keeps belting out, "Welcome Dana and Jessica from New York." *In case anyone was curious where the only two gringas were from.*

In Guayaquil they learn about Montanita, a nearby party town on the beach, and quickly head there on New Year's Day to catch the buzz on a bus. They meet a jewelry vendor they befriend, who lives in a humble apartment right on the shore, with a hammock! He invites them over for sunsets and chilling around.

They also discover an Israeli Shakshuka place, just down the street from their quaint $7 a night Airbnb. As they are walking "home" to their safe little hut off the main road, they see a sign for parapuente (para gliding). They quickly sign up and pay for para-gliding the next day.

The carefree bliss of flying like a seagull over the beautiful coastal cliffs is so divine- they do it again. They get picked up on a motorcycle, yes both of them, and the driver, all on one bike, and enjoy the ride, maybe even as much as the glide.

The second paragliding day, Yaya decides she wants to do an A to B glide, which leaves from the top of the cliff and lands on the beach! They ride back up on a motorcycle to find Jessica being interviewed by a local TV crew. Jessica speaks zero Spanish, and they are capturing her happy exclamations of how much fun she is having before landing.

A few days in, Yaya gives Jessica some magic mushrooms, or 'veggies' as she calls them, in a yogurt parfait. Jessica decides the few crumbs are too much for her, and the couple get in a fight and head back to the room. All dressed up and nowhere to go. Jessica wants to stay in the room listening to headphones looking at the ceiling. Yaya goes into the mosquito hammock and tries to enjoy the moon and the stars. She doesn't like it when people are upset with her.

Finally, after five full days of partying in Montanita, they wake up early and head straight to the internet cafe to book their bus out of town, and their flight to Galapagos. Montanita is a kind of Vortex that sucks party girls right in. They had been enjoying the spa, dancing, laughing, and flirting. After a lackluster New Year's Eve in the capital, they happily were indulging in the nightlife in Montanita.

They booked their trips and then went to have a classic Ecuadorian breakfast. They loved the food there, fresh fruit and vegetables, lots of plantains, rice, and fresh fish, which all worked well for their gluten free, pescatarian lifestyle. Oh, plus the coffee. It was all delish.

Once in Galapagos, they took a flight to a boat, to a bus, to a place- and got acquainted and booked some upcoming day trips.

They spent a full-day with the Giant Galapagos tortoises, the largest species of tortoise in the world. They watched them play in the mud, munch on plants, and crawl through caves. The whole encounter was majestic. They seemed prehistoric in their careful demeanor. On the way out, they somehow got to ride in the back of a pickup truck, definitely per their request, back to the hotel.

Yaya looked at her beloved Jessica, and said, "It's like you're my kryptonite."

"I can't believe you just said that," uttered Jessica, in a bit of a shock.

They had been together as a romantic couple for four months, after knowing one another for almost one year. Kryptonite can seriously weaken or harm a particular person or thing.

The next day they go island-hopping by boat to snorkel and see the sea, land, and air creatures of the magical Galapagos. They have rental equipment, and Yaya has brought her own light-pink snorkel and matching mask. As they speed off to sea with a local captain and a few other tourists, Jessica makes Yaya melt one more time with pity or love bombing, or some swirling dangerous combination, and Yaya let's Jessica use her home-brought snorkel set while Yaya uses the rental gear. Again, putting Jessica's needs before her own.

Jessica is afraid of swimming in the ocean and it's her first time snorkeling, she doesn't usually desire to mess up her makeup or lose her sunscreen. However, it seems like a once-in-a-lifetime opportunity, so everyone aboard jumps in the warmish crystal-blue water with their flippers, flailing around. Yaya holds Jessica's hand and escorts her around the leopard sharks and seals. They even watch a mama seal birthing a baby seal right in front of them. *Nature, wow.*

One of the days in Ecuador, on one of the Galapagos islands, they rose before the sun to climb a volcano. Yaya gets ready fast and goes to hunt for coffees in the local area, while The Doctor finishes getting ready.

As Yaya was around the block to get them both coffee, she watched the bus leave without her! Jessica, was sitting in the window. Yaya was furious and sad. All of her abandonment issues were flaring up all at once. She couldn't believe Jessica didn't ask or demand that they stop. Yaya said under her breath "If she had dropped a hair-clip out the window it would have been a whole different scenario." The van ends up picking-up another passenger and coming back for Yaya, just in time to bring the coffees for the two of them.

They arrive at the trail head, and deboard the van. It's dark, cool, and eerie. They find a spot to pop-a-squat and take-a-bump before the full day hike. While they are both fairly athletic from their natural movement regime of dance, sex, yoga and active walking, somehow they were in the rear of the pack, chatting and sightseeing, and admiring all the local plants. As they ascend, they take off more layers of clothing, getting hotter as they get closer to the sun and the top of the active volcano. They continue to climb for hours, to the dry crusty peak of the volcano, until they reach the place to enjoy the 360 view from the top.

In the rush to get on the bus in the early morning, they left the dodgy place without all the essentials. As Burners, they definitely could have been better prepared with more hiking survival supplies.

When they finally reached the bottom, they were dropped off at the travel agent's store, a couple of blocks away from their lodging. Jessica and Yaya were both sunburned and physically exhausted, hungry, thirsty, and tired.

Yaya wanted to inquire about a ferry back to the mainland the following day, as transport seemed to take a while here, and Jessica wanted to hire a taxi to immediately go home. At this point, Yaya thought, *What are two more blocks to walk?*

This tiff resulted in the silent treatment towards Yaya for the next 36 hours.

They leave their shitty accommodations and check in at a really nice hotel. Yaya keeps trying to ask silent Jessica, "What is the issue?"

They go off on their own beach walks. Yaya exploring the coast one way and Jessica another. They pick up sea stars and find flamingos. Yaya swims with a seal. She eventually goes in to shower and to get ready for dinner. Jessica is still not back. So Yaya goes back out, walking around the town, and finds some yellow panties, apparently they are known to be 'lucky' in Ecuador. She is craving a hit of dopamine to feel better and buys a few things in shop therapy; pear lotion, and some hair accessories.

She returns and quietly opens the front door to see the cascading sunset before her on the terrace of their hotel room, she sees Jessica in the corner of the balcony, who lets out a big sigh, apparently unhappy with Yaya's return. Yaya asks her if she would like to go to dinner. Jessica surprisingly says "yes". They stay rather quiet at dinner and eventually over dessert Yaya asks her what she did to offend her.

Jessica tells her that when they were done with the hike, Jessica expressed that she might be sunburned, apparently her least favorite state to be in, and Yaya appeared to not care. Yaya is happy to know this, but also finds it petty, she too is sunburned and yes, in that moment, she didn't care, there were many things going on.

They miss their flight out of Galapagos by a few minutes and get rerouted, thanks to Yaya's persistence on the phone and Jessica's encouragement, eventually making it to their destination, Los Baños. Sometimes they made a good team.

In Los Baños, they find a cute Airbnb from the guidebook, and immediately go for a dip in the hot pool spa near their accommodations. They wear creamy face masques and soak outdoors and indoors, in the sauna, in the steam room, and in the hot tubs. Yaya, of course, the thrill seeker she is, finds the water slide and escapes for a few rides down, while Jessica, wears an extra special hydrating face masque in the sauna.

That night the girls meet two guys, from the hotel, that want to take them salsa dancing, fun! They salsa dance for an hour or so and get bored of the repetitive steps. They were never big on structured partnered dances.

As they say good night to the salsa boys, they meet the town's notorious coke dealer and follow him to an after-hours party. He is flirting with Jessica, and his friend is flirting with Yaya. After a few hours, the four decide to go back to an abandoned building and have an orgy. As the roosters start to welcome in the day, the girl's decide it's time to walk home. The bad boys walk them back to their Airbnb and head off into the morning.

It's now a few days later in Los Banos, mid January 2018, Yaya's 35th birthday, and she wakes up alone, tossing in the sheets.. She pushes down the feelings of sadness, trying to call in the feelings of birthday exuberance, as she sees her girlfriend hasn't yet returned from her late night tryst with the local drug dealer.

The day before, Jessica commanded that Yaya not leave the hostel until she returned, under the guise of the issue around the keys. Yaya goes to the front desk and speaks in speckled Spanish in her half-waked state, to ask about the possibility of another key. *Score!* The guy behind the computer happily gives her another key. *That was easy,* she thinks, like the sound of the Easy Button.

So she heads up to the roof and gets some coffee, chilling in the light morning sun, and overlooking the foggy landscape filled with greens and shanty roofs. It's early, so many of the other tourists in the villa haven't risen yet. She antsily explores around, rechecking all the parts of the five-story lodge.

She heads to the downstairs outside, which is rocky, dark, and shaded by a few trees and laundry supplies. She lowers her head down to avoid the tree branch, and heads into the hammock, which sinks lower than she expected. She is interested in neurotically checking her phone for any incoming birthday messages, however the Wi-fi is frustratingly weak down here. So she restlessly stays for a few minutes, probably four, and then bounces up and heads back to their stuffy room complete with a Queen bed and bathroom and their personal belongings, and stronger internet.

She was traveling with a backpack, borrowed from Sophiane, and its contents were strewn about all over the floor. Yaya sat on the bed and refreshed the Wi-fi. A few happy birthday texts pop in with smiley faces and balloons.

She scrolls through and smiles, but the urge to go outside overcomes her and she goes downstairs again. As a female born in North America in the 80s, she loves any excuse to workout and burn some calories. She goes to leave the new found extra key at the front desk, in case SHE decides to come back in. Yaya heads directly across the cobbled street to talk to the tourism place about options on what to do locally. They have river-rafting, rock-climbing, and other amazing adventures.

As Yaya is sitting in the open-air office on their couch, frustratingly browsing the options, Jessica comes walking back, make-up-less and with a look of dismay, which Yaya interprets to mean, she has seen that she has disobeyed her, and left the hostel. There are many unspoken conversations in their relationship.

Yaya shows her a menu of options that strike her fancy, including a jungle trek and amazon hike. Jessica says, "What about horseback riding?"

That was the one thing Yaya wasn't up for, based on experience. But at that moment, she felt so torn, wanting so much to please her, even on her own birthday.

The last time she rode horses was the scary time with Adil, so she was frightened and didn't really want to ride horses. Eventually she would overcome this fear on a trail ride with a trusted friend from the pet industry.

Meanwhile, at that moment, Jessica's drug-dealer boyfriend (who speaks zero English) walks by, holding-hands with his five- year-old daughter. The drug dealer asks Jessica for some money to buy his daughter some soup, and to Yaya's surprise, she gives him a couple of dollars.

Later that morning, after Jessica was finally ready, they left the hostel, hand in hand, to find some birthday breakfast for Yaya. They sat outdoors at a hammock-table-situation in a restaurant's yard with many plants and birds. They ordered some cappuccinos, juices, pastries, and eggs. Yaya spoke to her family on the phone and Jessica posted on Instagram, from her private account. Jessica didn't allow Yaya to follow her on social media, however she approved a local Ecuadorian dentist to follow her.

They had a long, leisurely stay at the cafe. Jessica paid this bill, and asked Yaya "What is your intention for this year?"

"Responsibility," she answered with conviction. Jessica smiles.

The girls had been contemplating doing a sacred plant medicine journey, if the time was right. They signed up for a temescal ceremony on the roof of their hostel, however, it was a drumming and sweating journey, sans medicine- to their dismay. The activity place across the street offered jungle tours to the Amazon, and neither of them had been into the jungle before. The tour guide casually mentions that they could spend the night with a local tribe in the jungle and drink ayahuasca medicine. Yaya's ears perked up. "That sounds easy," said Jessica. They were in.

They departed early in the morning to make the drive to the Amazon in the open air Jeep their trusty guide provided. They stop along the way to buy essentials, like honey and earrings.

Once they arrive to the parking lot for the trail head of the Amazon jungle, Yaya obediently rescues Jessica from the two big dogs looming in the parking lot. She still hasn't overcome her fear of dogs. They picked up on her energy immediately.

The girls both strip down to their bikinis to prepare for their jungle hike. Their guide smirks a bit, but says nothing. He provides them each with a big long pair of rubber boots, which go past their knees, and equips them each with a machete. Ready for the jungle trek!

They each wear a small backpack with goodies like water, a Chapstick, and their phone cameras, and they embark on their jungle hike. Their guide stops and points out various trees and medicinal plants and flowers. The jungle is alive with noise, they even hear the 'cuckqua, cuckqua' of the rainbow camouflage Toucan in the distance.

They studied the local trees that move with aerial roots, always seeking the moving streams of water. It reminded Yaya of her own roots, easily able to pivot and relocate.

They stop to pose with their machetes, and take photos in the trees. At one stream, the girls are laughing and walking and Yaya's boot is not coming out of the sandy bottom. She laughs- and it sinks further. The boot sinks all the way into the quicksand, and the guide has to grab her arm to lift her out. Afterwards they rescue the boot. While it was mildly scary, she continued to laugh through it all.

Eventually they make it to a cool pool of water, where the guide recommends that they swim. It is dark and still. Yaya immediately fears leeches and snakes in the stagnant body of water. However, they are dressed for the occasion so they go for it and jump in. The cool refreshing water feels good on their sweaty bodies. After the dunk, Jessica has had enough of the adventure and asks if there is any other way back. There is. They follow the cow trail back and end up in a big field where they sit to meditate.

They get back to the car and drive another hour or so to a drawbridge. They park and get their belongings for the overnight stay, and walk across the bridge to the other side of the river. They are greeted by little kids with no shoes, running around and smiling. The women are in the casitas stirring big pots of orange liquid, the ayahuasca plant medicine that they will drink later that night.

The girls are shown to their humble cabin with bunk beds where they dress warmer for the evening. They meet the shaman who will be serving them the medicine, and it starts to rain. They drink the ayahuasca, with no pomp and circumstance. A parrot and a monkey are both hanging around and they simply drink the medicine. They each have a hammock to lay in to contemplate the psychedelic visions.

Yaya is shown in the journey, how if she made different decisions in her family, she could have more peace. It's like a 360 visual around her, similar to being at an Imax, but the movie playing is her life.

Yaya is shown from Great Spirit during the ceremony, how if she peacefully grounds herself and takes care of herself before meeting up with her family, she will experience less negativity- as everything has a ripple effect. She is shown the ripples from her own actions, and sees what could have been. It is in technicolor and feels extremely real, on the replay.

Jessica 'gets well' and purges, deep into the night. Overall, the two of them have a thorough and peaceful journey. Yaya decides it can't get much better than that and she is done with 'grandma medicine', at least for a while.

Back in New York City, it's time for the Dance Parade Showcase Gala. Yaya is on the committee for the Dance Parade, as a PR person, and Jessica gets to attend as Yaya's plus-one. Jessica drives them to the city on this wet Sunday night for the occasion, and the girls are both dressed up. They walk into the venue and order champagne from the bartender. He procures two small bottles of bubbly rosé, and they happily "cheers".

159

Someone is going around recruiting $50 sponsors for underprivileged dance teams and Jessica becomes a sponsor. Things are going swimmingly well. They must be in the cycle of love-bombing again.

After the fabulous showcase, featuring dancers from all around the five boroughs, the girls get their photo taken by a local media person, before heading next door to a fancy French dinner. They enjoy small bites of delicious French delicacies over lovely conversation and laughter.

Jessica didn't cook, she made most of her meals in the microwave, and was used to having someone cook homemade food for her. Jessica would often call Yaya from the line at the grocery store, on her phone, like a hopeless husband, wondering if she picked out the right food provisions.

Over St. Patrick's day weekend, Yaya goes to Washington DC on a road trip with Connie to visit a pet show, and have a table of cool pet products for "The Pet Lady". During this time, Yaya and Jessica get into a fight. As a result, Jessica decides that Yaya, no longer gets to be privy to her selective Facebook posts, and blocks her indefinitely from all of her social media channels.

However, they had never actually been friends on Instagram. "I save it for random strangers that I don't know," Jessica had told her. *Well, that's normal*, Yaya thought sarcastically.

A few months go by, and it's May, and time for the actual Dance Parade in the streets. Yaya wakes up with enthusiasm. It's raining out of Jessica's windows in Rockaway. *Hmmm*, she thinks, *maybe it will be bright and sunny in the city?* She hops in the guest shower, which has really become her domain, and does a quick body-scrub and towels off. She saunters into the kitchen to test out the new gift she got The Doctor, a big-ass blender. She likes to cook naked anyway. Her long brown hair drips onto the tiled kitchen floor as she opens the new box and tries to figure it out.

Yaya doesn't have a lot of time so she hurriedly applies some makeup, throws her hair up in a bun and slides on her one-piece-spandex-multi colored-dance-costume. She grabs her Burning Man goggles, which have been painted and bedazzled and adds them around her forehead. *Ready*, she thinks.

Now, just how to make breakfast? She plugs in the massive black-and-clear blender and tosses in a peeled banana, some cold-brew coffee, and some powdered super food supplements and presses play. *Hmmm nothing is happening.* She messes around for a few more minutes and the blender slowly churns the liquids together. It's not exactly blended.

She leaves it on the counter to deal with later, for now she must run to catch the ferry! She plops on her pink high heel converse with purple sparkly laces and heads out the door, locking it behind her so Jessica may get a bit more rest.

This Dance Parade is a rainy one. She goes to the media check-in center, where most people are huddled under the tent.

Photographers have their cameras protected in plastic bags. They go ahead with the ribbon cutting and the parade is off!

Yaya joins the Five Rhythms float, and dances on top of it with a friend. Eventually, she meets up with her buddies Gabriela and Jeff, who find her near Union Square. They finish the parade at Tompkins Square Park as usual, and head to the House Music corner, after posing with the painted ballerinas. A few hours into it, she gets a text from Jessica saying that she is on her way!

Eventually a very soaking wet Jessica shows up to Tompkins Square Park. Jessica and Yaya and their friend go back to her place nearby to dry off and regroup.

Jessica is in a foul mood, and accuses Yaya of trying to poison her. She wasn't sure what to do with the half-ass smoothie when she woke up and that enraged her. She thought since the blender hadn't been properly washed first that Yaya was indeed trying to kill her, and poison her via smoothie.

Yaya calmly and patiently reassures her that that was not her intention. The three of them follow the host's lead and wash their feet in the kitchen sink before collectively enjoying a much needed joint together to relax.

Later on that night at a Burner Bar in Brooklyn (a bar that was owned and operated by people that attended Burning Man), Jessica and Yaya were dancing on the small checkered dance floor in the front by the DJ, among the dusty weird items including porcelain dolls, rotary phones and antique children's bikes, randomly perched and hung all-around the venue. A tall woman wanted to meet her, and Jessica introduces them.

The tall woman proceeded to tell Yaya how Jessica was a witch and put a spell on her to lick her pussy 1,000 times. She went on and on and on. In some way it helped her explain the weirdness of their relationship. She felt relieved that she wasn't the only one. However, in Chinese tradition, Yaya was born in the Year of the Dog, as loyal as can be.

Yaya remembers thinking that Jessica was worried that night. The whole thing really didn't phase Yaya, and it also seemed like a bit of a setup.

Jessica told Yaya that the tall woman would be happy to host her at her Astoria apartment, and smoke-Yaya-out and tell her all about it. She thought she was being a good partner by staying true to Jessica, despite this seemingly nasty rumor and invitation.

* * *

On this particular Saturday, it was sunny, yet rather windy, and the beach was vacant *just for them*. They walked hand in hand for a while, chatting and stopping to smooch under the epic cloudage. Then they paused at the summer's leftover lifeguard chair, looked at each other and climbed up. They sat and listened to an exercise from 'Fulfilled,' by Anna Yusim on Audible.

Jessica wanted Yaya to share a secret with her, to "get it off her chest and release some baggage" all for Yaya's benefit, of course.

Jessica is a covert narcissist, and was always on the quest to get some juicy vulnerable bits of information from Yaya, to later use against her. Yaya was compromised and looking for healing when she had met Jessica.

At the time Yaya was naive and shared a secret, about being a child and charging her neighbor $1 extra for the fourth grade gift catalog item. It was actually a relief off her chest, to share with her and felt vulnerable at the time. In return, Jessica, told Yaya some lame story about lying to an ex about shaving her teeth, which was a joke.

This was part of the slow drip of the grooming process, to the dark slave/master relationship that was building between them. Similar to the way Michael Jackson would allegedly groom his youthful guests.

They had been just friends for about eight months, which transitioned into her calling her "Babe," and starting to do three-way kisses with men. Then they were girlfriends for about eighteen months, which is exactly the time of the honeymoon period in a relationship.

There had been an article in the New York Times about how to get someone to fall in love with you, and Jessica seemed overly fascinated by it.

Yaya and Jessica fly to Florida to attend 'Splash Mocha', a hotel takeover play party with two big, black male lovers as roommates.

Jessica had been telling Yaya about this epic sex party for a while, and they are excited to be there. All the hotel rooms are rented by 'Splash Mocha' guests, and the ballrooms had been transformed into various play areas with colors and themes and sex-play set ups, with condoms, lube, and hand sanitizer.

One night, they are in the BDSM room playing with the Sybian, a machine to ride, where they meet Jerome with the really big dick. They are less interested in going back to people's rooms as there is more safety to stay in the big rooms with everyone, as two females.

They play, and play, and play, until they both 'tap out' and go back to the room to shower and snuggle, feeling blissed out. The next morning, they meet Jerome for breakfast and Jessica surprisingly forgets her wallet. Yaya pays again.

They check out the pool party and select a few guys to make a private play party, in the cabana off the pool. The next night, they check out the vendors and buy some floggers and some cute booty-shorts, and play some more.

Sunday is now their last day and they have to check-out and fly home. They get all packed-up and decide to go for a walk around the golf course they are staying on. They go for a walk, slowly chatting and holding hands. Yaya's favorite time of day. They see birds and Florida wildlife out and about.

It starts raining horribly in a downpour, unexpectedly, and they run for cover under a big oak tree. Yaya meditates and shares her sense of peace and calm with Jessica.

Before going out for the walk, Yaya had prepared some water bottles and drinks with ice from the machine for when they returned from the walk. What she didn't count on was the ice melting and leaking onto everything and getting their clothes wet.

They are planning on quickly changing into their dry clothes after the rain walk and flying home, but everything has ice water on it. Jessica is furious and stops talking to Yaya for the next few hours, even when Yaya offers to dry the clothes in the dryer or let her wear some of her dry clothes.

Once they arrive at JFK, Jessica turns to Yaya and stiffly asks, "Will you be coming home with me, or going to your home?"

Yaya says, "If you are going to forgive me for getting your clothes wet and move on, I will gladly come over. However, if you are going to hold a grudge against me and continue to not talk to me, I'll go home."

The girls hop in the shuttle to go pick up Jessica's car in the parking lot. Jessica goes to pay for parking and snags Yaya an orange from the front desk. "See, I take care of you too," she says and tosses Yaya the orange. They ride back to Rockaway hand in hand.

Weeks later, Yaya flies to Vegas for the pet conference she attends every year. Her Polish friend from NYC has moved to Vegas, and he has a boat. He takes her out for a sunrise joyride and they pop some champagne and cruise. Back at the diner for breakfast, all before the conference, Jessica calls Yaya to let her know that there has been a problem with the upcoming festival tickets, and basically, she doesn't have them.

They had made a deal that Yaya would get and pay for the Burning Man tickets that year, if Jessica would get and pay for these festival tickets, including the cabin for accommodation and driving. However, it turns out Jessica has done none of this, and forgot. Yaya confirms that yes she would still like to go to the festival and Jessica says she will try to figure it out.

Yaya finishes the conference and wearily flies back to New York City after walking laps around the casino on the trade show floor for three full days. Jessica has managed to find them some tickets and a cabin and has secured them bus tickets, so she doesn't have to drive the two and a half hour trip. Jessica has road rage anyway, so Yaya agrees this is a mighty fine plan. Yaya finishes packing at home, and makes a snack. She lights some candles, as her place smells a bit like mouse droppings. Her pet closet has been having a mouse infestation and she hasn't properly dealt with it. Jessica says she is ten minutes away.

Thirty minutes later Jessica comes up to get a snack, and uses the potty. The girls are meeting to get a taxi to midtown together to catch the bus.

When mouse or rat animal totems crosses your path, you are being asked to assert yourself in new areas that you have not yet explored. This symbolism warns you to evaluate the clutter around you. It's time for spring cleaning.

Luckily the bus hasn't left yet, as Jessica and Yaya are very late, and the girls are the last to board.

To enter the festival there is a big line. Yaya and Jessica casually go up to the front, past everyone and snag two hot pink wristbands amidst the clutter of people and chaos at check in. The girls put on their wristbands and walk into their cabins, past security and everyone at bag check.

At the festival, they are offered some lovely hot cacao to drink, they make art and dance, and wear costumes. At one point, while they are both under a triage of enhancements; Jessica has an epiphany, that the problem with society is that everyone is too entitled.

They run into Jessica's ex and his friend, who are scheming to get a nitrous oxide machine inside. The two guys miss each other by about two minutes so Yaya helps them connect the dots. She is surprised when Jessica makes no effort to help them. She thought they were friends.

The next day, there was a water fight out on the lake. It's hot, and the girls are dancing in bikinis, drinking seltzer, and not minding the light spray of water that comes on shore every once in a while from the water balloon and water gun fight on various rafts and pirate ships.

Back in New York, Yaya hosts a Latihan night and is impressed with the practice yet again. Yaya wants to further her exploration and knowledge of Latihan and goes for a twelve- week introduction at the Subud Center in midtown Manhattan in order to get 'opened.'

Every Friday, she goes and meets with the center's women, talking and reading about the teachings of Subud, which means 'practice' in Indonesian. They practice with men and women separately, which is very different from the 'naughty-han' version, or 'body-han' she learned from the tantra teachers at ISTA.

Tony and Yaya decide to host a few Latihan events at Valencia, the fifteen person community house that Tony runs. They have a big upstairs community room that works well for connection events. It's a potluck event, and Yaya brings some Pad Thai. Tony is very punctual and likes to start on time. They are expecting twenty guests, and the last two to arrive are Jessica, The Doctor and her friend Gabriela. There is no way that Yaya is locking either one of them out, so she stalls and delays as best she can manage until they both arrive, within minutes of each other.

Everyone is given a blindfold and instructions on what kind of touch to use when they encounter another body. Tony and Yaya are going to be the 'Latihan angels," keeping their eyes open and watching out for any funky-play, or consent and safety issues. They press play on the Spotify playlist they have happily co-created and let the Latihan begin in the pillowed-in area. Jessica is by herself in the corner happily touching the air, while everyone else is energetically connecting.

Immediately afterwards, Jessica leaves to go home while Yaya stays to hang out with her friends, and go to an after party. The next night when they are together, Jessica tells Yaya to "stop hosting those ridiculous events," as it makes her look bad to be dating someone who is posturing to be an expert in leading community functions.

Yaya accepts this controlling message, and tells Tony she won't be collaborating on any more Latihans for a while.

Yaya flies to San Francisco to meet up with Will and a few others to drive to Reno. They stop off at BJs and Walmart to get supplies for themselves and for Jessica. Will tells Yaya in Walmart, as she searches every aisle for a box-cutter for Jessica, "You have been whipped."

The group of shoppers go into The Burn early, and start building sturdy cardboard yurts for their community.

Yaya has started her day with coffee and stretching, a joint and some veggies (magic mushrooms), and is helping to build yurts and wooden bike racks in the camp. It's hot, and at one point she sets down her hammer and her water bottle to get some shade. She comes back twenty minutes later completely freaking out that someone has stolen her water bottle. This is a special water bottle that keeps cold things cold and hot things hot. She starts crying. She has a meltdown in the middle of the unbuilt camp, thinking that she is going to die of thirst now that her lifeline, her water source, is missing.

Will offers her one of his plastic water bottles. She grumpily refuses. About ten minutes later she goes back to work and finds the black bottle next to the tools she set down. *Aha! Found.*

She finishes building the wooden bike racks with pride and moves on to helping the yurt builders. She offers to do the doors, which require a special amount of two sided Velcro to withstand the wind and dust. She also assembles a few Air conditioning coolers in buckets that successfully operate with ice.

The first night she sleeps in the yurt alone with a mattress that Will has brought for them. The next night Jessica arrives, as does their roommate Jeff. The three party and dance and come into the yurt in the morning to rest. The AC works so well that Jeff's date gets too cold and storms off in the early morning complaining that she has no warmth. It was blowing directly on her.

Yaya and Jessica found the slow dancing camp in Center Camp, and melted into each other even further, becoming completely enmeshed in Jessica's bubble.

This year, Yaya was supposed to meet up with Dean, a guy she was dating, to join the Mile High Club at the Burning Man airport, a special flight with a mattress where lovers can connect, but she was too occupied with Jessica to ever find Dean, to meet up with him on Wednesday, or to return the note he left for her at their yurt.

When Yaya returns to NYC, it's election time. Yaya works the polls as her meditation, she enjoys the challenge of working alongside a varied population for long hours and remain her cool. They arrive at 5am and are on teams of four. Some checking people in, some handing out ballots, and some handing out 'I voted' stickers.

Dean and Yaya go for a drink after Yaya works the polls all day, at 10pm. They laugh and share some jokes at a local bar in her neighborhood. She apologizes for missing him and his note, and he understands. He was busy getting up to his own shenanigans at the Burn.

He looks at her and asks Yaya to be his girlfriend. Yaya thinks, *Well, it would be cool to have a girlfriend AND a boyfriend.*

However, Yaya has never even been to Dean's apartment. Somehow, after Adil, she feels seeing someone's digs is pretty important before moving forward with a label like that.

She challenges Dean. "What would you want to happen, that's not happening now, if we were officially labeled in that way?" He can't answer. He has just come out of a long marriage, so maybe he feels ownership is the way to love.

Jessica's gay friend comes to visit from Uruguay for a week and Yaya makes him some black wings, with clothes hangers, tights, and black spray paint, for him to wear for Halloween. The four of them, Yaya and Jessica, dressed as matching witches from Bahia (an island off of Brazil), the visiting friend dressed as a fallen angel,' and Dean, wearing a bondage hood subordinate mask, attend an all-night Halloween rave party.

They take a bunch of group photos on the stairs of the fabulous mansion that they are at on Jessica's camera - so they never see them again - she has a knack for capturing special moments in pictures on her phone and then never sharing them.

When they end up all crashing back at Jessica's pad, just after sunrise, Dean and their Uruguayan guest sleep in the living room while Yaya and Jessica cuddle in her bedroom.

A few days later, after their morning ritual of sun salutations at yoga, the girls were next door getting coffee when Chaya, the yoga teacher, popped in to pick up her breakfast bowl. She asked Jessica how it was going with her drug dealer boyfriend in Ecuador? Jessica looked her right in the eyes and declared that he was not a drug dealer. Yaya covered her mouth and looked away.

She couldn't believe that Jessica was lying to Chaya to her face! It was too much to take in. He literally had a five pound bag of cocaine in his bedroom, in the same room where his little daughter slept, and Chaya was their friend!

CHAPTER TEN

Yaya Decides to Stay

A dangling carrot keeps the donkey wanting more.

Yaya sees an 'Open House' sign in the street as she leaves Jessica's place one morning. She pops in to meet the Realtor and see the spot. It's on the 4th floor overlooking the ocean. It's a big bright, sunny studio with a cute little captain's kitchen. There is a little side hallway near the bathroom that she has ideas for and a big walk in closet; all the essentials. It's not even listed on the market yet. Plus, there is a big palm tree in the corner. Yaya wants it all.

She places an offer, a bit under. Denied. She places another offer, on the same day. Denied. Her third offer, also on the same-day, is accepted! The beach view window is marvelous, and Yaya can envision pulling off the blinds completely to have curtain-less access to the sun and moon.

The co-op building is just four blocks away from Jessica's place. *Perfect! She is finally actualizing her fantasy to be neighbors with her partner!* She is ecstatic and feels like things are really coming together. The seller agrees to let her keep the big palm tree too.

Originally, Yaya had started the real estate search, as Jessica suggested they buy a place together. Yaya was proud of herself for not going along with what Jessica wanted, and for standing her ground and getting her own place. They weren't married and a shared property would entangle them too much.

Meanwhile, the dean from FIT called Yaya to let her know that they were terminating the Pet Product Marketing program, and she would no longer be able to teach there - it had been the only pet product program in the world.

Her ego was bruised. She quickly put together an email proposal to send to all the local colleges and universities offering them this one of a kind curriculum. She got zero response.

Then just a few weeks before the Fall semester was starting, she got a call from Baruch College. They were inviting her to teach in their international Master's program teaching Luxury Marketing, would she want to do it? Yaya said yes.

She dresses up and has her 'teacher bag,' a baby blue, nice crisp purse she bought in Charleston, and stands in front of the podium to get ready to lecture them about following their heart, passion, and dreams. The mid 20s French kids all can't wait until their next cigarette break, as it's mid-afternoon on Friday. Yaya just hopes she doesn't run into any of them at The House of Yes, or any other cool Brooklyn dance clubs, *now that would be awkward!*

* * *

The girls spent every weekend together. Yaya always slept over at Jessica's unless they were ridiculously close to Yaya's place. One time when sleeping over at Yaya's Astoria Heights apartment, Yaya woke up to Jessica reading her journal.

That night, Yaya had wanted to go back to her Astoria home, alone, after they were out dancing, so she could get up and go to Voice Cult the next morning. Jessica didn't like to sing, so she thought she would plan to go without her, an unprecedented weekend occurrence.

They were pretty codependent at that point, so Yaya had felt bad that Jessica was spending the day, all alone. So after Voice Cult, Yaya rode her bike from Bushwick to Rockaway, and let Jessica know she was coming as an afternoon surprise. Jessica seemed happy about it. Yaya arrived and they smooched and hung out in the ways that they usually did.

She had been preparing dinner for them in Jessica's tiny kitchen, after a beach day acid walk. She jumped in the shower and washed herself in the guest bathroom, which had been pretty much taken over by her makeup, toiletries, and extra clothing.

She was still damp, as she walked on the carpet, down the hallway, naked, and into Jessica's bedroom, which was completely painted in a space-ship motif (by her ex-boyfriend), to let her know that dinner was almost ready.

Jessica seductively pushed Yaya onto her bed and suggested that they mess around first. Yaya was usually hornier than her, but this one time, she was not feeling it. She had just rode her bike twenty plus miles and her hoo-ha was sore, to be frank. Yaya said "No, not right now."

Yaya thinks she is with her life partner, when Jessica looks Yaya straight in the eye and says, "You don't get to say no to me."

Oh snap.

They quietly move food around their plates and then Jessica disappears for hours to get ready.

Later on that night, they were supposed to be going to dance at a boat party. Yaya was pissed off, and she still wanted to go, and she probably had bought the tickets for both of them. She thought she was choosing love over fear, by deciding to stay with her girlfriend through this appalling statement.

As soon as they arrived, one of Jessica's other lover's, the bouncer said, "I love you so much, it hurts." He then offered to go down on both of them in a private room on the boat. Jessica said to him that they were in a bit of a fight, and now might not be the best time.

Yaya was wearing a black mesh see-through skirt, with red panties and a matching belly dancer bra, and matte red lipstick. She liked to bend over and shake her booty in general in life and especially, when she was mad or had extra emotions to release.

Janet J. was there, and contemplating how she could get her favorite brands like the pretzel company to pay for her life. Jessica recommends that she talk to Yaya.

It was 9am, and the girls had all been partying all night. They sipped on coffee that a pirate on the ship had made and smoked joints, still bobbing their heads to the music.

The girls pretended everything was okay, brushing their previous disagreement under the rug, and stood in line for the bathroom together and took some selfies in the mirror. Yaya did some strange things in her mind to distort the truth to be okay with it.

She didn't know that the sex was a form of abuse. She accepted the calculated manipulation.

The following weekend Jessica hid away in Rockaway at a three-day meditation retreat. Yaya already had plans one day that weekend so decided not to join. There was a monk visiting to share his wisdom. The retreat goers were challenged to bring in their favorite book to give him as an offering. Jessica quickly grabbed Yaya's special earmarked copy of 'Power vs. Force' and gave that to the monk. When Yaya asked about it, since she was midway reading it, Jessica ordered her a replacement copy on Amazon.

On November 6th, Yaya hires a 'man with a van' and moves from East Astoria to her new studio apartment in Rockaway. A few weeks later, the girls hosted Thanksgiving at Jessica's place, a new tradition, for the third year in a row, this time with a fun older burner couple. At this point, the Thanksgiving formula is that they invite guests over, they take some acid, they go for a magic beach walk and then Yaya cooks. Then they all eat on the carpet as a picnic, and then they watch a scary movie.

Their mature female guest wasn't exactly comfortable eating on the floor, so they Jerry-rigged a table for her. After dinner, Yaya and one of the guests were making tea for everyone, and Yaya in a bout of laughter, drops one of the mugs full of hot water and honey on the tiny kitchen floor. It breaks and spills. The two women start cleaning it up when Jessica comes in and completely flips out, yelling and hissing.

"Oh harsh" says the woman. Jessica is completely reaming-out Yaya with shame and punishment, and then collapses into a pile on the floor and busts into a sob.

It was an accident.

A few weeks later, after Yaya showers Jessica with Hanukkah gifts every day for eight days, they fly to Cabo, Mexico together to meet Tom and Leila Humphrey for Christmas.

"See you later," Yaya calls to her Mom as she grabs the keys for Hank, to the big white van. Jessica and Yaya are going to downtown Cabo.

They have been staying with Yaya's parents in San Jose del Cabo, which is a cute quaint town, and they are going to the big city of Cabo about forty minutes away, where you can find Senior Frogs and Cabo Wabo. The girls are going to have lunch, and then go on a boat cruise to see the natural magic arch.

They park and walk to book their boat cruise tickets and then hit-up the ATM. They find a taco shop and enjoy the salsa bar and their almuerzo (lunch in Spanish). Half way through lunch, Jessica looks up at Yaya and declares she has lost her phone. She rushes back to the ATM, thinking she may have left it there. No phone.

They board the booze cruise and take some pictures, and Jessica, is sulking the entire time. Yaya has done this boat trip a few times already, so she doesn't really need to see the arch, and the current vibe is a bit lackluster.

After the boat cruise, they walk around the mall and Jessica buys a watch so she can know what time it is, without her phone. They visit the empty shops and eventually stop for a drink. Around 9pm once the sun has set, the two return back.

The next day, Jessica and Yaya's Mom are having a legitimate stare down before dinner.

Jessica has hope that her phone is still findable in Cabo. They finish dinner and check Tom's computer for Jessica's phone's exact location. Leila, Yaya's Mom, was hoping the four of them would play her favorite competitive game, Scrabble, that night. Instead, Tom, Yaya's Dad, offers to drive them, and go with them to find the phone.

I guess it's true, every man just wants to be a hero.

The three of them drive to downtown Cabo. They have Tom's laptop in tow. They park on the street in a neighborhood where the phone is indicated to be. They pass a family having a 'pinata party' in the dark. Next door, some dudes are out front playing video games. It's the day before Christmas Eve. They ask the dudes, who suggest the three muskateers go upstairs.

Tom, Jessica and Yaya walk upstairs to a door that is open, and Tom barges right-in demanding they give them the phone. The girls are taken aback. The guys living in this home immediately get defensive, rightly so, and ask them to leave. It was a bit of a scary situation and any Mexican guys who are not with their family on Christmas may be troubled, Yaya assumed. Tom eventually backs down, and the trio leave and go to the police department to file a report.

The police couldn't care less about their predicament, so they go home, empty handed.

Over the next few days, Jessica is beyond forlorn. She borrows Yaya's phone to call her parents and is generally sad, although they are in a warm paradise.

Andrea comes for a few days and they go to a fun festive party with body painting, lights, and an awesome band.

On the way out, when Yaya and Jessica are going to the airport, Leila asks Yaya to sweep the floor. The girls are literally walking down the stairs with their bags and about to hop in Hank, the van, with Tom to go to the airport.

Andrea just spent a few nights there too and she was not asked to sweep the floor.

Yaya said, "No," to her Mom, and left.

She received the silent treatment for the next three months. Yaya eventually wrote a letter to apologize, and her Mom started talking to her again - like nothing happened. Always brushing it under the rug.

* * *

Jason was one of their lovers. He had a nice big dick and he was good at sharing and playing. He lived in New Jersey and was even-tempered, sober, and quick to please. He was one of their regulars for play parties.

Jason had a sub (submissive) name Carly. Carly played dirty. Sometimes she would do blow jobs without condoms, and the girls didn't like that. As sexually wild as they were, they did uphold safer sex practices.

However, Jessica was on a mission for them to play with more women.

One night, when the girls are chilling in the kitchen, Jessica is trying to read her mail and Yaya is trying to give her smooches everywhere, Jessica announced that she wanted to invite Carly to play with them, the following Tuesday.

Tuesday rolls around and Yaya hasn't heard from Jessica all day. She calls her around 8pm. "What do you want? I'm out," said Jessica ,not offering any other details although Yaya clearly hears a play party in the background.

Later on, when Yaya was brave and confronted Jessica about it, she quickly denied it. Just one subtle example of the way that Jessica would undermine Yaya's sense of reality by routinely gaslighting her. Plus, since narcissists never think they're wrong, they never apologize.

CHAPTER ELEVEN

Yaya Takes a Break

Sometimes, the only way is back on the road again.

Yaya wakes up early at Jessica's place. She has rented a car and will be driving to Hartford soon to make it for an 11am live TV segment on NBC. Sometimes, Yaya does her hair and makeup in CT, sometimes before. This day she whips up some make-up at Jessica's place, in the guest bathroom. They had been out late the night before in Astoria at a sound bath, followed by a movie. Jessica had asked casually before the movie, if she could hypnotize Yaya, again. It may have been wearing off. Yaya declined.

Jessica walks in to grab her coffee from the counter, and exclaims that one of these days she should do Yaya's makeup, suggesting it could be better. Jessica is a self- taught expert at makeup as her appearance is critical for her well-being.

Yaya agrees and says, "That would be great, how about right now?"

Jessica responds that she needs to book it into her calendar in advance with her assistant. Yaya has watched Jessica do the makeup of countless acquaintances, but alas never her own, and they have been dating now for eighteen months. *She doesn't want to make an appointment.*

Yaya leaves the Doctor's place in Rockaway feeling disappointed, and wondering if her very own partner will ever do her makeup.

She races to the segment and gets a speeding ticket in her rented green Fiat, and ends up arriving a few minutes late. The crew from NBC are not impressed- but they squeeze her in - at the end.

That night, Yaya has a date planned with Dean to sleepover. Jessica is texting Yaya like crazy and says she wants to see her. So, Yaya agrees to stop by on her way home, now that they are neighbors, it's easy to stop by for a hug and a kiss.

They smooch and chat and Jessica mentions that there is a store by her work, the hospital in Brooklyn with amazing sparkly jackets on sale. They make a plan to visit together on Friday.

Yaya heads home to get ready for Dean. Now, the girls are in an open relationship, anyone was allowed and encouraged to sleep with anyone, but Yaya is still a bit upset that Jessica lied about Carly, so she decided to keep the fact that Dean was sleeping over - a secret. Jessica finds out, upon pressuring Yaya to sleepover that night, and tells Yaya that she is offended.

Friday morning, they go to a yoga class not speaking to one another. Yaya writes a note to Jessica and drops it off on her car window.

They had plans to go shopping and then to see, 'To Kill a Mockingbird,' a new Broadway show that Yaya got them tickets for. Instead, Jessica texts her to "find a date, and pick up the tickets from her assistant," as she is too upset to go to the show with her.

Instead of dealing with Jessica's assistant and going all the way to Brooklyn, Yaya calls the theater and has the ticket status changed to 'will call.' She follows Jessica's instructions, as usual, and asks a date, Aaron, to go to the show with her and he says "yes." Aaron and Yaya meet at Junior's restaurant next door first for a snack and chat a bit before the show.

They arrive and start walking into the show. Jessica walks up as well at the same time, sees Yaya there with Aaron and screams, "You have now ruined my evening- you stupid CUNT!"

180

She runs off and follows this up with photos of vomit texted to Yaya's phone.

After the show, Aaron and Yaya go for some hot chocolate. Aaron asks Yaya, "Does she always talk to you like that?"

Yaya's initial reaction was stressing and thinking about *How can she make things better? How can she 'fix' this problem?* Being with Aaron during this quest helped her see things through his perspective, which was through a loving and compassionate lens.

Yaya is finally building up the strength and courage to choose herself, and love herself first.

She has a moment of clarity where all the fucked up things that Jessica has done to her over the last eighteen months flash before her eyes. All the inconsistencies, the lies, the manipulation, the gaslighting. She remembers conversations they had that were twisted and plagued with inaccuracies. She recalls the looks of contempt Jessica would wear when Yaya shared some of her good news with her.

She also remembers the conversation with someone at Burning Man, that they had had about falling in love, and how the honeymoon period lasts about eighteen months. The rose-colored glasses were wearing off.

The next morning Yaya is distraught.

Jessica suggests via text message that Yaya read a book called, 'Lies'. So, Yaya immediately downloads it on Audible and goes for a long beach walk to listen to it.

This propels her to read 'The Power' next, which is about narcissism. She spends all day and all night on Saturday listening to books.

The next day on Sunday, Yaya is hosting her 36th birthday party and housewarming party at her new Rockaway place.

She makes a few things for people to munch-on and some warm-mulled-wine, and generally feels like a zombie. About thirty of her friends pop through, throughout the day, but not Jessica. In her reading and research, Yaya is learning that it's hard for narcissists to celebrate other's birthdays.

Yaya decides to break-up with Jessica, and to not travel with her.

Vacations were usually the happy part of their relationship, where she would benefit from some heavy love bombing after this type of familiar discard. They had planned a three-week vacation together to southeast Asia, departing in just a few days.

The following night, Jessica calls Yaya on the phone, to no answer. So she then comes over and knocks on the door. Yaya peers through her locked door chain, afraid, and knowing it's her.

Jessica asks, "where are we going to stay in Dubai?" Yaya says she doesn't care and that she is not traveling with her.

"Oh," exclaims the Doctor, "Well, in that case we should trade back keys." Yaya sighs in relief. *That's actually a good idea.*

They walk back to Jessica's place together in silence. Yaya takes out her baskets of things from the guest bathroom and pours them all into a big yellow laundry bag.

After learning about NPD (Narcissistic Personality Disorder) Yaya decided to go 'no contact' with Jessica. Going no contact is one of the most effective ways to escape the claws of a narcissist. However, it's not as easy as just blocking their number. No contact is a strategy that works if you want to dissolve a relationship with a narcissist, someone with NPD, narcissistic personality disorder. If they are a narcissist, then going 'grayrock' or stonewall means you are setting yourself up for success from getting sucked back in, or 'hoovered' by them. Individuals suffering from personality disorders such as narcissistic personality disorder, generally hoover on their victims.

A few signs of being hoovered are re-establishing communication, perhaps contacting you out of the blue, and pretending that nothing has happened. Twisting the conversation and asking, for instance, if you still have something that once belonged to them, or saying they dreamt about you, is a manipulation tactic.

'The Power,' spurred her onto a trail of books about narcissism including, 'The Human Magnet Syndrome' and many others.

Jessica saw Yaya like a coffee machine. She was useful, she liked having her around, she missed her when she was gone, and she didn't care how she was feeling.

Yaya had been burnt in a relationship with a hyper-sensitive, gaslighting narcissistic toxic woman.

After the painful break-up, Yaya had trouble moving on. She had been addicted to a person who didn't care for her. She felt stuck and miserable. She had thought she had found 'the one.'

At the airport the girls see each other. Both attention-loving brunettes with sparkly apparel and sequined accessories, they are both hard to miss. They conveniently avoid each other, and Yaya gets her seats changed to sit far behind her for the long flight to Dubai.

Yaya's friend in Dubai is on a business trip to UAE for a few days. Yaya stands at the airport not sure what to do, when she learns that Emirates, the airline she flew on, has a free shuttle from Dubai to UAE, leaving in forty minutes. She gets in touch with Mona, who says, "Yes, come!" Mona is being hosted by her client at a seven-star hotel there. Yaya felt like things were finally starting to work out.

The next morning, Yaya discovers the hotel's mighty breakfast and is completely satisfied. It may have been the best, most robust breakfast of her life. There is food from East and West and all kinds of teas and cappuccinos. It is truly decadent. When she finishes, while Mona is working, she goes across the street to check out the spa.

She books herself a massage and enjoys the amenities, a hot tub and sauna in the women's locker room. However, she is taken aback by a huge sign in the locker room reading, 'Nudity prohibited.' Apparently they were supposed to change in the tiny stalls. *Wow, this place was pretty homophobic,* thought Yaya. Luckily she was the only one in there.

That night Mona and Yaya meet for dinner, it was Mona's treat for Yaya's birthday, and they enjoy a fabulous Italian place on the water next to their hotel.

She got to chill and be pampered, and to enjoy the company of her longtime friend Mona from their Istanbul days.

The stay over in UAE is short, but exactly the respite she needed, and the next day Yaya has to return to the Dubai airport.

At the airport, Yaya sees Jessica near the gate, buying psychology magazines and decides to dodge her death-stare, and check out the massage store. Yaya ends up leaving with a very expensive travel massager for her back and neck. It feels like real hands applying pressure to the muscles.

When Yaya experiences emotional pain, it shows up in her body.

Once they land in Sri Lanka, Yaya takes an Uber to her Airbnb and plans her trip to the land of hot air balloons, to finally check it off her bucket-list. Apparently, sunrise-ballooning happens in the North, so she sets off on a long bus ride with her handy massager - to the North.

She communicates with the hot air balloon people via email and arranges a pick up at 5am at her little bed and breakfast. She stays in a private room in a house with an elderly couple who don't speak much English.

She is putting on her socks and shoes after making her bed as she hears the roosters rise in the distance, when she gets notification that the balloon ride won't be happening that day, maybe tomorrow. The wind conditions aren't right. She is slightly disappointed and raring-to-go.

She uses her up-and-at-em morning energy to walk to the Golden Temple and hikes to the very top. Along the way, she passes naughty monkeys and bats and some stray dogs, all looking for a snack.

She passed the ticket counter for the Golden Temple around 5am and no one was there, so she kept hiking up the stairs. When she made it to the top, she had to check-in her gray converse at the shoe counter, and borrow a shawl to be properly covered before entering the temple. Just as she was going to enter, a guard starts yelling and screaming at her that she has no ticket and she may not enter.

A vendor selling wooden boxes nearby sees the ruckus and comes gently beside Yaya and says, "It's okay, you must just go back down the stairs and pay for a ticket and return. I do it barefoot all the time," he says, waving his left-bare-foot back and forth.

Yaya's nervous system is on high alert after the past two years of emotional abuse, and she is grateful that this man came to her aid. With confidence and grace, she returns down the stairs, shoeless like the locals.

She finally makes payment and gets her ticket, and is able to explore the attraction. There are ruins and artifacts from the Golden Buddha inside. It is very cool and she enjoys herself. She takes photos of the lotus flowers and the typical Tibetan Buddhist prayer flags in the trees.

After touring the temple, the same vendor invites Yaya to meditate on the rock. He is really looking out for her that morning and she goes with it. After meditating for about forty-five minutes, he brings her a vegan Sri Lankan noodle breakfast to enjoy from her view point, and a fork!

He sells two wooden boxes and decides that Yaya is his lucky charm for the day.

He hands her one of his trick wooden boxes to open. He says if she can open it she can keep it. She drops it at one point and nudges one side to slide a fraction down. She goes with that movement and ends up opening the box! It becomes her special distance Reiki box.

They walk to a site he wants to show her, and they meet up with his friend, the tuktuk driver. He negotiates with him in Sri Lankan and they pile in and head off to the trees.

She has a moment of hesitation, accepting to go to the woods with a 'stranger-danger man,' however, she decides this is what travel is all about and says yes to the potentially threatening adventure.

Sometimes when you are at the bottom, the only thing left is hope.

It's still early in the morning and they have the whole day ahead of them. They go through town to somewhere secluded and into the great wide open space. They turn down a dusty path speckled with grass, that is really more of a one-way than a two-way road. The tuktuk driver stays in the open-air-vehicle and Yaya's new friend takes her to the trail head.

He invites her to drop her despair and sadness at a very special old tree in the woods by the mountain.

There are many kinds of plants and trees, which make for beautiful shade patterns in the interesting woods. The path is strewn with varied leaves, long skinny ones and short circular ones, green ones, and beige and brown ones. They walk past a family getting some fresh air and hiking in the woods, and they make it to a very big, light colored tree.

He recommends that Yaya give the tree a 'pelvis-to-tree hug,' and really let the tree take all her sadness. He encourages her to give it all to the tree. She is wearing a light pink scarf and white and she embraces the tree with love and tender gratitude and stays in her eco-sexual position against the big tree for a while. She feels very content, just being one with nature and the forgiving tree.

Afterwards, they take the tuktuk to one more place, first stopping to get some lunch for the three of them. Her new friend pays, and Yaya likes that the driver is included in the meal. They enjoy some typical rice with various spicy curries, all yummy and vegetarian. As Sri Lankans are either Buddhist or Muslim, Yaya feels safe traveling around here in a spiritually and religious minded place.

Next, they enter what seems like a national park, Sigiriya. There is a big road surrounding a body of water, covered in large, water monitor lizards, until they get to the base of the mountain. They pay the guard a bit to get in, and must take off their shoes to walk through a special monastery to get to the trail.

At the trail, they tie their shoes back on and start the ascent. They climb and climb for about an hour, reaching the top of the peak just in time for sunset. They see the sun's lingering light over the whole lush area full of limes, and greens, and trees.

They hike back down and after a luxuriously exhausting day they drop Yaya off back in town, to find her accommodations. Her new friend keeps offering her a special naked healing massage on meditation rock, but she declines and chooses to go home to safety, comfort, and sleep.

The next day she wakes up early, has a conference call with Facebook, at 3am Sri Lankan time, one of her current PR clients, and then gets ready to go hot air ballooning.

After two days of waiting, she finally gets a chance to go up into the sky. She gets to fly with the only Sri Lankan pilot in the country, and funnily enough she matched with him on Tinder.

They have a few little baskets to stand in on the hot air balloon. It's still dark out when she hops in the van to go to the take-off section. They blow up the balloons with huge tubes. The two French couples she was paired with, and her, each hop in their baskets and up they go. Slowly and steadily they transfuse gravity and lift off. It is just before dawn and still pretty misty.

They go over luscious farmer's fields and see cows and horses and birds, and little kids jumping up-and -down to wave at them. After what feels like a nice long ride, they decide to descend on the field and are warned to watch out for field snakes while deboarding. The van from the hot air balloon company is on walkie talkies trying to follow the balloons and to come in for support.

They have a set-up of champagne and snacks for an impromptu landing picnic! The sun has recently risen and its beautiful warmth lands on their skin, and they get to enjoy a morning cocktail. It's absolutely picturesque.

They drop her off back at her place, and she decides to pack up her things and head towards the safari park.

Yaya researches the train schedule and tries to make it for the long train, apparently it's the preferred one as you see more of the countryside and the tea plantations. While waiting for the train, Yaya gets her haircut at a little salon run by three Sri Lankan women. She has a blast with them, chatting and pointing, and laughing. They don't speak much English, nor does she speak any Sri Lankan, just enough to get the haircut done.

On the train, Yaya is looking out the window and also using her massager. After a few hours she gets bored and starts 'playing' Tinder. At one point, she matches with an Israeli in Sri Lanka and starts chatting with him on the app. She convinces him to come to the next town she is headed to, so he gets off the train he is on and turns back to the town he had just come from!

The two of them are now on the same train and he comes to find her! It is now dark and she is becoming more and more sleepy, but also anticipatory with excitement to meet this guy. They meet and chat, and decide to get some dinner together in town and stay in a hotel together. They eat and have a few drinks and then go back to their room.

They hook up and then cuddle and fall asleep for the night. The next day they go for a hike. Yaya has spent her first few days in the country alone and in a very meditative state, so it's weird having company. He gives her space on the mountaintop to breathe and meditate.

It was such a long train ride there, over nine hours, so she wanted to stay here in this town, for at least two nights to ground and not be in constant transit. It was a small tourist town, bigger than where she had been so far, and they had a variety of cuisine options, which she liked.

That night, she just wanted to sleep and he was eager to repeat last night's activity. They fooled around a bit and eventually got some rest. The next day after a lovely Sri Lankan breakfast with coffee on the terrace and lots of fruit and yummies, they talked about heading to the safari area. They had slept in and had to pack.

At the bus station, they could really feel the afternoon heat. They decided to get a chocolate covered ice cream for themselves and there was a blonde French girl also ordering herself an ice cream. The three of them hit it off and decided to travel together by taxi to the safari, this way they wouldn't have to wait indefinitely for the bus.

The French woman was full of ideas on how to travel inexpensively and was very happy to have their companionship to make things cheaper. The Israeli was playing with ideas in his head about having two women- at the same time. Yaya was interested in both, the discounted pricing, the group to travel with, and the potential threesome option, now that she identified as bi-sexual! After this was expressed by the Israeli, the French woman made it clear that it was not her intention at all. Yaya found this comical.

They made it to the area where the safari would be the next morning and found a guest house for about $10 a night to accommodate all three of them. For a few dollars more their hosts would prepare them dinner too. What a deal!

The next morning, they were picked up bright and early by their Safari driver. He let them stop off at a roadside store to get bread, instant coffee, and bananas to snack on. They then pulled into the queue at the safari park entrance. They were about twenty jeeps deep. The safari jeep was lifted and had a nice view. The Israeli guy was trying to hide his disappointment for not sleeping with the two ladies in a menage a trois. It was gradually working.

They finally made it in. They pulled-in to buy their individual tickets and off they went. They saw elephant families walking through the long grass. They saw alligators sunning themselves in the shallow ends of the pond. They saw many varieties of birds; the French woman was very knowledgeable on the various kinds of avian. It all worked out, and they took each other's photos and generally had fun watching the animals together in their natural habitat.

After the safari, the three of them parted ways. Yaya heads towards the beach and the other's elsewhere. She was going to spend her last three days in Sri Lanka, beach bound.

After beaching in Sri Lanka, she flies to the Maldives. She spends a night on a small island before heading to her timeshare resort, the original impetus for this entire trip, for her and her ex. The island is so small it doesn't even have its own ATM.

There are two hostels and two restaurants on the island, and one is closed. Luckily she booked her accommodation in advance, and they arranged a water taxi for her to arrive. Otherwise there would have been no way to get there. Three young cousins run the bed and breakfast, and they are all in their mid-teens. They hangout and wait for customers and smoke cigarettes and share a motorcycle. One of them offers Yaya a tour of the island, and she gladly accepts. The whole tour takes less than thirty minutes.

The next day she goes back to the airport before taking a tiny plane, with a total of seven passengers, one of them being Jessica, to an even tinier island. The Maldives have over 1,000 islands. Jessica had booked herself at the same exact island and resort.

The staff mix the two girls up with each other right away. Two brunette solo travelers from New York. Most of the guests here are couples from around the world on their honeymoons. *What was Jessica doing here anyway?* Yaya wondered.

They get greeted with a welcome beverage and get to enjoy the main section of the lodge in the waterfront cabanas before being shown to their rooms. The last person on earth that Yaya wants to see at that moment is Jessica. Yet, there she is.

Yaya's room is complete with a chair swing on the beach, a porch, and an outdoor shower, she loves it. Later that night, she enjoys the buffet dinner meal plan, and makes herself a whole plate of cheeses. They have a variety of fish and vegetables, so many offerings to choose from.

Later that night at the resort, Yaya is dancing to 'Empire State of Mind,' by Jay Z and Alicia Keys in the club - the club is in the main lodge and Yaya is the only one dancing. It's fairly empty in general and there are not a lot of people.

Yaya see's Jessica and her newly wedded friends coming in and trying to video her in-action dancing solo. Yaya stops and leaves when they enter.

Dancing has always been one of her ways to express her emotions and move through difficult times, and now it was being threatened with the presence of her manipulative ex and a barrage of video cameras.

She goes back to her room, arranges all the pillows all around her and indulges in Emotional Release, which she had learned from ISTA, for hours. This is a tool to move energy and unwanted emotions through the body. She slams her pelvis into the pillows, wails to the heavens, muffled her screams into the pillows and waves her arms and legs around in a messy, screaming, crying, tantrum until she eventually passes out from sheer exhaustion- and no more tears to cry.

The next day Yaya wakes up, a bit dehydrated, to take part in the snorkel adventure. There is a boat that heads out after breakfast and takes about forty passengers snorkeling for about an hour. Yaya is prepared, as usual, with her gear from home. She also brings her cell phone with her in case she wants to take any photos. She sits in the boat and finds a sunny spot to soak in the rays and waits for it to leave. The sun recharges her.

She sees Jessica and her newlywed friends approach the boat and Yaya immediately gets off. The activities captain asks her what's wrong and she shrugs and just walks back to her room. There is no way she is going to risk any phone shenanigans on the boat while she is out trying to enjoy the fish. Yaya doesn't trust Jessica, or her motives.

After a few days of snorkeling, Yaya decides to spice things up a bit. She swims to the next island. A boat from the resort follows her and asks her to come back. *Fail.*

She visits the dive shop. The poor Austrian woman working there says she hasn't been diving in months as there hasn't been much interest from the tourists. Yaya books a dive for the next day. They do an alternative approach of jumping in and heading straight to the bottom, and grabbing a rock. Usually the method is to go down slowly and acclimate to the water and balance your ears. Yaya found no balance in this method and was also always trained to not touch the bottom of the sea. She didn't like the idea of grabbing a rock, but she did it anyway because she didn't really see an alternative, she just wished she had gloves on. Right away they started to see large sharks and some dolphins. It was exciting. However, the current was strong, which is why they had to rock climb the bottom of the sea.

After that miserable dive it takes Yaya about two hours of calming music, meditation, chamomile tea, and grounding with her feet in the sand, to come down from that havoc of a dive. Her nervous system was shot from the last two years with Jessica and she was in no shape to be scuba diving. She decided then and there in her mid-thirties that she was retired from diving. It was no longer relaxing or fun.

The next day at breakfast, Jessica sees Yaya and approaches her at the buffet. She tells her that she "had a dream about her and she hopes she is okay. Also, she was available at any time for closure."

A few hours later, after some successful snorkeling, Yaya marches straight to Jessica's room, still dripping wet and in her bikini, and in a moment full of courage - knocks on the door. Jessica is surprised and wonders how Yaya knows what room she is in? *Duh, she paid attention at check-in.* Yaya notices everything.

Yaya bravely gives Jessica a hug and says she is happy to give her closure. Jessica talks and talks, "shooting the salad" as Yaya patiently listens, one last time.

Yaya says goodbye and leaves the island early, that afternoon actually, on a tiny jet and spends a few nights back at her first place in the Maldives on another tiny island. It is not relaxing for her to be in the same resort as Jessica. It's pure paradise, however anywhere else would be better.

She visits the official Maldives museum, where they show the infamous tsunami damage and various heritage artifacts of the lands and the people. Yaya has a nice time chatting with a museum worker and eats some interesting local foods in town.

Within two days, she flies back to New York in the morning with enough time to make it to 9am yoga. She watches a movie about a hypnotist taking advantage of her patients called, 'Trance' and becomes even more leery about hypnosis.

Chaya says to her, "You are our hero!" Yaya is not sure if they are talking about making it to yoga after a long flight, or for breaking up with Jessica.

Yaya found this yoga studio thanks to Jessica, so she is very happy to see that there have not been any sides taken, or at least that she is still welcome.

Yaya keeps attending yoga to center her body, mind and spirit. At one point in their relationship Jessica had said to Yaya, "I hope we can still both take yoga here if we are not together. I think we can." It was an agreement that they had made when things were still seemingly happy between them.

At this point, Yaya is watching Lisa A. Romano videos on YouTube about narcissism daily. She has been down many rabbit holes online, watching various discussions about the topics: forgiveness, narcissism, and codependency. One video she stumbles upon is a forgiveness coach specializing in ho'oponopono, which means, "I'm sorry. Please forgive me. I love you. Thank you." She hires him on the spot. He uses hypnotism in his practice. While this now scares her a bit, she thinks she needs hypnotherapy to undo, and to combat whatever trance that Jessica had her in before.

He has a mattress in the living room set up for them to work. They dance and shake it out before he asks her to lay down on her back and takes her down the steps into a hypnotic dream-like state for healing.

* * *

Green lasers flung across the ceiling as sequin-clad dancers, sexily hung from hoops in the sky. It was March, and Yaya was at a Brooklyn dance party, feeling happy and blissed-out upstairs, when she got a clear message from her intuition that she should go three flights downstairs and find Jessica on the dance floor and give her a hug. Yaya was on MDMA and had her heart wide open.

She turned to her friend Jeff and told him the plan. He looked at her surprised, brow-furrowed and said, "Are you sure about that?"

She had always wondered if they could be *those* kind of exes, you know, the friendly kind. She followed her heart's open urge to go to the basement of the building. She marched down the stairs on a mission and found Jessica, exactly where she intuitively expected her to be, on the middle of the dance floor by herself.

Yaya made eye contact with the black sparkling Doctor, and slowly and gently went in for the hug. Jessica grabbed the thin part of skin between Yaya's ribs and side with a hard deep pinch of her fingernails. Yaya grimaced, looked at her and slowly backed away.

Yaya got confirmation at that moment that her decision to avoid Jessica and stay 'no contact' was best.

In Rockaway, there is a group of women who meet monthly, the Women's Business Association. Yaya knows a few people in the group like the Goddess Witch, and The Money Mermaid, both characters from the House of Yes party and mermaid scene.

She walked into the kitchen at the meeting to add her homemade sangria as an offering to the potluck. There were two pints of MUD, which was her favorite coconut plant based ice cream, and some homemade cookies. She grabbed a bowl and placed a cookie in the bottom and proceeded to make a big ice cream sundae with both flavors as scoops of ice cream. There were two women watching her, and the blonde leaned in and asked, "Can we take a photo of you with that?" Yaya sheepishly agreed. It turned out she was the owner and inventor of MUD.

Later on in the evening, everyone went around the room and introduced themselves with a trinity: a brag, a gratitude, and a desire. She happily walked home on the boardwalk in the windy

March winter night under the stars, and thanked herself for living in such a special community and for making some new friends.

The next morning at yoga, a woman said to her, "So I heard you went to the Women's Business Association last night." News travels fast around here. "Yep," she replied and hurriedly got her yoga mat out.

Rockaway has about 200,000 people living on the peninsula, and she was starting to understand that they were all very connected. It was like living in a small town again, similar to her hometown, Danville, where she was raised. The more she got to know people, the more she realized everyone was someone's mom, neighbor, son or landlord etc.

She decided to take a break from dating altogether. She deleted Hinge, OK Cupid, Dig Dates, Meet Mindful and Tinder apps off of her phone to focus solely on herself and her healing.

She started participating in group breathwork, and practicing with a friend she met at Burning Man. They started meeting once a week in the evenings to do thirty minutes breathwork sessions together, chat, hangout and share some food.

Yaya was getting to the point in her research where she was recognizing her own involvement in this pattern of dating unavailable people. While she was eager to point the finger outward to her parents and to Jessica, as being narcissistic, she was starting to accept her own Codependency as a common denominator and a big piece in the puzzle.

She had decided to commit to one year of celibacy. Of course in Yaya's mind there were a few loopholes to this policy. Celibacy to her at this time meant there were no new lovers in the mix. A few old timer lovers got to come by on Sundays to visit for a good booty call, but it was limited.

In May of 2019, Yaya decided to take on the thirty day yoga challenge at Yin and Yang Yoga Studio. She was already going most days, what was a few more? She thought by the end of it she would feel amazing. It was a total mind fuck. Chaya, the owner and main instructor celebrated her like crazy on the 30th day, with a balloon, a certificate, a free one week pass, a trophy, and a photo for the bulletin board.

However, that whole day, her expectation of completion and the actual feeling of completion, didn't match, and this led her down a path of despair. For the first time, her outside world reality didn't match her inner world's reality. She was beginning to track that her feelings of depression weren't affected by outside factors. She should have felt on top of the world.

The day after the challenge she decided to not go to yoga, instead she called her sister and rolled around in bed weeping.

Don't I have any tools? she thought, completely exacerbated. Yaya writhed in self-pity and wonders if she should hire a coach, when she remembers she has one! Sometimes in the fog its challenging to find a moment of clarity. She recalls her message from her journey in Canada, to turn her pain into beauty. Inspired, she busts out the crafts.

Desperate energy is best used in her life towards creation, or else it leads to destruction.

Yes, okay, I have a life coach, and I can take a bath and I can make art, she told herself. Regrouping and getting herself together.

Normally Yaya's addicted coping skills would be to smoke marijuana and numb out all day, and she adamantly decided not to do that and to learn to self-soothe. It was a beautiful sunny day in May and she lives on the beach. Yaya locked herself inside, decided to not to go to her singing group at the House of Yes, and instead started to bedazzle her door frame.

A few weeks earlier, she had been to Philly to visit her friend, for a morning dance party and he gifted her a gallon sized zip lock full of clear silver gems. She moved on from bedazzling the door frame she finished, to the light switches, using nail polish to affix the gems to the wall.

She wailed. She cried on the floor. She prayed.

She asked God, *"What else?" What else could she do to heal and move through this?*

She felt shitty. She had hoped to feel on top of the world.

Was this as good as it gets?

She resisted her urges and kept crafting, one gem at a time and the despair passed.

The next day she decided to go back to yoga. Chaya asked her, "Did you think about not coming back?"

"Yeah," responded Yaya.

"Fuck you!" said Chaya, seriously. Yaya laughed. She loved her teacher.

Yaya's friends, Connie and Alice had both been recently attending AA and CODA (for codependency) meetings and shared about it vulnerably and with hope. With their success stories Yaya thought maybe she could give the Al-anon CODA method a try, *plus it was free.* She had attended a few AA meetings back when she had a DUI, but it was mandatory and not out of personal interest.

She kept up with yoga and beach walks and had no contact with Jessica.

One Tuesday evening, she gets up the gusto to attend her first CODA meeting in her Rockaway neighborhood. She had attended one farther away in Queens, but it was only a few women and it had taken her an hour on the bus each way, making it a four- hour experience.

She was scared to go-local in case she would see someone she knew, as again Rockaway was a tight community. Of course as soon as everyone is settled at the meeting, one of her yoga instructors walks in and joins the meeting. They had just reviewed the principles that everything was confidential and that it was a safe space.

The yoga teacher was friends with Jessica, and Yaya was paranoid about sharing out loud in case anything got back to her. Narcissists usually had 'flying monkeys' lurking around gathering information.

Each person shared a bit about how they were doing or their history with codependency. When it got to Yaya's turn - she took a pass. After the meeting she quietly bought a copy of 'Courage to Change" and made it part of her morning routine to read the daily passage. The yoga teacher offered her a ride home and she accepted. That normalized things between them a bit.

Also during this time, Yaya had completed Reiki Level 1 and Reiki Level 2, a tradition passed down orally for energy healing. Yaya loved deepening her Reiki practice, and really enjoyed the meditations and energy attunements in these sessions.

In the late Spring, they offered a community Reiki day. It was a chance for the new practitioners to offer Reiki to the public. The twenty attendees sat in a circle around the yoga room on the floor on cushions, while the practitioners each found a spot, they were to each give Reiki to six people. Yaya counts it out and sees that Jessica is in her lineup. She quickly asks another Reiki practitioner to switch spots with her, and she agrees.

This spot is starting with Kim, a woman from the Women's Business Association. Kim is beyond excited, thinking that Yaya switched to pick her. Life's perceptions are funny.

While giving Reiki to Kim, Yaya sees deep maroon, the color associated with the root chakra, representing safety. Yaya sees colors on most people that she gives reiki to. Afterwards, they share and Kim is super happy to have had Yaya for her "Reiki reading," as she called it.

Chapter Twelve

Yaya Takes Learning into Her Own Hands

The real parts of our selves are often the shadiest.

In the summer of 2019, Yaya assisted at Level 1 for ISTA, and attended Level 2 for the first time at Easton Mountain, a beautiful retreat center near Albany, New York. She rode the bus up with her soul-tribe brother, a poet from California. He was at her first ISTA training a few years' prior in Arizona, and during their bus chat, they discovered they had a medicine community in common as well.

As they abruptly pulled into the Greyhound station and whisked themselves off the vehicle, they found themselves in a rainy parking lot in Albany. They quickly ordered an Uber to take them to Easton Mountain.

Easton Mountain had been a gay man's retreat center for years in response to the AIDS crisis in the 80's, and they were testing out having co-ed groups in their space. There were hiking trails and trees, and grass and swamps, snakes and birds, and wild rabbits and frogs.

Yaya was put in the yurt to stay with two other female bodied assistants to co-habitate for the coming week.

Yaya lay on the thin mattress pad staring up at the roof of the yurt, praying for sleep. She feels a swirling of energy coming from beneath her and she desperately wants to change out her mattress. It's the wee hours of the night, potentially 1am, and she decides it's worth it. She tosses off the blankets, gets up quietly so as to not wake her two sleeping yurt-mates, and drags the mattress out the door and onto the dewy grass back to the main lodge. She wants to switch it out for a different one - with less swirly energy.

The mattresses had all been used for a powerful ritual that day. Yaya had a feeling hers didn't make it to the energy-cleaning smudging station.

The next morning, Yaya rose early to hit the hot outdoor showers and make it for the first cup of coffee before the kundalini session was being offered at 7am. Her other roommate always joked that their main love language was coffee, so Yaya got them a hot cuppa too.

Later that day, during mid-morning break, Yaya and another participant decide to go on a hike in the woods. Her hiking buddy is a therapist and a social worker, and has been in two narcissistic marriages. The two of them get into a deep conversation, deep in the woods. They walk, and talk and walk, and get really lost. They have no idea how to return back to the retreat center. Eventually, they hear a road and make their way toward it.

The venue had a pond, a sauna, a pool, and sprawling lawns for outdoor nakedness.

At Port Authority just before she boarded the bus, she realized she wanted to buy some deodorant, so she stopped at the drug store in the station and was completely overwhelmed by the variety of selection. She usually buys a favorite aluminum-free one online. She stood in the very bright aisle, paralyzed with choice and finally just grabbed a pink and white one and quickly checked out.

Their Canadian yurt-mate was carefully unpacking her bags, and Yaya noticed she had the same exact deodorant - and it became a whole thing, a bonding moment for them, it was rose-scented, which represents love. She recognized this as a sign from the universe that she was in the right place at the right time, a little bit of synchronicity.

It was a large group of sixty humans at the retreat. One special Texan and Yaya ended up having long heady porch chats about Quantum Physics, after the sun had gone down and the tantric transmissions and lessons were over. She was swatting off mosquitoes here and there and he told her his philosophy on bugs. He embraced the notion 'may all beings be fed.' Yaya took this on for herself.

Here is the explanation for you, the part that causes itchiness and irritation after a bug bite— is the resistance. If you drop the resistance and let them get nourished by your blood, it's an easy breezy transaction. They get what they need *and* there's no hassle.

It's a meditation that Yaya adopted that night and still lives to this day. It has also helped her in making space for Jessica, in her day-to-day life, in various overlapping communities, post-breakup and going 'no contact.'

Jessica and Yaya often find themselves at the same event, dance, or workshop. Yaya finds that if she is able to center herself and really believe 'may all beings be fed,' she is able to drop her irritation from Jessica's presence, and understand that they can all use healing work and be fed and nourished by the activity at hand.

At the assistants meeting at ISTA, they are expected to share their crushes. If they want to act on any of these crushes they must declare them among leadership first. It's part of the authenticity work that they are there to do. It also disrupts any misplaced power in a sexual dynamic by having this structure in place. Yaya shares that she is coming out of one year of celibacy and gently easing her way back into intimacy in that way. Each night at the temple night she happily volunteered to run the Cuddle Puddle Station, usually followed by a hot sauna and bedtime.

* * *

202

For the Burn (Burning Man) this year, Yaya goes 'poly-camp-erous' with three different camps. She was originally going to be in one camp, she had applied and they let her in and gave her a spot. About two days later, she saw that someone named Jessica from New York was added to that particular Facebook group. It was the Doctor, all right.

Yaya decided to change camps, not letting Jessica's presence 'fuck her burn'. Yaya ended up getting a ticket through Planet Earth camp, located right on the esplanade, so she went for it. She did a ride-share with 'Marty who likes to party,' and got dropped off at her friend's camp in the suburbs around Avenue J. Black Rock City is a grid.

She exhales a deep breath and feels 'Home.' She helps make a big sign for the camp in bright colors, and then grabs her pink bike to head to the esplanade to find her other camps. She picks up her black and yellow Loews bins that have been shipped from New York with Kostume Kult and sets up her tent in her main camp. Planet Earth is a disco club with "songs with words" in a sea of EDM (electronic dance music).

A few nights in, Yaya is out exploring by herself and hears some music that she wants to dance to. She is judging herself and telling herself "this must be psytrance." She stays and dances from about 11pm until the light of morning starts changing the sky. She sees an older woman in a purple fuzzy jacket come out to dance and she feels inspired.

I want to be dancing to psytrance at Burning Man at sunrise in a purple jacket when I'm 80, thinks Yaya.

The next night Yaya is out cruising again and finds an art car to jam out to. A tall Asian man with a white furry coat locks eyes with her through the dark, and they start dancing together until the art car with the music moves. They start chatting and walk towards an outdoor lounge to smoke a joint, and it turns out he is also from Danville and they went to the same high school. Yaya is wearing bright red lipstick to match her red robot-themed top. They make out and stumble across an umbrella photo shoot, inspiring them to get undressed. They oblige.

As the sun rises yet again, Yaya remembers that it is the morning dance party on the playa. Yaya and the guy from her high school are on top of a lookout when another girl walks up, and she has a map. She helps them locate the morning dance party. Yaya dances at this early morning dance party in New York City bimonthly, she is excited to connect with her dancing buddies from back home, out here on the playa.

He leaves to go get some water and she doesn't see him again for a few days. Yaya dances despite her tiredness, and when she eventually makes it back to her camp she realizes she has red lipstick all over her face from smooching and mask-wearing to keep the dust away.

The tall Asian man and Yaya reconvene a few days later to walk, dance, chill, and fuck.

They come across the wooden human wheel, it's not open, and the guy who made it is out sipping some coffee. Yaya expresses her desire to go in it and she gets strapped in and goes for a spin on the human wheel! This was one of her dreams since her first burn. She also makes it out to the Black Rock City airport for the first time for a visit, and runs into an ISTA buddy.

She runs into Jessica a couple of times, which startles her and affects her nervous system, however, she successfully avoids her for the most part and they have no altercations.

Back in New York City, a bunch of Yaya's friends from the ISTA community are registered for 'Tantra meets BDSM Level 1.' Yaya is scared shitless of this. She sees forty of her mates go to take the weekend course and happily doesn't go, she still thinks she wants to avoid pain and is afraid of kink.

After a sold out workshop, the teacher adds another one, two weeks later. Yaya knows not one person going, and decides to register. She likes the idea of anonymity to practice this work, as she is uncertain what will come up.

Each day they read materials, practice domination and submission positions, with all their clothes on. Yaya really feels the impact without even diving into anything sexual yet. At lunch, they order mass amounts of vegetarian Indian food for everyone to enjoy and continue learning about this hot practice. She is seeing a pattern in her life involving fiery practices, such as ayahuasca, Burning Man yoga and now BDSM.

Even though they say to not make any rash decisions within six months of attending Burning Man, Yaya decides it is time to switch careers, go back to school, and get a masters in social work. When she sets her mind to something she is determined. She contacts admissions, books a few open house appointments and figures out the financing. All during this one-week period, four women who she knows randomly pop into her life, all of them former social workers. They all were now doing different things and recommended that she NOT move ahead with it.

Yaya invited Connie over for pumpkin painting and she brought her friend. Her friend worked at an ad agency, however she used to be a social worker, she straight up said, "Don't do it."

Yaya reconnected with her life coach and psychotherapist, Apolline, who has the whole alphabet of titles behind her name, and she also said, "Don't do it." Instead, Yaya hired Apolline as her life coach and they got started right away.

She had been wanting to work with Apolline for years and the feeling was mutual. Yaya's desire is to have a profession that helps people, and to be living with purpose in the 'right livelihood.' Right Livelihood is an important aspect of the Buddha's Noble Eightfold Path. The idea of right livelihood is an ancient one. It embodies the principle that each person should follow an honest occupation, which fully respects other people and the natural world. It means being responsible for the consequences of our actions and taking only a fair share of the earth's resources.

Yaya believes that marketing, public relations, and pushing consumerism is not part of this path.

After "Tantra meets BDSM Level 1," she wants more. She signs up for 'Tantra meets BDSM level 2' with her beloved teachers.

This time, a bunch of friends from the community rent a house in New Jersey and Yaya plans on staying for the weekend with them. Molly and Yaya get assigned the living room to share an air mattress, but 2am they are completely sunken into each other with a deflated mattress beneath them, and Molly moves to the couch.

One of the theories at this BDSM training is to 'trust your Dom'. The teacher is offering Latihan as part of this workshop and at first Yaya thinks, *I know this already*. Then she remembers the new teaching to try on is to trust your Dom.

After these workshops, Yaya sees life as one big exercise in domination and submission. When you are in a student role you are the submissive. It serves you and the teacher, or the Dom better if you trust them to handle you well. If you add doubt and skepticism, you set yourself up for failure.

They have a beautiful Latihan and Yaya shares in her blissed-out state of submission how much she loves this practice. Then they move on to Humiliation play.

Yaya asks another to give her the phrase, 'You are a fat slut.' The practice is to thank the person after hearing your selected phrase and ask for it again. The concept being that when you consensually ask for your humiliation you can reach a point where it no longer triggers you. This was hot. Yaya got all red on her chest, neck, and head and became rosy and turned on.

Yaya enjoyed being in the surrender or submission position, and allowing a trusted Dom to take her into her chaos in a safe and held way.

After the first day, they all go back to the rented house and get food at the local grocery store to munch on and share. Yaya gets chips and ice cream. That night, Yaya moved into a room with an empty bed in it so Molly could enjoy the living room to herself. On the last day of the workshop they get to practice a directed scene with rope, and Yaya takes the role of Dom in her scene. She likes this too. *I guess I am a switch,* she thinks.

* * *

Yaya has a session with Apolline, and has been learning a lot about the DSM 5 in her own research, studying narcissism. One of the personality disorders she is intrigued by for herself is BPD, borderline personality disorder. Apolline suggests that Yaya research 'codependent empath' instead, which she also identifies with.

Apolline is hesitant to diagnose Yaya with BPD, but after constant pressure she asks Yaya some questions. Based on the black and white thinking that Yaya has about the concepts 'always' and 'never,' and 'good' and 'bad' she agrees that yes Yaya has BPD.

Some of the traits of BPD include spontaneity around sex, shopping, and bursts of rage. It's in the Cluster B of mental health, and NPD is in the same cluster according to the DSM 5.

The week after the BDSM training, a man Yaya has heard about, but never met, invites her over for a community Sunday dinner night at his place. She has been to this community house in Brooklyn many times for events. He cooks pasta and serves wine, although there are a few AA members present, and many gluten-free eaters.

Yaya made a deal with herself on the subway ride there to take a break from all her food rules, and she happily indulges and eats the glutinous pasta that night, and enjoys some wine.

The host and Yaya end up chatting, and chatting, and chatting. By the end of the night, the two are washing dishes together and bidding the others adieu, but not ready to call it quits. They move down to his temporarily rented bedroom and make out. They end up dry humping until the wee hours of the morning when Yaya finally decides to go home.

The next few days she can't sleep, she can't work, he is on her mind. She texts him to ask if he is sending her energetic sex? He is. She decides she can't take it anymore and insists he come over.

Their brief fling is driving her wild, and she begins to trip out for a few days on the highs of this new connection. He is super polyamorous, and they talk a lot over coffee the mornings after their fun sex-capades.

Before the first penetration they have a safer-sex talk about boundaries, fears and desires, which is a common language they use in their ISTA community. Yaya bravely expresses a fear that she is afraid that once they have sex, she won't ever see him again, and she likes him. He reassures her that he wants to see her again, and they have amazing sex-magic infused, morning sex.

Months later in January, he and Yaya attend a fundraiser for the ocean together at this very cool venue in Manhattan. When he walks in, he sees Yaya in a blue one piece, painting a giant octopus on a group mural. They make eye contact and walk towards each other and smooch in the middle of the museum.

She has a tab of acid in her mouth that she asks him while they are kissing if he would like to share it with her. He would. They spend the rest of the night together frolicking between rooms, dancing, sitting, talking, meeting friends, until about 2am when he really has had enough partying and wants to head home.

They bust out into 34th street and there are many other party goers jammed up on a one-way street with a big trash truck. The two lovebirds escape down the street and find a cabbie that is willing to illegally back up for at least two blocks, passing cops, no problem. They make it back to Brooklyn to his new community rental place.

They go up to his room and light candles and make love for hours, and hours, and hours. Yaya cums, and moans and writhes in ecstasy. At one point they realize that she has started her period, and there is a bit of menstrual blood on both of them. They don a towel wrap, and head downstairs to the bathroom, with no shower but a big tub.

He rigs up the very special porcelain tub and scrubs her down, body part by body part with much care. They eventually head back upstairs and pass out. They sleep in and eat at a diner nearby for a late brunch, as it snows out the window. They come back to his place, and end up watching a movie, 'Spirited Away' on a big projector in the living room.

After that weekend Yaya ends up sick as a dog, on the floor, for about a week. She has the flu big time. Finally, after a few days, she has the strength to visit the doctor. Her building's super sees her, and gives her a ride to the clinic down the block.

In the medical office, she watches TV and sees that there is a Covid outbreak and she is sure that she has it. The staff assure her that she doesn't and sends her home with antibiotics. Her friend, a veterinarian, kindly sends her soups to nourish her out of this swampy sickness.

She is too tired to even watch movies, to eat or do anything but rest and recover. Yaya blames her new poly lover and decides to go no contact with him too. She doesn't want to be with someone so poly and sharing so many germs. He had told her that one of his beloveds had the flu the week prior and that he visited her twice, as Yaya was saying goodbye during their last hangout.

She didn't quite get yet that smoother endings led to smoother new beginnings.

After attending the BDSM courses, students are invited to attend 'directed scenes' nights at the teacher's penthouse. He hosts them a few Wednesdays per month, and it's a chance for the students to meet each other and share their desires, and to practice Dominance and Submission.

Plus, he has a full dungeon with whips and ropes, riding crops, and all the toys.

It was winter. Yaya had taken the PATH train to New Jersey. She got out at Jersey City square and there was a holiday market on, in full-force with food vendors and festive things lit up all around. She landed in a coat shop, and found the perfect purple coat she had been looking for. One morning at Burning Man the year prior, she danced into the dawn with a fabulous older woman in a purple fuzzy coat. All year she had been looking to get herself one.

The designer was there and her jovial team, most likely her husband and son, happily assisted Yaya into the soft, well-made luxurious purple coat. She bought it, always happy to support female entrepreneurs. She rounded the corner of the market and bummed a cigarette from some foreign boys. Yaya doesn't usually smoke, however, the rare craving was on. Maybe it was anxiety, maybe it was her rebel teen's desire to be seen.

From there, she regrouped in her new jacket, on the bench, and hired an Uber to take her to the penthouse.

She was nervous. As she entered the building, a tall handsome man and another woman were also there. Many people lived in this apartment complex, but as they walked to the elevator she was sure that they were all going to the same place. They de-shoe-ed and hugged familiar faces, ending up in a circle on the hardwood floor in the living room. The format for the opening circle was for each person to share their desires. If any desires matched up, they would be partnered for their directed scene.

210

Yaya knew almost everyone in the circle, except the two she walked in with, from various New York City communities, dance, medicine, and tantra.

She shared that she had a desire for Humiliation Play. She wanted to be told a potentially triggering phrase, so as to let the heat in and dissipate. However, no one wanted to play humiliation with Yaya. As usual for these directed scenes nights, there were many more women present than men.

She ended up being matched in a three some, with the man she walked in with, and an experienced sub.

Attracted to both the man and the woman, Yaya was happy with the arrangement. They reviewed their boundaries, fears and desires on a paper checklist and headed down to the dungeon. The beautiful thing about BDSM in this community is that the boundaries are very clear and explicit.

The other woman they were paired with had asked for a lot of pain, whereas Yaya had asked for just a little bit. Once he got to spanking each of them, Jacob told Yaya she was taking much more pain than the pain-seeking sub.

During the scene, Jacob got an inkling to bite Yaya, but it wasn't agreed upon in their boundary conversation so he refrains. Later on, as they are recapping the scene, Yaya notices that yes she would have actually loved a big bite on her butt.

The scene finished and Yaya was in sub-space (a happy natural high from the dopamine and other love drugs released during the play) and wanted to be a 'good bottom" and thank her Dom. She was trying to use her phone and get his number. While no external substances were consumed, she was absolutely altered from the chemistry from the scene and entered it incorrectly.

Yaya ended up getting a ride home from the Goddess Witch who also lived in Rockaway. The next morning, she texted her Dom. It turned out she got her humiliation play after all, instead of texting Jacob, she accidentally texted a graphic thank you message to someone from the women's chapter of the Masons that she was a member of.

The following night the Goddess Witch invited Yaya over for a 'chilled out kirtan' singing session at her house. It was a singer with her music box, the Goddess Witch and Yaya happily chanting some kirtan, when Jacob walks in. He looks right at Yaya and is like, "You didn't text me?"

So she explains to him what happened, and he ends up giving her his correct number and a ride home. They briefly talk about ISTA, and he goes home and registers that night for an upcoming week-long training in Ireland. Yaya likes that kind of action.

Jacob is over six foot tall and a pretty serious, beastly looking guy. He surfs and does many outdoor sports, and he is very big and strong. They decide to be 'play and massage buddies' to practice some scenes, when not traveling to New Jersey.

Usually, Jacob doms Yaya. One night, they were at his house and they decided that she was going to Dom him. She thinks that things are going well in their scene, when he grabs her by the legs, throws her over his shoulder and flips her around, mid scene!

So, in this case, Yaya is not Dom-ing him. Rather, he is still the Dom and she is still the Sub archetype in their dynamic. However, they have decided to switch roles, where she is on top and he is on the bottom.

* * *

A few days later, Yaya attends the New York City Pet Fashion show at the iconic, but disgusting, Hotel Pennsylvania for the tenth year in a row, and declares to her pet friends that she is going to adopt a cat. They all tell her that if you get one, it's really better to get two, especially a bonded pair.

Yaya gets home after the pet fashion show to find out that Jacob and Yaya have gotten Burning Man tickets to camp for 2020!

That weekend, Yaya and Jacob go to the House of Yes. They dance all night and celebrate, and close the place down in their alien and cowboy costumes and end up going home together. Jacob gets his first rim job.

On Sunday morning, Yaya makes it to yoga and has a conversation with another yogi about South America. He shared about his memories driving through Central and South America in his twenties and remembers being in Tikal fondly. Yaya is about to embark on a trip to Guatemala, and he begs her to stop off at Tikal. Yaya is supposed to travel with friends and she asks them about making it to the Tikal ruins. They are not interested in the long trek up there on this trip, maybe next time.

CHAPTER THIRTEEN

Yaya Dances into the Sunset

Everything feels better after a haircut.

Yaya was supposed to fly to Guatemala on March 18th, 2020. She was flying to Lake Atitlan for a retreat, to repeat ISTA level 2 to enjoy one more try at a proper 'ego death'.

On the morning of the 14th, she woke up and went to yoga and came home, drank her coffee and smoked a joint.

She saw on Facebook that the Guatemalan government was going to close the border at midnight to Americans and Canadians due to the Covid pandemic. She called United Airlines and decided to get on the next flight out of LGA, instead of waiting for her scheduled flight in a few days.

When she left her studio apartment before noon that day, to fly to Guatemala - the retreat was still on. She arrived safely to Guatemala City that night.

They took her temperature with a thermometer on the plane. She was wearing her pink and purple tie dyed Burning Man mask, which she grabbed at the last second.

She then took an Uber to her Airbnb where the Wi-Fi password was WINSTON and she knew she was where she was supposed to be. Winston was the name of her childhood dog. She took this as another sign from the universe.

Despite growing concerns surrounding the Covid-19 crisis, she was excited when organizers of the retreat told Yaya the event was still on. After spending her first day in the capital, she had a few extra days now, so she took a bus to Tikal. Her other friends were no longer joining her, they were staying in Mexico to stay healthy and work on their new house, so she thought this was her chance to visit the ancient ruins

Upon arrival to Tikal, she realized it was closed.

She found an Airbnb on the water to stay at that night, and in the morning she rose and enjoyed a traditional Guatemalan breakfast next door. A few minutes after she returned to the hotel, the owner dramatically informed her that there would be no more food served in the country. She told him, "It's okay. I am sure you can get some breakfast next door."

What he meant was that there had been a government advisory closing down all restaurants and travel, effective immediately. Yaya had been on a very long bus ride to get to Tikal and decided she better take the bus back if she was ever going to make it to Lake Atitlan for the retreat.

She started making her way to Lake Atitlan for the event. The bus guards insisted that all passengers spray their feet with Clorox bleach before entering the crowded bus. She sat next to an older man who was coughing and hacking the whole way, she was worried.

She arrived in Guatemala City at midnight, and then the second leg of her bus ticket to Antigua was canceled. She had taken the last legal operating bus in the country! Luckily, she took an Uber the rest of the way.

The Uber drops Yaya off at the hotel name she had programmed in, the hotel that her friends had booked for them starting March

20th. She was a few days early and she was alone, and it was 6am. She had an email from her friends saying that they were not coming, and yes she could stay there, as they had pre-paid for the room.

Yaya has been on a bus all night and looked disheveled. In addition to her luggage and backpack, she has a black plastic bag, complete with a can of regular Pringles and a few bananas for nourishment, since all the restaurants were now closed.

The staff looked at Yaya, and looked at the email and the reservation, eventually permitting her to enter. They gave her a beautiful room off the garden and pool with two big queen beds and a fireplace. That night she gave herself a mud mask treatment and walked around the grounds. There were parrots and a sauna.

A volunteer from ISTA helped arrange for an unlicensed taxi to take her the rest of the three-hour drive to Lake Atitlan. After the drive, she was supposed to transfer to a boat that would take her to the retreat location.

When she finally arrived to the retreat, the volunteer greeted her on the dock with a cold hand shake and asked her to leave. He told her she couldn't be there.

Yaya was confused. Then it started to sink in: the retreat, ISTA Level 2, was canceled. They were just finishing up the Level 1 and the event space was not allowed to take on any new guests on the premises due to the new scare of the pandemic.

Yaya took the boat taxi to San Marcos, another part of the lake, where she met a Canadian woman with dreadlocks in the same situation. She helped Yaya find a yurt with a small bathroom, kitchen, and even Wi-Fi, to stay in for the next couple of nights.

Yaya spent a few days on her own in the yurt with a black cat named Shadow and her laptop computer. She met with the Canadian woman once a day and socially-distance-chatted and sometimes walked to town for provisions. Yaya had power and Wi-Fi, her laptop and a French press to make coffee, plus a gorgeous view of the two volcanoes and a jungle. She had what she needed.

After a few days, attendees from the first part of the retreat returned to San Marcos, where Yaya was, a 500-person-town on Lake Atitlan.

Yaya patiently waited on the dock for their arrival. The local police asked her to please go get her temperature checked at the twenty-four-hour health center on top of the hill. She obliged. The health center had no supplies, no pens (just tiny little library pencils), no masks, no gloves etc. An older woman came and took her temperature. It was 37 degrees Celsius, an indication of health.

She walked back to the dock, which was closed. She received a message that it may take a bit longer than expected for the group to arrive and that she should just go to the house. They gave Yaya directions to go to a big house on the lake with a big yard, and to wait for them there.

She arrived at the beautiful big house on the lake and made herself at home on the lawn furniture. The guardian of the place came and introduced himself. He kept asking where the others were, in Spanish, and within two hours the rest of the crew arrived. All eleven of them.

She moved in with this group of strangers, and they became one big family of 12 in a five-bedroom house. They split rent and household chores but most importantly, looked after each other. They hailed from different countries — the U.S., Mexico, U.K., Belgium, Spain, Israel, and Australia — but English was their common language. There were four men and eight women between the ages of 23 and 40. Yaya was the oldest female. They made a plan to stick together until it was safe to travel again.

They were interested in a concept called, 'radical discontinuity,' or the idea that you can reprogram your mind with simple unfamiliar life changes, like brushing your teeth with the other hand. Because of this, they switched bedrooms every ten days, rotated the jobs they're all responsible for, and cooked different meals. This practice is what she considered to be the most powerful part of living in the house.

They would meet every morning at 9am to gather in a circle to talk about how they're feeling and discuss logistics for the day. They would use a timer to give each person two minutes to honestly and vulnerably share how they are doing.

One of the rooms, the suite in the house, was complete with a large king bed, bunk beds and a large bathtub and sink area - also had many hats on the wall. Each day they would arrange pillows and the many hats in a circle, and each person could choose a hat to fit their mood. It added a certain fun flavor to the morning routine.

They had many different roles, including the 'activities queen' who figured out what they wanted to do as a group each evening or weekend. There was also the 'movement mango,' who might organize a morning yoga session. The 'logistics ladybug', handled daily and future tasks, like delegating who will make a grocery run that day, who would cook lunch and dinner, who would clean dishes after both meals, and decide whether they want to upgrade the house Wi-Fi, or what they're doing for another housemate's birthday.

They also had the position of someone who spoke to the guardian about issues dealing with the property. Yaya liked to have this position, however many of the housemates were leery of this, as Yaya's Spanish was not fluent. Yaya and the guardian would chat for hours, he was calm and mellow and had a slow cadence to his speech, so Yaya could understand him, unlike some Spanish speakers who spoke much faster.

The roomies also pooled their money and had a 'kitty' to pay for daily expenses, like food and water and coconuts. They had fresh coconuts delivered to the house weekly. Luckily, they all ate the same way, they were all vegetarian and gluten-free. They also had copious amounts of tahini delivered regularly.

Breakfast was on their own. They enjoyed papaya, pineapple, mango, oatmeal, cacao, and granola. There was even a 'laundry fairy' who sorted and cleaned communal laundry.

They would nominate one person per day to go out with a mask on and buy groceries with a suitcase. There was a bit of a panic in town that there might not be enough food for everyone, now that there was no transportation between towns. All boat-taxis, cars, and tuktuks were not permitted to move. The food was to be bought in rations for that day only.

The fruit and vegetable vendors were still around and available for the most part in the mornings. As they were twelve adults, they went through quite a bit of food each day. After a while the town became familiar with them, and learned that they would bring suitcases not to stash the food, but to carry it back for the main house. Only one person was allowed to go out on a food mission at a time. This also limited access to things like walks or hikes.

They were on curfew, just like the rest of the country, and the world, during these strange, unprecedented quarantine times. Even the lake was closed. Yaya used to get in trouble with the local female official who would blow her whistle and ask Yaya to get out of the lake for her afternoon swim.

Every day, local health workers visited the house to measure every member of the house's temperature and blood pressure.

During the first two weeks, Yaya's blood pressure was high. She was stressed and worried about the pandemic, and about her situation. Her younger sister, Andrea, a nurse, suggested she stop drinking coffee for a while. She did. Once Yaya decided to stay in Guatemala and paid her rent for April, her blood pressure went back down. When she was vacillating around the decision to stay or go, was when her stress levels were high.

They were mostly healthy, although they weren't immune to other issues like a water parasite that went around. It is known as 'Parasite Lake' after all.

Some of them had lost their jobs, and others were self-employed and worked from there remotely. They also designated a room filled with pillows as the emotional release room, a safe space for anyone to rage, release tears, or chill out with their own music.

Yaya liked to say that she is "S.I.P.," which in Corona times meant 'stuck in place,' or in her case 'stranded in paradise'. There were no regular flights from Guatemala to New York, only emergency flights. They were on strict lock-down, and there was a national curfew between 4pm and 4am. You could get an $800 consales fine if you are out after this time - which is about $80 USD.

For the most part though, Yaya thought they were all really happy and grateful to be there. They really grew to love each other and she saw everyone in the house as her brothers and sisters. They worked as a strong team and they felt lucky to have each other.

One roommate had been studying with a Mayan elder on the lake for a few years. He learned about the Mayan calendar and how to do chart readings based on people's birthdays. He completed a constellation chart of everyone in the house and they had some significant overlaps. Yaya and a twenty-five year old lad from the UK had the exact same chart.

He told Yaya that at age thirty-seven in Mayan tradition, is when you come into your last energy. Hers was the hummingbird, and she had just turned thirty-seven.

They were living and quarantining in-community. Their story was unique and ended up being featured on Today.com in an article, thanks to Yaya's public relations pitching skills.

A few weeks into living together the crew decided to have a cacao inspired ecstatic dance. There was already a lot of energy flying around with so many young people in one place, so they tended to avoid altering substances. They all got dressed for the occasion and the Mimis (the only couple in the mix), gave them all strands of brightly colored pom poms to wear.

Yaya wore a yellow and red, one shoulder strapped, dancer's one-piece that arrived in the mail the same day she left for Guatemala. It was thrown in her bag at the last moment to come along. It was festive.

Yaya played music, and one roommate requested her favorite DJ, Buho. Yaya refused, and she started to cry. Yaya disliked when the music was constantly changing, she preferred to choose one set by any DJ and stick to it. In a group of twelve, this was challenging as everyone wanted their own music. However, Yaya also didn't like it when people were crying.

They made-up and decided to tie the pom pom strings together and make a double-dutch jump rope. This game lasted for a while.

The ceremonial cacao was really affecting them. They were laughing, jumping, and dancing, and being silly. It was their first 'real' party.

Yaya shared a room with many of the different roommates as they rotated rooms, after ten-day increments, during their three months together. Then Shannon and Yaya started sharing the king bed in the suite. Shannon was going through a breakup with a narcissistic DJ in Paraguay.

Yaya shared about her exes. She told Shannon that when she had told Dean about breaking up with Jessica, all he responded was, "Holy Fuck." That was the last she had heard from him, almost a year before. Shannon said, "Yeah, I can imagine that wasn't exactly the support you were looking for."

The roommates teamed up with some neighbors up the hill, and decided to do a unified magic mushroom ceremony between the two houses. They sat in ceremony in the big living room at the lake house and each shared their intention before eating the psilocybin chocolate. The neighbors lived in a house called the 'Secret Garden'.

Yaya hadn't been there before. After the morning dance party at their house, they made pairs to stealthily walk through locked down town to move to the Secret Garden.

It was extremely beautiful with trees and birds, and flowers and plants. Yaya sat in the garden and enjoyed the magnificence of nature, watching the tiny ants crawl through the grass and noticing the butterflies flitting through the air. Finally, her favorite roomies showed up. It was one of the roommate's first mushroom journeys and Yaya wanted to be with her. She was a young Israeli woman whose name means 'morning dew'.

As it drew to 4pm, they knew they had to make a decision, either walk home or commit to sleeping over, due to the curfew in town. It had just started to sprinkle a bit of rain. Each person made their own decision to stay or go and to the group's delight, they reunited at the lake house at sunset, all twelve of them. They celebrated that they had all actually wanted to be together.

They also started the process of coming up with a house name. Everyone put suggestions on a bit of paper and submitted it to a jar. Then two papers were chosen at a time by each person to come up with names. The top three names went on the white board and they landed on Casita Wa'a Ba'a - mainly because people were always in hot pursuit of their water bottles to stay hydrated.

That night Casita Wa'a Ba'a decided to eat chili for dinner. One hungry woman was the main instigator to have someone cook the chili, and they took on the chili challenge.

The Mimis and Yaya had made chili a few nights before for dinner, but it wasn't cooked enough, so they had made an emergency-extra-soup to feed everyone that night.

The chili had been brewing and stewing for a few days and they were stirring it up in a huge pot with a big wooden spoon. She was using all of her elbow strength to stir the concoction. It was hilarious. Yaya laughed hysterically for hours about the chili, and it became a joke in the house, that all chili should be 'triple-baked'.

Later on that night, 'freestyle cookies' were born. They wanted something sweet, so Yaya decided to just take a bunch of cookie-like ingredients out of the big pantry and throw together some cookies. She was still not in a place energetically to use her phone or look up recipes so she just eyeballed the amounts of flour, oil, eggs, and chocolate chips. They came out amazingly well.

One of the roomies loved hot food, and would always linger around the oven when treats of any kind were being made.

In early April, one roommate turned forty years old. As part of the birthday celebration, they blindfolded him and took him on a voyage to another neighbor's house up in the woods of the jungle, where they would all be sleeping over.

They hosted a wild play party temple night for him, with the intention to make all his desires come true. Yaya and friends helped to roll forty sacred joints, as one of the birthday boys' dreams was that everyone would have a sovereign joint. However, the hostess didn't allow marijuana to be smoked at her house, so they were all placed on the altar. Around the property you had to watch out for duck poop, as there was a paddle of ducks living there.

Yaya and Tim shared a cacao cup and ended up fooling around on the couch downstairs. They eventually tried to sleep together there, but it was a challenge to share the small surface, and early in the morning Tim got up and walked home. The others had cake for breakfast -- it was delicious.

Soon after, another roommate wanted to leave, she had been triggered about the night and didn't want to talk about it. Yaya and her hiked back together in silence.

For some, the party was so much fun. They talked about whose party would be next. Another roommate's 40th birthday was coming up soon in early May.

Yaya's hair was getting pretty poofy and she joked that if they were still in Guatemala for his birthday, on the full moon, she would shave her head.

Well, the weeks passed in April, and they inched closer and closer to May. She met another neighbor, a man from Ecuador who had had long hair. He had done a ceremony to shave his head releasing the past, present, and future of his hair - and she was inspired.

Eventually they paid for May's rent for the lake house, and on May 7, in conjunction with the Super Flower Full Moon, Yaya shaved her head.

She asked a friend from the Secret Garden to facilitate the ceremony, and she asked one of the roommates to man the fire, one to capture the event, and the rest to show up that morning at 7am, wearing all-white.

Yaya made three braids with her long dark brown hair, one for the past, one for the present, and one for the future. She buried the past, she burned the present, and she donated the braid (to a place that accepted dyed hair) to represent the future.

Her British housemate did the honor of shaving her head with some borrowed clippers from the neighbor. After the ceremony they put on some psytrance and danced it out to celebrate Yaya's new look.

Accidentally, during the ceremony they burned a patch of grass. Luckily, the guardian on the property, didn't mind too much.

On the property they also have a Temescal. Once a week they are permitted to fire up the temescal and enjoy the sweat. The first few times, cramming all twelve of them in there was a bit rowdy, and involved yelling and screaming, singing, fighting, and purging – but eventually they learned how to sweat in peace together.

One night, Yaya had just finished a big release of clearing some energy in the small red temescal and came outside to the starry sky. She wrapped herself in a towel and gently collapsed on the damp grass, staring up at the cosmos. She rested and enjoyed the moment for a few minutes, cooling down her body from the hot temperature she was just in. She goes in to take a shower and looks at her phone. She has a message that Burning Man is canceled.

She crumbles. She cries. She spends the next few hours on the bench under the bungalow outside the house, mourning this loss. She was supposed to go to Burning Man with Jacob! She thought it was kismet. They already had tickets.

Yaya was still stuck in black-and-white thinking. She applied meaning and took signs from everything. She had thought that because Jacob and her had got tickets to go together with such ease and grace, that it meant something promising about them.

She feels that this cancellation signifies it's over with Jacob and this makes her doubly sadder. It's the end of her favorite desert party and her current situation-ship. She cried for hours.

In addition, during the hair shaving ceremony, Yaya makes a commitment to herself to stop doing the seductive task of marketing. As her business partner says, "public relations will make you wealthy, but miserable." Instead, she commits to a life of service, to help people with her life-force energy through light-work.

For the upcoming surprise birthday, they acted like monkeys, in honor of the birthday monkey, and made a slip and slide on the front lawn. It was an amazing surprise. They went to the hardware store and got big sheets of plastic and special tape that they secured together and ran down the hill, next came the hose and the dish soap to make it nice and slippery.

The entire house donned their bathing suits and jumped in for some slippery fun. The birthday boy was asked to show up in a bikini, just for fun. The guardian of the property had two grandsons who wanted to play, so they were invited to slip and slide too. The laughter, drone videos, and slipping went on for a while.

When they tired down from the waterworks, it was time for face-and-body painting, this was Yaya's department. She laid out a tarp by the empty hot tub (there was not enough water to keep it full) and they asked people to lay down to get covered in designs. Everyone got playful colors on their body and face, depending on time and interest. Meanwhile, back in the kitchen, another cohort was making pizza, the birthday boy's favorite food. They ended up in the 'dorm,' the big room with a pool table and many of the bunk beds with balloons, and a fun birthday video that all his friends from around the world had submitted for.

That night Yaya and the other Californian, consensually dosed everyone with a tiny bit of MDMA, which they nicknamed H.O. (Heart Opener). With powerful intention there was enough to go around and melt everyone nicely.

Tim and Yaya had been flirting a bit after the first birthday party and gave each other a Reiki and massage exchange. After dancing quite a bit at the heart opener party, they decide to find some privacy in the Temescal.

They make out and get turned on, and decide to have sex. There are a ton of cozy blankets and pillows in there making it comfy, however there are also a ton of red ants! They are thrusting missionary style, while literally getting bitten by ants in their pants! The condom comes off and Tim ends up cumming inside her. Yaya was not on birth control. Eventually, Tim couldn't stand the ants anymore and had to leave.

The next day he showed up with a morning-after-pill that he had procured at the local pharmacy. Yaya was relieved. She thought she might have to take a coveted boat across the lake and get a special doctor's note to get across, to get the contraception- and this made it all much easier.

Before ever meeting Tim, Yaya had a dream about having sex with him. She had wanted to follow this premonition.

One day, Tim comes over to their lake house to have a few drinks and watch his favorite movie - Apocalypto. The Mimi's take photos of Yaya and Tim snuggling together with their matching bald heads.

Later that night a few of the roomies lead them all in an intro to BDSM workshop. Yaya and Tim are partners and do a simple 'follow the leader' exercise. Yaya realizes in this demonstration that she doesn't want Tim to touch her anymore or Dom her ever again. Maybe it's the BPD and black-and-white thinking or her attitude, but she decides to cut him out of her life as well.

* * *

All the women of Casita Wa'a Ba'a were invited over to a woman's house in town for a yoni egg workshop. They gathered downstairs around the cacao and made themselves a warm mug of liquid to bring upstairs. Yaya bought a yoni egg, it was a medium-sized Jade egg. The host played some lovely music and the women laid in a circle and introduced themselves before being led into the practice.

It was a really beautiful self-massage of the belly, thighs, and pelvic area before ever penetrating the yoni with the egg. Some women had obsidian eggs, which are said to be more powerful. After the workshop, the roommates had yoni egg sessions back at the suite and they often would set up a table under the full moon to charge them up overnight.

The housemates also split the cost of the ISTA online tantra festival, and set up the living room for twenty-four hour streaming, so anyone could participate in any of the workshops streaming from around the world at any time. Yaya decided to join in on the Sex Magic workshop. Yaya had a beautiful self-pleasure release in which she had some amazing visuals she hopes will come true! She saw herself becoming a Mom and for the first time in her life, she was really open to it, in this way, with the person revealed to her. She had never wanted children before this moment.

Meanwhile, two of the other roommates announced they were leaving the house. Going to live at a nearby hotel with a helicopter pad, and from there they left for France.

At their going-away party it was a tantric multi-course home-made French dinner followed by an online short film festival, a streaming, amateur-porn, queer-friendly, short-film competition.

Shannon played the character, 'Madame Fuckabye' and led the tantric dinner. Each course was paired with a sexy morsel and invitation to participate in. At the first course they were inspired to kiss their partners. During the second course, a sherry-based mushroom soup, they found interesting places to slurp it from. Each course was also paired with a different type of wine.

Some of them had a lot of fun and it was an epically wild night at the house. A pair of the housemates had been hooking up for weeks, and that night they decided not to be together. The male from that pair ended up having sex with a different female roommate in the middle of the dinner. The woman from that pair cried. Others were drunk with wine and desire.

Another of the roommate's going away parties had an eco-sexual vibe. Everyone was invited to make wings out of egg cartons and add plants to become fairies. It was a surprise for their dear ringleader. Yaya set up a secret wing-making station in the Temescal, and housemates were encouraged to take a visit there to make their personalized eco-fairy wings.

He was crying with excitement when they led him through the rain out to the Temescal to meet his wings. They were the wildest and fiercest wings of them all. He was leaving to go back to Tsunana, the next town on the lake. Yaya had bonded with him when she went to help him stain his roof with one more coat of paint, just in time before the rainy season began.

His party was also a temple night play party. So there was a voyeur section on the bench, there was an appetizer section where you had to ask someone to feed you, if you wanted a taste, not self-serve. There was a full on sexy-time-station, and a rope station. A friend asked to tie up Yaya and she said yes. She carefully wrapped the brown rope around Yaya's chest and pulled her limp surrendered body into a few ovals.

There was a white and black cat who hung around. The guardian said she was the neighbor's. Casita Wa'a Ba'a named her Regina.

A few of the roomies loved dogs and cats of all kinds and would feed Regina cans of tuna.

The first night they were there, they met a big dog that smelled like fish, they named him Pescado. He would visit them daily for a belly rub or a Frisbee toss. He started to smell better, and he got neutered. A few months later he was wearing a collar and tags.

At the house, they would eat shakshuka, and celebrate Ramadan and other food-based holidays. Weekends often were pancakes.

The day of the eco-sexual, going-away party, Yaya had two visitors. A friend of a friend from Israel from New York City, and she was coming over for lunch.

The other was a friend dropping off some mushroom chocolates for them to buy. Of course these two showed up on the big lawn at the same moment and Yaya was not sure how it would go. Luckily they knew each other, and she picked up a chocolate for herself. Easy Breezy.

During that visit, Yaya learned that he was going to fly to New Orleans in June to visit his family. He casually mentioned that he was flying United Airlines. Later that day, Yaya called United on Skype and learned that regular flights were happening again, come June!

Ever since the sexy tantric dinner, things hadn't been right in the house. It had started to be the rainy season and they had to spend more time inside. The woman hurt from the tryst was spending more time by herself. There was talk of people moving out of the house and into other places.

Yaya decided her time had come. She booked a regular flight on June 7th from Guatemala City back to New York City. She got to use her same confirmation number and everything from back in April, no change fees either.

After the morning circle, the housemates were going to have a big talk about the housing situation. Yaya was leaving, so she proceeded to have her own dance party under the tree instead of participating in this discussion. She ended up getting a huge thorn in her foot from the grass, which the roommates helped her excavate.

About five minutes later, she got hit with a heavy sharp piece of tree right on her nose, she started bleeding and crying and had a scar for a few weeks. This was the beginning of the end for Yaya.

She was going to move to Eagles Nest for one week before departing back to her home in New York City.

Back in New York, there were riots with Black Lives Matter (BLM) and a newly imposed curfew. Yaya started getting messages from friends saying, "Don't come back." They were the same friends who thought she was crazy for leaving in March.

She knew it was the perfect time to come back. She felt a sense of obligation that her city needed her, and she was ready to go home. On the last day of May, the housemates sadly packed up their things and put back the hats.

It was a big rearrange of all the things they had displaced over the three months of staying there. Yaya took her things and hiked up the hill to Eagles Nest to get settled in the Baobab room, a wooden treehouse overlooking the lake.

Eagles Nest was rustic and had an outdoor heated shower and a very cool temescal perched above a walkway. The Wi-Fi didn't always work, and someone could make a hot tea and bust the electric outlet for the day.

It was chilly in her little cabin, but she had a hammock. There were a few cats and a dog named Daisy who lived there, and the whole place was Little Prince themed. It was cute, not too cozy, and she was happy to be leaving sooner rather than later.

The housemates were invited to an underground Kirtan party on a Thursday afternoon at a big house in the woods. A few of them walked there together. Usually it was recommended that females be escorted by males or carry machetes for walks in the woods, but they decided to take a chance without these precautions.

Yaya met an ayahuasca medicine woman from California. It was serendipitous as a few of the housemates were feeling called to drink the plant medicine. Yaya was still a "no" to it.

Some of the Peruvian and Colombian male bodied 'shamans' she had worked with in the past had committed sexual misconduct, not against her, however, she was skeptical.

She liked the idea of grandmother medicine being served by a woman shaman.

At the Kirtan, they enjoyed cacao and singing, and the medicine woman played some beautiful kirtan bells. On the hike back, the jungle spoke to Yaya inviting her to drink medicine with them. She asked the medicine woman if she could come too, and there was one more spot that had opened up and yes she could attend!

After a week of dieta, they walked to the gated yard around dusk. They were let in by the medicine woman's guardian. They walked up to the medicine cabana and dropped off their pillows and personal items. It was a beautiful sanctuary with all kinds of gems and instruments at the front making a big altar.

That night it would be almost all women drinking medicine, led by a female medicine woman. For grandmother medicine Yaya appreciated the feminine energy that was present. She had always sat with male medicine men before.

During the dieta, a routine in preparation for a ceremony, usually avoiding sex, processed food, allergy medication, news, tv and marijuana, it finally clicked for Yaya that it was like preparing to go sit with your Grandma, you don't bring these distractions or addictions to chat with an older, wise woman.

There was one man from Iceland, and the medicine woman's partner who were both holding the masculine polarity.

They sat, they drank, listening to the amazing live music to encourage them on their medicine journey. In the morning, Yaya rose early with a German woman making coffee. The two shared some caffeine and nicotine and chatted about life. She was partnered with the women's cacao collective and her wife was the matriarch there. They chatted about cacao, real estate, and New York for a few hours before the others rose.

Yaya visited their cacao place and brought a few pounds of cacao back to Queens.

* * *

They walked back up to Eagle's Nest together, after having a full moon fire ceremony sleepover the night before, with just the girls. They each had whiskers painted on their face and fun cat ears on their heads. They chatted lightly as they breathed with a bit more heaviness as each step got steeper up the hill. When they arrived, they were greeted by the larger community. For Yaya's going away party, they were having a surprise at Eagle's Nest.

The DJ played music for the party, and a few people hung from the acro yoga silks. A few more guests arrived, and they popped the champagne. Yaya and a few others dabbled a bit of acid. It was one of their first times. A few hours into the party someone ordered a lot of pizza for the bunch and this coincided with a robbery, so the police came.

Yaya was in the back in the volunteer kitchen making some vegetarian, gluten-free food with a few others. They stayed up there until the police left, trying to show as least amount of people as possible at the 'party,' as they were still in quarantine times. The event started early so people would have a chance to get home before the 6pm curfew. The curfew time would change from 4pm, to 6pm, to full lockdown, depending on the week. The up to date curfew news was delivered on a loudspeaker on a truck, which would drive around town on Sunday nights.

After the police and pizza robbery escapade, the party winded down and ended up on Yaya's balcony surrounding the hammock that she laid in, cozied up with a couple of roommates. The others sat around on chairs and benches, and on the balcony itself wrapped in blankets and sharing joints.

The next morning, she was off to the airport in Guatemala City and shared a taxi with the mushroom friend. At the Houston international airport, Yaya experienced reverse culture shock. Most of the airport was closed due to Covid, however, there were a few Duty Free stores open. Yaya had to turn away from the bright lights highlighting the huge pile of M&M's candy. In San Marcos, there had been candy, but never showcased in this way.

Yaya flew to Newark in her mask, and took an Uber taxi all the way home to her vacant studio apartment in Rockaway Beach in Queens NY. She had forgotten about her big palm plant, it was not happy and had actually died while she was away. Otherwise everything looked proper as can be, and she enjoyed nights in her own cozy bed, and running hot water. She would never take a hot bath for granted again.

The Pet Lady Finally Finds Pets of Her Own

A few weeks after being home, her business partner forwarded her email newsletter to Yaya and said, "Hey did you see, Sassy?"

Yaya had already seen the newsletter and had checked out Sassy. She was a one –year-old calico cat (all calicos are female) available for adoption. Yaya thought what the heck and submitted an application. Within about four minutes she got a call from the shelter director at Paws Long Island saying she was approved after a glowing recommendation, and did she want to foster Sassy? Yaya asked if they had any bonded pairs.

So Sassy had gotten into a fight with a coyote in Texas and had her tail amputated. She came to New York City with her brother, Chance, a black male, and the two of them ended up in different foster homes, and neither one was working out. A few days later, Chance and Sassy were dropped off at Yaya's home by a shelter volunteer to reunite, and to meet their new human!

Chance had just been neutered, and Sassy had just been spayed. They were both supposed to wear a cone of shame. Within moments of being in Yaya's apartment, the black cat was hissing, and neither of them had their cones on. Yaya was asked to please keep their cones on and to keep them separated at night. It was a studio apartment, so that meant that one of them would have to sleep in their crate at night.

Yaya successfully coaxed Chance into his metal carrier and locked the door. After hours of meowing and lots of banging and scraping sounds, he was able to successfully unlock himself from his crate from the inside. He was determined.

Yaya then put him in the kitchen and closed the French doors and put furniture in front of them, attempting to block him in. This is now at about four in the morning. Chance leaped out from the kitchen through the tiny window into the living room, completely clearing it of all debris, like greeting cards and candles. He walked past Yaya as if to say, "Just try and confine me!"

The next day it was raining and Yaya didn't feel like going outside. She was allergic to cats and managed this by taking an antihistamine daily, keeping the window open and going outside every morning.

She called the shelter volunteer in desperation and said, "It's not working out. I think you need to pick up Chance."

They said it was impossible. The soonest they could come would be in five days.

After Yaya and Chance got through that morning- it was smooth sailing. Yaya no longer tried to confine Chance, and he no longer tried to escape. They had reached an understanding.

Yaya got it at a soul level, she didn't like to be limited herself. The shelter woman told Yaya she was learning about cats as 'baptism by fire.'

She walked out of her apartment with no shoes to do her regular weekend, summer beach walk to Riis beach. This day a local Burning Man crew were having a socially distanced party at the beach. She found them and danced, and danced, and danced. At one point, she stepped on a broken beer bottle which cut her foot and decided to check out the emergency services by the bathrooms. They happily wrapped up her foot for her.

* * *

Labor Day 2020, on the 13th anniversary of having moved to New York City, Yaya flew to Oregon to meet up with her sister and her parents for some hiking and family time, after a strange year of living in Guatemala, and enduring a COVID world-wide lock-down.

Yaya flew to Oregon, on a six-hour flight, wearing both a face-mask and a shield. Her parents picked her up at the airport, and they all went to stay at her sister's new residence in rural Oregon, in McMinnville.

It was the end of August, and before COVID-19 scratched everyone's plans, she would either have been at a trade show in Vegas or Burning Man in Reno at that time.

The four Humphrey's decided to go hiking on the Oregon coast. They had masks on as they climbed the rocky trail. Making it out to the epic seascape cliffs for a family photo op, and generously helping a few couples take some photos in return, delicately passing their phones back and forth as if that would prevent germs from spreading.

They were coming down the trail, getting closer to where they parked, hunger building for the packed lunch in the car which nobody wished to carry, and Yaya sees one of her favorite veterinarians and his wife and their daughter, and *her* daughter!

This veterinarian is one of the most well-known and respected vets in the country, an author, and Yaya's friend.

When Yaya first moved to New York City, he invited Yaya to the green room at Good Morning America, where he was a regular. She will never forget that morning, getting off the subway and walking into Times Square, moments before the sunrise, and having a New York Moment, where she was literally the only person there. This lasted for about forty-five seconds before it seemed to unfreeze and move back into its circadian rhythm of extreme movement and business.

So, here they are on the trail, normally Yaya would hug him, however, it's Covid times, so touching is basically inappropriate.

She is a bit struck by his out of place presence, and says something like, "This is my family." The good veterinarian proceeds to dish out some heartfelt compliments to Yaya. He calmly turns to her parents and says, "You really have a rockstar of a daughter over there."

Yaya was touched and took it all in. She really appreciated him saying that.

Her parents couldn't have moved the conversation along quicker. So they got to talking about who knows what, word salad some would say, and Yaya stood quietly, happy to know such a beautiful man and his family.

She was able to take in and really receive his praise. If her younger-self knew this moment was coming, she wouldn't have believed it. Instead, her higher self got to look down and see it all unfold.

For so long, Yaya had wanted validation, approval, and praise from her parents. They would brag to others about her behind her back, but never to her face.

Now she knows it's not their fault. They are who they are, and they brought her into the world, and she is grateful. Yaya can validate herself, and surround herself, and attract people who care for her and value her and her gifts. It's okay. She could accept her parents for who they were and love them anyway.

The girls say goodbye to their parents and close the Honda doors. They pile in for the highly anticipated kickoff for a camping road trip to the Alvord Hot Springs in Oregon, just north of the actual playa, where Burning Man takes place.

First stop is Portland to pick up Jane and some food. Their friend works for a community Food Pantry and has lots of fresh vegetables, fruits, and gluten-free snacks for them. Jane grabs her crate and many belongings, and piles into the already full four-door car. They have an eight- hour drive ahead to the hot springs.

They are caravanning with another crew behind them. Halfway, they pick a dispensary to stop at. Jane has her recent graduation money and Yaya and her have fun going shopping.

When Yaya arrived a few days before, Andrea told her sister that she had lots of weed. She had one and a half joints. Yaya laughed and insisted she hold on to "all that" and let her replenish.

Jane and Yaya were ready to party. On the way in, on the dirt path Yaya insisted that they stop and get some rocks to help with the upcoming camping wind factor, Andrea stood firm that they wouldn't need any rocks. Instead, Yaya convinced her to stop by some wildflowers and they picked yellow flowers to bring to camp.

They stopped at the little wooden pay-as-you-go box and made a donation, and then entered the barren desert. Far away in the distance, perhaps miles away, they saw other cars. They spied a spot with a patch of grass, a few rocks and a wheelbarrow and parked immediately. This solved the debate around rocks, they had a grassy knoll to dump excess water and they now had a safe vestibule for their camp fire. It was the ideal spot and walking distance to the hot springs, so no one had to drive.

About 100 yards away was a solo camper. Within two hours of them setting up and playing music, Graziela came over to introduce herself. She was a Burner and had come out to the desert for some peace and quiet.

She could see Jane getting riled up. Yaya motioned that she got this, and took Graziela on saying, "We do not have any big speakers for amplified sound, to my dismay, so this is as loud as we get."

The crew was laughing and joking, and cooking and hanging out, as they would be doing for the next week. Graziela tried to claim that she was there first. Yaya firmly stood her ground and said "We are Burners too, we will not be moving. You are welcome to join us, but we will not be leaving, thank you." The next night Graziela came over with a hard seltzer apologizing for her behavior and asking to hangout. She was warmly welcomed.

They ate magic mushrooms, and put up their tents, and made a latrine out of a bucket. Yaya's Burner husband, Will, his cousin, and his girlfriend came out to camp for a few nights and joined the group, making ten of them altogether.

The rest were Andrea's friends. They brought a lot of firewood. They wore costumes and danced around, and made camp food and art. The cousin brought a legitimate painting kit and they had fun painting rocks. They found an altar etched into the ground on their campsite, too.

One of the campers was a professional photographer for the *New York Times*, and he took their photos during the golden hour each evening before the sun downed behind the mountain range in front of them. As it became dark their solar-powered lights would illuminate the space adding vision to the camp. The nights were crisp and clear with excellent vision of the moon, planets, and stars.

Instead of driving all the way back to Andrea's place in McMinnville, they stopped in the woods for a night to shower and stay in cabins and decompress. It was mainly outdoors, with various hot and cold bath tubs from local thermal centers that the public could pay to use. They were at limited capacity due to Covid and the girls had a reservation. Plus, they got to enjoy some freshly prepared, hot vegetarian meals.

Yaya flew back to New York City and rejoined her cats in her sunny apartment. She had asked an acquaintance to stay at her place and cat-sit while she was gone. The cat sitter had lost some earrings during her stay and hopefully thought that Yaya would want to help her search for them, after her all night, red eye flight. She did not.

She left and the earrings showed up a few weeks later under the bed. *Maybe the cats had been playing with them?*

Yaya had been reading a few books about animal soul contracts and healing by Tammy Billups. She learned that Billups gave energy clearing sessions for the pet and the pet owner on the phone, so Yaya signed up for one with her male cat, Chance. Apparently there were two patterns in this life that they were both trying to heal, betrayal and abandonment. Betrayal shows up as in-your-face neediness, insatiable externally, and abandonment shows up as guarded and cautious.

Tammy recognized that Yaya had had patterns of being over-controlled in her life. She told Yaya that all three souls, the cats; Sassy, Chance and Yaya all knew each other from before and had gratitude for each other. She suggested the way to heal from control is through freedom.

Yaya decided to keep the cats, and the moment she posted the paperwork in the mail to officially adopt Chance and Sassy, they seemed to intuitively know and act differently towards her.

CHAPTER FOURTEEN

May All Beings Be Fed

Just like a prayer, our own words will take us where we need to be.

Jeremy and Yaya met on LinkedIn that summer. He is a dog trainer from Texas who claims he was mentored under Cesar Millan. He tells Yaya that he is launching a podcast and wants some good pet guests. Now Yaya has got guests. All her pet product clients became interviewees for the month of August.

On one of their video chats, he was showing her his Instagram and she saw a photo of him at Burning Man. He was telling Yaya about a dog party that he was hosting for BLM.

He even interviewed her ISTA teachers about tantra and her Reiki teacher. He sent her gifts of jewelry and thank you cards saying, "I love you."

Months of phone flirting go by and he invites Yaya to visit him in Mallorca, Spain when Covid is over. That fall, he came to New York City to visit. He was going to fly and stay at a hotel, and then it became a road trip and an Airbnb. *He talks a lot,* she thought

He gave Yaya the address to his Airbnb and asked her to meet him there in an hour. Yaya obliged. When she got there, right on time, he was still in Staten Island and running thirty minutes late, since he and his girlfriend both stopped to get their nails painted. *Hmmm.*

Yaya is starting to see the signs of grandiose narcissism in him. For example: the surprise girlfriend in tow and running behind on purpose - just to make her wait for him.

The New York City underground Burner crew happens to be throwing a tunnel party in Prospect Park that very night. The three of them walked from their Airbnb to the party. It was the holiday season, so they stopped to take photos in front of fancy wreaths and colorful lights along the way. It was a fun and enhanced walk.

Yaya has a Post-it note on her refrigerator reading: *I bless you with love - You are free - I am free - I release you.* It was a daily reminder for forgiveness and cord cutting, as she believed that energetic ties were created with people when a connection had taken place. This has been her intention for years now, and she says it often in her mind, mostly meant for her ex, Jessica, and to her Mom.

At the party, the three of them, Jeremy, his girlfriend and Yaya are sitting, taking a rest from their two mile walk there, before dancing, when Jessica and her current partner Jerome walk towards them and make-out behind a relatively close tree.

Yaya pointed them out. Later on, as the hostess for the party was hugging them, Jessica's partner Jerome and Jeremy, the only two big black guys at that party, at that time, introduced themselves to each other, and were chatting.

Jeremy misunderstood and thought that Jessica's partner was the ex. Not exactly the vibe that Yaya wanted them to be having.

Regardless, they dance and dance. At one point, a saxophone comes out and is playing with the DJ electronic dance music, among the lasers and hundreds of masked dancers. It was an epic party.

The three of them all really brought the dance moves and there were a few others at the party creating that beautiful swirly dance floor energy. As it gets towards the early morning, Jeremy and the girlfriend announce that they are leaving, and start walking towards the trees. Yaya doesn't want to leave yet, but decides to escort them out.

As she goes to grab her gold backpack and giant fuzzy bear coat, she sees Jessica is perusing her section of belongings. Yaya quickly snags her stuff and bounces while Jessica stands there with her hand over her mouth.

Yaya walks Jeremy and the girlfriend out of the park towards Grand Army Plaza. There she assumes they can take a car back to their Airbnb. It turns out they are in worse shape than she thinks and neither of them are capable of using their phones. Yaya calls an Uber for herself, and makes a stop to drop their messy asses off.

Jeremy talked a big game that he was a Dom, but in Yaya's opinion if he couldn't Dom himself, he would never Dom her. Jeremy getting so fucked up that he didn't know where he was, was a big turnoff for Yaya, pretty much forever more.

Maybe that was her BPD showing up, showing her black-and-white thinking, but once Yaya wrote someone off it was very hard to switch up that opinion.

Jeremy had had visions of a late night threesome, but his girlfriend wanted nothing to do with that, and neither did Yaya. There were supposed to be some dog training sessions the next two days, however Yaya decided to stay home.

She was learning to listen to herself and enforce her boundaries.

Over winter solstice, Yaya forms an ISTA Covid-cohort with seven others at a big mansion in Southampton that they rented for a week. The place is complete with tennis courts, a volleyball net, and a hot tub. It's ten minutes from the beach and a short walk from the bay. They all get Covid tested a few days in advance, followed by a rapid test at the door, for extra safety.

Two of the members of the cohort came to pick Yaya up, with a big gong and a drum in the SUV packed to the brim with

BDSM supplies like floggers and restraints. One of them had been studying his Greek pagan heritage and had a vision of making genital cookies. Yaya was excited about the idea of this ritual.

Another fantasy that they had was to celebrate one attendee's belated birthday, by having a really rich chocolate cake eaten off their naked body. Another member of the cohort really wanted to order Chinese food on Christmas Eve, so they paired this with watching, A Christmas Story in Yaya's camping tent, which they set up in the living room.

Downstairs they set up the dungeon, complete with mattresses and gong. They had many beautiful sound baths and Latihan practices down there. They even got to play Yes, No, More, one of Yaya's most favorite tantric games.

On the eve of the winter solstice, they dressed up and sent prayers up to the fire, enjoyed cigars on the shortest day of the year, right at 5:04 AM, in time for the magical solstice.

The next night they prepared a tantric dinner where they got to eat honey, homemade sushi, and juicy scallops off of one another. This special solstice celebration was fun and magical, and also chill and relaxing, ending Yaya's 2020 with bliss.

During the week in Southampton, Yaya studied Human Design over the hookah. They would read and chat and search online. A few of them had just come back from a six-week training on the West Coast learning about this method, which combines I-Ching, astrology, Kabbalah, and many other traditions into one understanding. Yaya's Human Design result is a Generator.

The four options are Manifestor, Reflector, Projector and Generator, there are also a few Manifesting Generators. Yaya learned that her strategy in life should be to respond, and that her particular brand is a heretic. The Heretics are the warriors and the guides. They play the role of someone who is able to step in from outside the situation to offer a solution no one involved has considered. She is also a builder.

This is just one more piece of understanding her own puzzle. After spending Christmas in this community she goes back to New York City for her tradition to dance on New Year's Eve.

During her study of CORE Shamanism, Yaya found that the practice, even across different cultures, greatly depends on working with compassionate energies. Yaya followed this path, and found light in the practice of this work.

During the pandemic, her friend Mo started a park pop-up dance party. Sometimes, it is complete ridiculousness. Mo and Yaya know each other from a dance party, which started with no talking, no drinks, no phones and from Ecstatic Dance.

Usually, Yaya and Mo see each other on the dance floor, as they are both regulars, Yaya by the front speaker shaking all over and jumping around, and him, aggressively wanting to 'box dance,' or known to go into a puddle or in the fetal position on the floor. He was an interesting character.

Mo lives by McCarren Park in Williamsburg and started bringing his speakers out to the park, set up in the middle of some circles laid out by ropes and hula hoops. It is socially distanced with the hula hoops at least six feet apart, and everyone wears a mask within the space designated by rope. When the cops or the parks department comes, Mo turns down the music and starts leading the dancers into a sequence of jumping jacks.

She had gone to Williamsburg earlier that evening with a giant metal pot to help Mo make the hot apple cider and hot chocolate for the dancers. They added cinnamon and sugar, and stirred in chunks of real apple. Yaya helped Mo wheel the rig of speakers and hot liquid about four blocks. It had snowed a few days prior, and at one point the entire rig fell into the snow. They calmly just lifted the rig up and kept on moving.

At one point, Yaya noticed her ex, Jessica The Doctor. She watched as Jessica waltzed over to the hot cocoa stand to refill her container. Just a few months before, Yaya knew she would have felt overwhelmed with strong feelings about this moment. However, she simply let it be and smiled with ease as Jessica became just another dancer in the party, enjoying the hot beverage that she had made with love. *May all beings be fed.*

That night, Mo celebrated Yaya and thanked her for her support. Things are different now, Yaya is not just an observer and a dancer, but a real contributing participant in the New York City dance community.

At another one of the Friday dance parties, Yaya was there taking a breather on a blanket with her friend, and they looked at the sight in front of them. Mo leading jumping jacks, little girls in princess costumes, adults in onesies to match their dogs, and a bag of golf clubs. Just the amount of ridiculous reprieve from the seriousness of the week that they were looking for.

One night, Jacob came out to McCarren Park, the one who was supposed to go to Burning Man with Yaya.

Yaya happily went up to Jacob and gave him a hug. She asked him if he was going to dance, remembering all the good times they had dancing at the House of Yes. "No," he replied. "I am more of a sit-on-the-blanket-kind-of-guy."

"Oh!" said Yaya and slowly backed away. He was gaslighting her. *Good riddance, Jacob.*

The park bathrooms were closed, and Yaya needed to pee. Most of the nearby bars required a purchase so she ducked into the kava place. The guy at the kava place was cute and wanted her number. He would let her use the bathrooms in between dances. He was in his late-twenties, similar to some of the guys she would match with on Tinder while really trying to meet women.

After the extreme sport of outdoor winter dancing, Yaya enjoys the extreme act of self-care involving hot baths. The observer and witness part of her life is activated, and she just said, *Thank you* and *You're Welcome* to herself for listening to the idea to take a bath. She is becoming more aware and therefore more free.

A few days after New Year, Yaya flies to Mexico to meet up with her parents and sister to celebrate the holidays, their annual tradition. After a week of staying with Mom and Dad, Yaya booked herself a hotel for four nights to celebrate her birthday, and to decompress after being with family for a whole week. After a taco birthday lunch and a few Tinder dates, Yaya returns from warm Cabo to winter in January in New York City.

She flies back on a Saturday, and on Sunday she has planned a birthday beach dance party with her friend DJ Ollie. His birthday was also in January, and the two of them want to dance to house music, safely outside. Yaya arranges for a friend to bring her solar powered generator so they have power, and Yaya brings a few crispy recycled Christmas trees to burn, so they have a big fire. After the power generator died, a juggler friend had a big speaker all charged up and ready to go.

They played longer. Then their friend from the Burner parties in the tunnel showed up with his amazing sound system and set up right there with lasers and everything. They played into the night.

She overheard a phone conversation while she was dancing by the fire, barefoot at the birthday party, "I'm at a beach rave." Yaya grinned under her mask, she was in her happy place.

As Yaya learns to focus and bring attention to her inner community, mind, body and spirit, she continues to heal and let the light in and out with more ease and grace.

After doing soul retrieval rituals in shamanic breathwork, Yaya is able to recall the parts of herself that were hidden away in childhood, and come back to wholeness. She no longer identifies with the broken BPD diagnosis, as she has healed with soul integration. She was lost and now she is found.

Yaya has embraced the Burner lifestyle, using carabiners to carry her phone, water bottle and backpacks, in order to live hands-free, and to be always ready and able to dance or climb on something. While 'home' was once a place, at the Burn, Yaya, this wild artist, gypsy, shaman with no roots realizes she is home everywhere, every day in the sacred temple of her body.

In 2021, Burning Man auspiciously announced that it is "not canceled, but in fact everywhere."

So there it is, Yaya's many lives written into wholeness.

> May I find love without the bombing,
> Truth without resentment.
> Compassion without a carrot,
> Companionship in human form.

My Prayer for us all: May you return all non-love, with love.

And as they say after each yoga class: loka samastha sukhino bhavanthu.

May the entire universe find peace, joy, love and light.

Namaste.

Recommended Reading List

POWER: Surviving and Thriving After Narcissistic Abuse by Shahida Arabi

Pathological mind games. Covert and overt put-downs. Triangulation. Gaslighting.

Projection. These are the manipulative tactics survivors of malignant narcissists are unfortunately all too familiar with. As victims of silent crimes where the perpetrators are rarely held accountable, survivors of narcissistic abuse have lived in a war zone of epic proportions, enduring an abuse cycle of love-bombing and devaluation-psychological violence on steroids. From how to heal our addiction to the narcissist to how to recognize a covert narcissist, Shahida Arabi's articles on narcissistic abuse have gained renown as some of the most accurate and in-depth depictions of this terrifying trauma, resonating with millions of survivors all over the world and receiving endorsements from numerous mental health professionals.

The Road Back to Me, by Lisa A. Romano

I was in my early thirties when I was told by a therapist that I was codependent and that my codependency was the result of being raised by two unrecovered adult children of alcoholics. At the time I was suffering from panic disorder, clinical depression, adult onset asthma and various other health issues.

Surviving Narcissistic Abuse, The Human Magnet Syndrome the Codependent Narcissist Trap, by Ross A. Rosenberg

The Human Magnet Syndrome provides a life-changing and brilliant explanation for why patient and sacrificing codependents fall head over heels in love with beautiful and exquisitely interesting selfish and self-centered narcissists. Since the dawn of civilization, men and women have been magnetically and irresistibly drawn together into romantic relationships, not so much by what they see, feel and think, but more by invisible forces.

Stories from Heaven. Lessons for the Living: The Light Between Us, by Laura Lynn Jackson

NEW YORK TIMES BESTSELLER • For readers of *Proof of Heaven*, the astonishing story of a woman with an extraordinary psychic gift—and a powerful message from the Other Side that can help us to live more beautifully in the here and now. *The Light Between Us* provides guideposts for living a rich and fulfilling life. In her beautiful worldview, Laura Lynne Jackson reminds us that our relationship to those we love endures across space and time; that we are all connected and invested in one another's lives; and that we are here to give and receive love selflessly. Her story offers a new understanding of the vast reach of our consciousness and enlarges our view of the human experience.

Healing Back Pain: The Mind-Body Connection, by Dr. John Sarno

Dr. John E. Sarno is a medical pioneer whose program has helped thousands upon thousands of people overcome their back conditions--without drugs or dangerous surgery.

Imperfectly Sane, by Stacy Lee Hoch.

Imperfectly Sane is a raw and explicit account of bravery and self-discovery on a journey of daring the world, with a whole lot of truth. A young girl with a fierce defense of escapism gives a bird's eye view of the healing transformations one must go through to overcome a hellish past, face our fears, and own the power we possess through it all. It's the air you need to breath.

Selfish: Permission to Pause, Live, Love and Laugh Your Way to Joy by, Naketa Thigpin

It's time to redefine... Selfish women get the life they want. Are you exhausted from work/life burnout? Do you lack balance, or does love always seem to pass you by no matter how hard you try to connect? Maybe it's time to get *Selfish*. Naketa Ren Thigpen, the #1 Balance and Relationship Advisor in the World, presents a book for ambitious women everywhere.

The G.R.E.A.T.E.S.T. Soul Journey, by Dr. Kathleen E. Walls

This is a workbook-style journal designed to assist you in taking an honest look at your life and your beliefs. This journal will provide you with clarity as you assess your life, your relationships, your thoughts and beliefs, and the ways in which you are working toward or against your goals. The journal follows the G.R.E.A.T.E.S.T. Model, designed by Dr. Kathleen E. Walls, which was created to assist you in restoring your understanding of who you are, encouraging you to use your gifts and talents, and motivating you to live your G.R.E.A.T.E.S.T. Life.

Break the Grip of Past Lovers: Reclaim Your Personal Power, Recover from Neglect, Manipulation, or Betrayal, Reawaken Your Emotional Intimacy, by Jumana Sophia

In *Break the Grip of Past Lovers*, author Jumana Sophia teaches women how to move beyond the lingering betrayals of past relationships to reclaim their personal power, reestablish healthy boundaries, and move forward into deeper and more intimate relationships with a renewed sense of sensual receptivity and emotional balance.

In an Unspoken Voice: How the Body Releases Trauma and Restores Goodness by Peter A. Levine and Gabor Mate

In this culmination of his life's work, Peter A. Levine draws on his broad experience as a clinician, a student of comparative brain research, a stress scientist and a keen observer of the naturalistic animal world to explain the nature and transformation of trauma in the body, brain and psyche. In an Unspoken Voice is based on the idea that trauma is neither a disease nor a disorder, but rather an injury caused by fright, helplessness and loss that can be healed by engaging our innate capacity to self-regulate high states of arousal and intense emotions. Enriched with a coherent theoretical framework and compelling case examples, the book elegantly blends the latest findings in biology, neuroscience and body-oriented psychotherapy to show that when we bring together animal instinct and reason, we can become more whole human beings.

You're Not Crazy - It's Your Mom - By Danu Morrigan

You're Not Crazy - It's Your Mom explains what that it is, and what it means to you in your life. It will help you to undertake a journey of recognition and recovery: of moving on, healing, and claiming your own self as the wonderful, vibrant woman you really are.

Women Who Love Too Much: When You Keep Wishing and Hoping He'll Change, by Robin Norwood

Robin Norwood's groundbreaking work will enable you to recognize the roots of your destructive patterns of relating and provide you with a step-by-step guide to a more rewarding way of living and loving. If being in love means being in pain, you need to read *Women Who Love Too Much*.

In Sheep's Clothing: Understanding and Dealing with Manipulative People, by George K Simon

Dr. George Simon knows how people push your buttons. Your children—especially teens—are expert at it, as is your mate. A coworker may quietly undermine your efforts while professing to be

252

helpful, or your boss may prey on your weaknesses. Manipulative people have two goals: to win and to look good doing it. Often those they abuse are only vaguely aware of what is happening to them.

Lying by Sam Harris

In *Lying*, bestselling author and neuroscientist Sam Harris argues that we can radically simplify our lives and improve society by merely telling the truth in situations where others often lie. He focuses on "white" lies—those lies we tell for the purpose of sparing people discomfort—for these are the lies that most often tempt us. And they tend to be the only lies that good people tell while imagining that they are being good in the process.

Broken Open: How Difficult Times Can Help Us Grow, by Elizabeth Lesser

This inspiring guide to healing and growth illuminates the richness and potential of every life, even in the face of loss and adversity.

In the Realm of Hungry Ghosts: Close Encounters with Addiction, by Dr. Gabor Mate

Based on Gabor Maté's two decades of experience as a medical doctor and his groundbreaking work with the severely addicted on Vancouver's skid row, in the Realm of Hungry Ghosts radically re-envisions this much misunderstood field by taking a holistic approach. Dr. Maté presents addiction not as a discrete phenomenon confined to an unfortunate or weak-willed few, but as a continuum that runs throughout (and perhaps underpins) our society; not a medical "condition" distinct from the lives it affects, rather the result of a complex interplay among personal history, emotional, and neurological development, brain chemistry, and the drugs (and behaviors) of addiction.

Life Will Be the Death of Me: ... and you too! by Chelsea Handler

The funny, sad, super-honest, all-true story of Chelsea Handler's year of self-discovery—featuring a nerdily brilliant psychiatrist, a shaman, four Chow Chows, some well-placed security cameras, various family members (living and departed), friends, assistants, and a lot of edibles.

We Need to Talk: How to Have Conversations That Matter, by Celest Headlee

Today most of us communicate from behind electronic screens, and studies show that Americans feel less connected and more divided than ever before. The blame for some of this disconnect can be attributed to our political landscape, but the erosion of our conversational skills as a society lies with us as individuals.

Propaganda, by Edwards Barnays

Concepts outlined in Bernays' *Propaganda* and other works enabled the development of the first "two-way model" of public relations, using elements of social science in order to better formulate public opinion. Bernays justified public relations as a profession by clearly emphasizing that no individual or group had a monopoly on the true understanding of the world. According to public relations expert Stuart Ewen, "What Lippman set out in grand, overview terms, Bernays is running through in how-to-do-it-terms. His techniques are now staples for public image creation and political campaigns.

The 5 Love Languages: The Secret to Love That Lasts, Dr. Gary Chapman

In the #1 New York Times bestselling book The 5 Love Languages, you'll discover the secret that has transformed millions of relationships worldwide. Whether your relationship is flourishing or failing, Dr. Gary Chapman's proven approach to showing and receiving love will help you experience deeper and richer levels of intimacy with your partner-starting today.

CPSIA information can be obtained
at www.ICGtesting.com
Printed in the USA
BVHW082013250122
627118BV00011BA/380